Workers from the North: Plantations, Bolivian Labor,
and the City in Northwest Argentina

Latin American Monographs, No. 54
Institute of Latin American Studies
The University of Texas at Austin

Workers from the North

Plantations, Bolivian Labor, and the City
in Northwest Argentina

by Scott Whiteford

University of Texas Press, Austin

Library of Congress Cataloging in Publication Data

Whiteford, Scott, 1942-
    Workers from the North.

    (Latin American monographs; no. 54)
    Bibliography: p.
    Includes index.
    1. Migrant labor—Argentine Republic—Salta
(Province) 2. Migrant labor—Argentine Republic—
Jujuy (Province) 3. Plantations—Argentine Republic—
Salta (Province) 4. Plantations—Argentine Republic—
Jujuy (Province) 5. Urbanization—Argentine Republic—
Salta (City) 6. Bolivians in the Argentine Republic.
I. Title. II. Series: Latin American monographs
(Austin, Tex); no. 54.
HD5856.A7W46   331.6'2'84082   80-26599
ISBN 0-292-79015-5

Requests for permission to reproduce material from
this work should be sent to:
    Permissions
    University of Texas Press
    P. O. Box 7819
    Austin, Texas 78712

Contents

Preface   ix

Introduction   3

2.   Historical Context of Bolivian Migration
to Argentina   17

3.   Sugar Production and Seasonal Labor:
Labor-Control Mechanisms   29

4.   Recruiters, Canecutters, and the Work Camp   41

5.   Working in the Fields, the Union,
and Postharvest Planning   57

6.   The Multiple Faces of the Labor Reserve   77

7.   Urbanization and Seasonal Migration   91

8.   The Search for Security   109

9.   Different Perspectives of the City   129

10.   Conclusion   151

Notes   157

Bibliography   169

Index   185

Illustrations

Maps

Argentina   13

Provinces of Jujuy and Salta   15

Figures

1. Major Interrelationships of General Proletarian Migration
    Patterns Linking Urbanization with the Zafra in Northwest
    Argentina   89

2. Factors in Development: Rural Seasonal Labor and
    Regional Urbanization   96

Tables

1. Population from Neighboring Countries Settled in
    Argentina 1869-1964   23

2. Percentage of Immigrants from Neighboring Countries
    in the Total Number of Foreigners in Argentina   23

3. Bolivian Emigration by Country, 1967   27

4. Populations of the City of Salta and the
    Province of Salta   94

5. Net Migratory Balance, 1947-1960   97

6. Distribution of the Economically Active in the
    Province of Salta   98

7. Major Planned Allocations of 1971 Zafra Income   126

Preface

The publication of this book has been delayed by my involvement in two events in Mexico. First, I had the good fortune to participate in a major research project with the Centro de Investigaciones Superiores del Instituto Nacional de Antropología e Historia. Second, I had the misfortune of being hit by a small truck in Arriaga, Mexico, and was hospitalized for an extended time. Because of the delay I gave serious thought to not publishing the manuscript. Whenever one allows time to pass between research and publication the contributions may become dated. The research was designed to address issues on social change and urbanization which have since shifted as our understanding and knowledge has grown. On a personal level, some of my assumptions and paradigms have been redefined. Subsequently many questions I would now ask were neglected during my research. In the end, however, I decided to publish the manuscript because the processes investigated remain significant, underexamined, and little changed.

Many people have contributed their talents to this book, although I alone am responsible for the data interpretations and conclusions. I have benefited enormously from the ideas, criticism, and encouragement of many colleagues and mentors. In an early stage Harley Browning, Chad Oliver, and Angel Palerm made valuable suggestions. Morgan Machlachlan and Henry Selby left the University of Texas before my research, but they had introduced me to many of the critical issues in anthropology. Anthony Leeds's pioneering work in urban research and migration forced me to repeatedly reexamine my data and assumptions and to ask new questions. Like many other graduate students at the University of Texas, I am indebted to Richard Schaedel for his continuing interest and wide-ranging knowledge of anthropology and Latin America. I owe a special debt to Richard N. Adams, whose creative analytical approach forced me to look harder and longer for both questions and answers. His friendship, patience, and humor were crucial for me during the research and writing. I would also like to thank the whole Adams family—Betty, Walter, Tani, and Gina—who shared with us their home in Argentina and Austin, as well as our love of Argentina. During the revision of the manuscript William Derman, Terry Hoops, Robert Kemper, Norman Long, Joseph Spielberg, and Douglas Uzzell made helpful comments on different segments.

The research on which this study is based was conducted in Argentina when conditions were more conducive than now for social-science research. It was a period when Argentine social scientists, many now in exile, were doing important research and contributing to the growth of social-science theory. We were fortunate to share in the friendship and knowledge of distinguished scholars such as Eduardo and Kristianne Archetti, Francisco Delich, Esther Hermitte, Carlos Herán, Luis Gatti, Leopoldo Bartolomé, Leleo Mármora, Manuel Martínez, Luis Sappia, and Hebe and Santiago Vessuri. Juan Villar, who has done extensive research on international migration to Argentina, generously shared his material with us. His friendship is greatly appreciated. I would also like to thank Tuco, Elena Oliver, Hector, Walter, Marion, and Padres Haas, Sweeney, and Scheeler for their help. Leon with his friendship and interest provided important support.

Because I wish them to retain their anonymity I cannot thank personally those many individuals on the plantations and in Salta who were so helpful during our research. To them I owe my deepest debt. I hope this book accurately describes the processes and structures of which their lives were a critical part.

A few words of gratitude are due my kin who work in Latin America. My parents patiently supported career changes and were always interested in discussing the research and writing. The insightful ideas of my father, Andrew H. Whiteford, who generously read large sections of the original thesis, not only contributed to this book but also to my love of Latin America and concern for the struggle of the poor. My anthropologically oriented siblings, Michael and Linda, and the one who escaped anthropology, Laurie, have been a constant source of support, criticism, and enjoyment.

From the research in Argentina to the last day of rewriting, my wife, Weegee, has been involved in the project. An accomplished writer in her own right, she has contributed to the book in many ways. She was my best critic and most patient friend. With many close Bolivian and Argentine friends, she has a special appreciation of Argentina in general and Salta in particular.

The research was made possible by a graduate research fellowship from the Ford Foundation and a grant from the National Institute of Mental Health, which funded the Adaptation and Development program at the University of Texas. A National Science Foundation grant made it possible to return to Argentina in the summer of 1974.

Support from the College of Social Science "Scholar Program" and the Department of Anthropology at Michigan State University contributed substantially to the completion of this manuscript. The typing of Ann Featherstone and Olga Muhammad made it possible to meet deadlines.

Finally, I would like to dedicate this book to the workers, Bolivian and Argentine, whose lives we shared and whose futures concern us. We are grateful for the long hours of conversation, for thoughtfully including us in their activities, and for sharing with us their thoughts, hopes, and experiences. I hope this book does justice to their expenditure of time and energy.

Workers from the North: Plantations, Bolivian Labor,
and the City in Northwest Argentina

1. Introduction

Each year in early June thousands of Bolivians and Argentines migrate to the sugar zone of Northwest Argentina, known as the Ramal, for the *zafra*—the five- to seven-month sugar harvest. On the vast plantations they cut and load the ripe cane, which is then taken to company mills for processing. The *lotes* (company work camps) become their temporary home. When the last stalk of cane has been cut, the workers and their families must pack their belongings and leave the plantation. For some this means returning to small landholdings and home. Many others, lacking either land of their own or other means of stable employment, must move to new locations in search of work. For them the postzafra period is a time of great insecurity.

The search for employment takes the workers in many different directions for varying periods of time. Harvesting crops that ripen in different seasons throughout Argentina provides temporary work for many. In the northwestern provinces of Salta and Jujuy workers find jobs on the tobacco, vegetable, and grape farms. Some go much further south to Mendoza, Río Negro, and Mar del Plata to harvest the vegetables, grapes, and apples that grow there. Other workers seek employment in the cities of Argentina. Often men and their families are forced to combine a variety of strategies during the postzafra season, taking work both in towns or cities and in the countryside. Regardless of the type of work or where it is done, however, the jobs are seldom stable or lucrative enough to keep the workers from returning to the zafra the following June. Locked into a cycle of poverty and insecurity, the migrants are victims of a pattern of capitalist development and change over which they have had no control.

This monograph is about Bolivian workers and their families who labor in the plantations, farms, and cities of Northwest Argentina and their struggle for dignity and survival. It is hoped that the ethnographic description will give the reader a sense of their daily life and concerns and of their attempts to cope with the transformations generated by capitalism. On another level the monograph is about the growth of capitalist agriculture and its recruitment of foreign labor, the reproduction and maintenance of a labor reserve, and urbanization.

International Migration

Although most studies of migratory labor or urbanization in Latin America have focused on internal migration, international migration is an important dimension in some areas, where it reflects unequal patterns of development between nations, as well as within nations. The best known case is that of Mexican migration to the United States, but international migration is significant in other parts of Latin America also. Bolivians migrate to Chile and Argentina, Nicaraguans to Costa Rica, Colombians to Venezuela, Haitians to the Dominican Republic (Díaz Santana 1976), Guatemalans to Mexico, and Salvadorans to Honduras. To date this migration has received little attention, either because much of it is clandestine and does not show up in official census material or because it presents methodological problems for the researcher. The same factors are not in play in all of these cases, and there is a need for more research in this area. Mary Kritz and Douglas Gurak (1979: 421) have pointed to the necessity as well as the difficulty of studying international migration between Latin American countries, and they specifically note the paucity of studies that link macrolevel factors with the micro level, which is one of the objectives here.

Foreign workers have played a major role in the expansion of the advanced capitalist countries. The workers usually accept lower wages and more-menial jobs than the native population and often do not collect many of the benefits paid by the host national government, such as pensions and health care, to which they may contribute from their wages. The foreign work force adds another important dimension to the capitalist economic system. It serves as a "regulator of capitalist crisis, cushioning the impact of expansion and contraction of capital" (Burawoy 1976: 1065). When labor needs are high, workers are brought in; when the market retracts, workers are sent home and mechanisms prohibit their reentrance. In this sense there are many important parallels between Bolivian labor in Argentina, Mexican labor in the United States (Cornelius 1978, Haney 1978), and southern Mediterranean workers in the industrialized countries of Europe (Bohning 1972). However, in Argentina foreign-labor immigration is viewed as a means of increasing the population (Torrado 1979: 432), an attitude that sharply contrasts with the policies of Saudi Arabia, for example, or of such European countries as West Germany and Switzerland, where foreign workers are admitted only on a temporary basis and where the possibility of citizenship is slight.

Development, Labor Migration, and Urbanization

Direct recruitment of Bolivian labor by the sugar plantations of Salta and Jujuy played an important role in attracting Bolivians to Argentina. For the plantations the recruitment of foreign labor was but one of a series of mechanisms used to gain access to cheap labor (these mechanisms are examined in chapter 3). As in capitalist agricultural enterprises in other parts of Latin America, the mechanisms included coercive forms of labor bondage, which gave way to semiproletarian wage labor when labor was no longer scarce (Pearse 1975).

In many parts of Latin America seasonal laborers circulate between peasant villages, where they cultivate their subsistence crops, and the plantations or haciendas, where they work for part of the year (Donahue 1975). Often the peasants' ancestors had been forced off the best lands or lost the irrigation waters to the expanding *latifundios* (Whiteford and Henao 1980). As a result their descendants have had to hire out as laborers to supplement their income during the dry or cold seasons. Increased demographic pressures coupled with inaccessibility of new lands and credit have intensified the process.

The circular migration reflects patterns of uneven development associated with dependent capitalism.[1] Some development theorists hypothesized that there was a mutually beneficial relationship between modern and traditional sectors. The traditional sector, characterized by underemployment, limited or nonexistent capital accumulation, and subsistence-oriented production would develop as the modern sector absorbed excess labor and provided capital (Schmid 1967). The modernization paradigm had overlooked the nature of the articulation between the two sectors and the important fact that underdevelopment of the traditional sector, or periphery, is often a product of the development of the center, or metropolitan areas, a pattern that can be traced back to the colonial period (Mafeje 1973, Stavenhagen 1978).

Semiproletarian labor has important advantages for the commercial producer. He can pay the worker only when he needs him; during the rest of the year the worker's family maintains itself by subsistence farming. Despite fluctuations in productivity and the market, labor is reserved for the employer who can easily expand or reduce the number of laborers hired. In order for the producer to receive maximum benefits of this system the state must support and even facilitate the control of the labor force by not enacting or enforcing regulations that protect labor's ability to organize, articulate grievances, or institute reforms. Usually the governments of host countries are less concerned with the plight of foreign workers than with the work conditions of their own citizens. Chapter 3 examines the different mechanisms used by the plantations of Salta and Jujuy to recruit and control seasonal labor. The recruiting of Bolivians was a logical step, initiated when government support for plantation labor policies waned, which resulted in a series of reforms for Argentine workers.

Alain de Janvry (n.d.: 39) points out that the relationship between capitalist agriculture and the peasant sector (which he calls functional dualism) "constitutes temporarily a functional system that symptomizes and embodies the contradictions of peripheral capitalism." He proceeds to suggest that demographic pressure and deterioration of the resource base will generate increasing proletarianization and pauperization.

This process is reflected in the changing character of the labor reserve from which commercial agriculture in Argentina recruits its seasonal workers. Increasingly Argentine plantations are hiring laborers that are proletarians instead of semiproletarians. The former, in contrast to the latter, cannot depend upon the family plot for subsistence after the harvest season. Consequently they are forced to move from one temporary job to another. Many of these families are forced to settle in cities during part of the year, although they remain part of the labor reserve available to rural employers.

This structure and process which links the countryside and city, has received little study in the rich literature on Latin American urbanization, a literature that often fails to discuss the nature of rural-urban linkages beyond the physical act of moving.[2] Similarly, social scientists have generally treated seasonal labor migration as separate and distinct from rural-urban migration. In many cases the two processes may indeed be separate; but they are often generated by the same structural factors and reflect, for many families or individuals, similar tactics. The consequences may also be the same—the population becomes part of a rural-urban labor reserve which can be tapped by rural or urban employers.

The second part of this book focuses on Bolivian seasonal agricultural workers, most without access to land in Bolivia or Argentina, who have moved to the city of Salta.[3] They are compelled to seek a livelihood in a variety of environments in a variety of ways. Most have remained part of a labor reserve for the plantations, yet reside in the city during the post-harvest season.

Here the mixed household economic strategies so crucial for the survival of the peasant and the maintenance of the labor reserve continue to play an important role, although they assume new forms. Mixed strategies are a necessary adaptation to conditions of low pay and underemployment and serve to support a large population at a precarious subsistence level. Most families would prefer to be fully employed but have not been able to get the jobs. Thus the adaptations necessary to cope with the problems of the dependent capitalist economy generate the responses that perpetuate the system. "It is the extremity of their needs, the necessity of taking, if not willingness to take, any wage labor that may become available that renders them a pool of reserve labor"

(Uzzell 1980: 11). While production is individualized (wages are paid to individuals), both consumption and reproduction fall within the domain of the household. Wages of family members are often pooled to maintain the family, including those members who are unemployed (children, the temporarily unemployed, the sick). This system provides security for the individual laborer. Equally important is the role of the family as a unit of reproduction of labor, in terms of both daily subsistence and the biological reproduction of labor.

The Bolivians in Salta would fit many of the traditional definitions of *marginal.* They are excluded from the political decision-making process and do not participate in industrial production and its benefits. Explicitly or implicitly the term *marginal* carries the assumption of a nonfunctional population.[4] Yet the families described in this book are an integral, not marginal, part of the economic structure for both urban and rural employers, providing them with a flexible source of labor.

It has been argued that the unemployed and underemployed in Latin American cities do not promote the expansion of capitalism: they lack the education or skills necessary to compete for industrial jobs, therefore they do not influence the wage structure of the capitalist enterprises. Other authors have pointed out the importance of the underemployed in supporting the expansion of capitalist production by reducing costs in both the service sector and the construction sector of the economy. By maintaining themselves with low-return jobs, constructing their own housing, cultivating subsistence gardens, relying on manual transportation, and engaging in other labor-intensive, low-paying activities, the labor-reserve population plays an important role in subsidizing the expansion of the primary and secondary sectors of the economy (Roberts 1979, Stavenhagen 1978).[5] In many parts of Latin America and Africa, segments of the rural population are more important to the economy for the reproduction of labor than for the production of commodities (Cliffe 1978, Burawoy 1976). In regions such as Northwest Argentina, low-income segments of the urban population increasingly play this same reproductive role. Equally important, families based in a city may be an important source of labor for large farms and plantations, as are many Bolivians and Argentines who live in Salta. Their presence has been used by growers to curb unionization and to keep wages and benefits low.

Ethnography of Migrant Life

The descriptive analysis of migrant life in this study focuses on the concerns and activities of Bolivian migrants, particularly those who have moved to the city of Salta during the postzafra period.[6] Central to their lives are the problems created by the social structure and political economy—specifically unemployment, prolonged periods of disruptive migration, poor housing and health, insecure employment, and limited opportunities for their children. Although the constraints on the poor impose harsher limitations on them than many studies of dynamic marginal neighborhoods and populations indicate, they have not forced those described here to become pawns trapped in a culture of poverty. Rather, the migrants repeatedly demonstrate a creative, enterprising ability to cope.

For the Bolivian migrant, city and countryside have distinctive resources and constraints that require different types of strategies. At the same time most of the migrants remain part of a labor reserve whether their residence is urban or rural. The constraints which structure the labor reserve traverse these boundaries, as do the lives of most migrants. Chapter 5 focuses on families which have taken up temporary residence in the city, most of whom continue to work on the plantations and farms when not laboring in the city. In some cases a family may split up, some working in the countryside while others work in the city. This suggests that the move to the city often is not as abrupt a change of socioeconomic environment as some theorists would lead us to believe.

Decisions made by the Bolivian families in Salta are important in this analysis because they help define the migrants' view of constraints and how they cope with them. The process by which individuals or groups adjust to obtain and use resources in the environment and to cope with the problems confronting them is referred to in the text as adaptation. Adaptation is a process which includes many decisions at varying levels of complexity. Why individuals make different decisions is examined in terms of goals, values, family size, age, information, and resources. Some decisions are made unconsciously (Ortiz 1967); yet as choices are made they in turn influence the types of future choices that are possible (Garbett and Kapferer 1970: 188).

Information is critical for migrants in a new environment. Part of the ethnography considers what type of information the migrants feel is important, how they try to obtain it, and how they deal with risk and uncertainty. This approach leads to examination of the culturally defined alternatives—or distribution of choices—in coping with the constraints, as well as the factors which influence the alternative means or strategies. This approach suggests a basic rational-choice model which if left unmodified would be unacceptable, but the analysis and description presented here take into consideration the non-decision-making context as well.

More importantly, the migrants' decisions and strategies, as the ethnographic material suggests, are not based entirely on monetary calculations. They are made within the context of a social field of relationships, not just in the city but also in the countryside (Garbett and Kapferer 1970). These relationships with friends and family are crucial in an irregular economy in which employment is often short term, low paying, unprotected by insurance or enforcement of labor laws, and possibly illegal. Information about job opportunities, the character of employers, work conditions, and other factors becomes critical in this context. Networks are important sources for this information, as well as being a form of social insurance during periods of unemployment. In addition, they significantly affect ethnic and social identity—important elements in successful adjustment to new environments.

The analysis of social networks provides the social scientist with a "middle-range level of abstraction situated between the large-scale social structure and the individual" (Wolf 1970: 227). Networks are seldom native categories (Lomnitz 1977: 132), yet the individuals and families described on the following pages did not have terms for key people in what were, in essence, social networks. They made conscious efforts to develop social capital and were acutely aware of its significance in their lives. Different qualities of networks can be measured using a variety of interactional or structural criteria (Boissevain 1974, Mitchell 1969a). This measurement can be most useful for comparative purposes or to show change over time, but the crucial dimension of change in network structure is what the change means to the people involved (Mayer 1961). In this study it was not possible to quantify changes in networks over time. Instead networks were used to focus the analysis on the exchange of goods and services between friends, including family, and the subsequent significance this played in the adaptive process.

Underlying the behavior of many low-income Bolivians in Salta is the belief that there are ways to reduce, but not eliminate, their vulnerability to the socioeconomic conditions. This belief was expressed in many ways, both verbally and in terms of actions. Their adaptations that are predicated on this belief are referred to as the "strategy of least vulnerability." Formal and informal organizations as well as networks play a potentially important role in this strategy. The possibility that an individual will participate in groups depends on a number of factors, including individual trust (Roberts 1973), efficacy or trust in group leadership (Gamson 1968), a sense of class consciousness, the individual's economic condition, and the characteristics of the environment. Robert Dirks (1972: 566), in his study of an Afro-Caribbean community in the British Virgin Islands, suggests that "networks and groups comprise the structural framework for a balanced set of adaptive strategies geared to the exploitation of fundamentally different sorts of resources present in the same environment." The materials in this study show that although different types of cooperation are necessary to exploit different environments, in some cases the amount of cooperation that individuals can generate is influenced by the characteristics of the socioeconomic environment as well as their culture. Stable residence permits a greater degree of organization, just as the higher the income is, the more time and effort can be put into organizations. The ability to participate in stronger associations enhances one's ability to survive in the environment (Whiteford and Adams 1975).

Most patterns of rural-urban migration reported in the literature enhance the migrants' ability to maintain close ties with family and friends. The studies on urbanization document the strong ties the migrants maintain with their home communities and with fellow villagers living in the city, ties maintained through social networks and associations. In these cases the migrants are villagers who have moved directly or in a limited number of steps to the city.[7] Yet some migrants do not come from cohesive nuclear settlements and have been highly mobile with a high degree of geographic unpredictability over a prolonged period of time. How and why this happens to some Bolivian families in Argentina and not to others and its effect upon these families is examined in chapters 6 and 9, drawing together once more the macro and micro levels of analysis.

Research

Many anthropologists doing field work in Latin America have continued to use the "community study method," focusing on relatively small, spatially delineated residence units such as villages or neighborhoods. Generally the field work has been oriented toward participant observation, based on close personal contact with the informants and long residence in the community. Although this approach has produced a wealth of information, it has tended to restrict the types of problems that can be successfully delineated. The method has stressed "localized internal factors" at the expense of "external variables" (Devons and Gluckman 1964: 200). The limitations of this approach have been aptly discussed by Steward (1955), Leeds (1965 and 1969), and Adams (1967), among others. This is not to say that the community study method has not contributed nor will not contribute insightful material; to the contrary, it is an important approach to research.

An ethnography of migrant life that would contribute to the understanding of the migrants' daily lives and social organization, as well as of the factors generating contraints, required participant observation and close relationships. Yet to focus on a limited number of families in a single locality for an entire year was out of the question. If this had been done, the migrant worker would have been available only during the time he was "passing through" the designated spot. Thus I had to use another approach, which could accommodate limited time, energy, and resources.

One method employed in a study of African migration used questionnaires and caught migrants as they passed through transportation points (Caldwell

1969). Although this approach provided a great deal of data, I decided not to use it because I did not want to give up what I feel is one of the key aspects of anthropological research: prolonged personal contact and observation. If one is to study migrant agricultural workers, then one must himself migrate. But this requires a tactical decision. With whom does one migrate, and how does this affect the data?

One approach would have been to do a study of a Bolivian village and then follow migrants from the village to the Argentine zafra. Because of the constraints of time and resources and the nature of the research problem, this idea was discarded. Although some migrants maintained close contact with their home villages, others had never had contact with specific villages or their contact was insignificant. For many rural proletarians in the process of urbanization, the work camps and the city were the two most important parts of their social field. For this reason I decided on a compromise, dividing my time between a plantation and a city. While living on the plantation work camp I tried to gather as much information as possible about the different postzafra destinations of the migrant families. Then after the zafra, I selected one postzafra work site for intensive study: the city of Salta. We lived there for the duration of the postzafra season, returning to the plantation the following year. My wife and I also visited people we had known on the plantation in their home villages in southern Bolivia, on farms in Northwest Argentina, and in other Argentine communities. While living in Salta I regularly visited farms in the province where Salta-based Bolivians worked.

The field-work methods ranged from participant observation to structured interviews. A considerable amount of time was allocated to gathering and analyzing census material, studies by provincial governments, and historical records. Throughout the study I relied heavily on detailed life histories and in-depth, detailed open-ended interviews to gather data about the whole migratory process and to link and differentiate various migratory and adaptive patterns. Genealogies and family budgets were taken for selected families. A short questionnaire was given to a random sample of heads of households in plantation work camps. Another was given to rural semiproletarians who returned to one village in Bolivia after the zafra. In Salta questionnaires were administered to a random sample in three low-income neighborhoods and to a sample of rural-urban *zafreros* (sugar-cane cutters). Including additional interviews with permanent plantation workers, former zafreros, foremen, labor recruiters, agronomists, farm owners and administrators, city officials and urban employers, more than two thousand interviews were conducted over an eighteen-month period.

The Region

The provinces of Salta and Jujuy are the northernmost provinces in Argentina, which along with Tucumán, Santiago del Estero, and Catamarca make up the area known as the Northwest. Salta and Jujuy are the only Argentine provinces to border Bolivia. In addition they share widely diverse geographical features. Peaks of the arid, rugged Andes reach more than nineteen thousand feet above sea level. Broad valleys cut through the Andean mountains in places and are the primary sites of peasant agriculture. A long subtropical tongue known as the Ramal extends through both Salta and Jujuy. Bordered on the west by a chain of the Andes, this fertile valley stretches roughly north to south from the town of Tartagal in the northern extreme of Salta, past the foothills surrounding the booming little commercial town of San Pedro, Jujuy, to the town of Güemes, Salta. Besides being a hinterland for the provincial capital cities of Salta and Jujuy, as well as Buenos Aires, it is one of the two main sugar zones of Argentina.

The oldest and more important sugar zone is Tucumán, but the Ramal of Salta and Jujuy, known in the sugar industry as El Norte, is growing faster. These two competing sugar zones are very different from one another. In Tucumán most of the cane is grown by small, independent producers who own most of the land and sell their harvests to the mills. A large number of them are peasants who own small pieces of land (Delich 1970: 39-40, Vessuri 1977). In contrast, the sugar production of Salta and Jujuy is dominated by five major plantations that produce most of the cane they mill. Although there are thirty-six independent growers, their percentage of the total production in the region is minimal.

Agriculture of the Ramal is dominated by sugar cane. The main, two-lane highway that runs the length of the Ramal from Orán to Güemes is like a thin slash cut through an almost solid horizon of verdant cane fields. The borders of the towns in the region end abruptly as the vast sea of cane fields sweeps right up to their edges. Here and there, in small pockets not owned by the major plantations, are the little towns like Fraile Pintado, around which other crops such as flowers, tomatoes, onions, and citrus fruits are grown. Farmers in these areas must compete with the plantations for labor during the zafra, but in post-zafra periods, when their labor needs peak, there is a surplus of potential farm workers. Some of the major plantations also allocate a small percentage of their acreage to growing choice oranges, grapefruits, and avocados bound for the Buenos Aires market.

The economy of the Ramal is dominated by the major sugar plantations. The towns of San Pedro, Orán, Libertador, and to a lesser extent Güemes, are all in one way or another economically dependent on the neighboring plantations,

even though they are not themselves plantation towns. During the sweltering summer months of the postzafra season, these towns are relatively still and inactive. With the beginning of the zafra, vendors and workers, particularly those who work in the mills, pour into the towns seeking rooms, as do truckers hired by the companies to haul cane. In addition, both temporary and permanent workers come to these towns to buy clothing, kitchen equipment, some food items, and to be entertained.

The city of Salta (population 180,696 in 1970) is the capital of Salta province and the largest city in the Salta-Jujuy region. A major trade center during the colonial period, Salta's importance in Argentina has greatly diminished with the growth and development of distant Buenos Aires and the littoral region of the country. The elegant colonial architecture of many of the buildings surrounding the lovely central plaza indicates the power of the oligarchy, which has long dominated the Salta social structure. These owners of plantations, farms, haciendas, and urban businesses have historically played key roles in the economic and political history of the region.

In contrast to cities in well-known studies of urbanization (Monterrey, Mexico City, Lima, Rio de Janeiro, and Buenos Aires), Salta is neither large nor important industrially—a fact which is evident from the clean air and scarcity of permanent work for its low-income residents. Although the employment picture is not encouraging, the city offers other compensations, not least of which is its climate. The Lerma Valley, where the city is nestled, has perhaps the most delightful climate in Argentina. Summer days are warm but not uncomfortable, and nights are cool. Although winter weather is sometimes raw, it is not uncommon for midday temperatures to reach into the 70s as the sun warms the city. The rich and varied agricultural regions surrounding Salta, including the sugar zone already described, contribute to the thriving commercial activity in the city. Modern buses link Salta to the outlying regions, giving rural workers easy access to the city and urban residents access to the countryside.

Along with a steady stream of migrants from villages in the highlands and outlying valleys, Bolivian immigrants of diverse backgrounds have entered Salta. Some are political refugees, merchants, or temporary sojourners, but the vast majority are low-income families seeking work and hoping to settle in the city. Many have worked or still work on plantations and farms during periods of the year.

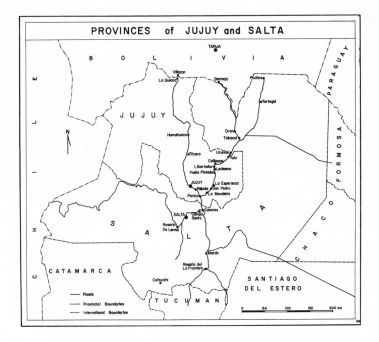

2. Historical Context of Bolivian Migration to Argentina

Large-scale immigration to Argentina during the last one hundred years has come from two different world areas: Europe and neighboring Latin American countries. Migrants from both areas were drawn to Argentina by the promise of participating in Argentina's economic prosperity and by dire conditions in their homelands. Agricultural developments coupled with government policies facilitating international migration drew foreign laborers, many of them seasonal, to harvest crops. The cultivation of the vast, rich pampas was the earliest and most important agricultural development in terms of numbers of laborers, primarily Italian and Spanish. Later, and of particular interest for this monograph, was the large-scale commercial cultivation of sugar cane and tobacco in the provinces of Salta and Jujuy, which created a demand for seasonal workers, many of whom were recruited in Bolivia. In both cases international seasonal migration evolved into permanent settlement of foreign laborers in Argentina.

Migration is a symptom of basic regional differences in resources. Factors which influence the distribution as well as the selective availability of specific resources such as employment opportunities within certain sectors of the economy are the focus of this chapter, not the migration per se.[1] International migration to Argentina, particularly Bolivian, is put into the macro-context of socioeconomic change in Argentina and abroad. It shows that the control of land, changing markets for agricultural produce, and technological developments played key roles in influencing immigration to Argentina.[2] A significant number of foreign migrants came to Argentina as seasonal laborers, remained in Argentina but—not finding opportunities in the countryside—moved to the city. (This process as it applies to Bolivian immigrants is more closely examined in later chapters.)

There were many differences between colonial Bolivia and colonial Argentina. Bolivia's highland population provided labor in the mines and for Spanish landlords, who dominated large parts of the country. A pattern of subordination and dependence on the part of the large native population was established during this period. In contrast, colonial Argentina had neither the vast quantities of precious metals nor a large aboriginal population the Spaniard could utilize as laborers. As a result, Argentina was not a center of early Spanish colonization. In 1776 the Viceroyalty of the Río de la Plata was created, which, coupled with the Free Trade Regulation of 1778, led to increasing involvement of the region in international trade. Nevertheless, at the time of independence in 1816 Argentina was a vast, sparsely populated country.

Argentine leaders such as Domingo Sarmiento felt that in order to modernize Argentina needed to increase its population. In the mid-1850s the country began a series of colonization projects, giving out land to attract European immigrants. But by the end of the nineteenth century a series of changes took place which altered this program and the subsequent pattern of migration and development. English industry had started to expand, rapidly increasing the demand for foodstuffs. Major technological breakthroughs occurred: refrigeration was developed as a means of preserving meat; barbed wire and the reaper and thresher were invented and marketed. Argentine agricultural producers could now utilize the great expanses of undeveloped land to produce food for the European market and were no longer willing to give land to immigrants.

Instead of agricultural colonization, they needed seasonal laborers and tenant farmers to work and develop their lands. Immigration policy was changed to bring workers from Europe to plow the pampas, plant wheat, and then convert the fields to alfalfa for the owners' cattle. When the task was completed they were forced to move along to repeat the process elsewhere. Between 1886 and 1890 more than 600,000 immigrants (mostly Spanish and Italian) were brought to Argentina to harvest crops. They earned five to ten times what they could have earned in their homeland (Scobie 1964b: 61). By the early twentieth century more than 100,000 migrated to Argentina annually.

After a brief recession during the 1890s, Argentina enjoyed economic growth until the beginning of World War I. Foreign capital poured into the country. Between 1857 and 1914 Argentina received a third of all foreign capital invested in Latin America (Ferrer 1967: 89). The economic booms of 1882-1889 and 1904-1912 in part were owing to the development of agriculture. Prior to 1870 Argentina had imported wheat; her only important exports had been wool, hides, and tallow. By 1914, however, Argentina had become the leading exporter of beef and mutton and the third largest exporter of wheat, mostly to England (Merkx 1968: 45).

During this period of economic growth the Argentine sugar industry expanded rapidly, partly in response to increased internal consumption. Despite early beginnings in Tucumán, possibly as early as 1646, sugar production did not become important until the nineteenth century. "The sugar industry began to develop only after national officials recognized Tucumán's military and commercial importance and made plans to extend the Córdoba railroad to Tucumán" (Guy 1973: 7). The Tucumán-Córdoba railroad was finished in 1877, and sugar production in Tucumán rose rapidly thereafter. In 1872 Tucumán produced 1,200 metric tons of sugar. By 1889 the production reached 40,843 metric tons; it peaked in 1896 with the production of 135,605 metric tons (Centro Azucarero Argentino 1954: 217).

At the time the railroad was being extended to Tucumán, Jujuy congressmen were making unsuccessful efforts to bring the railroad to their province. Sugar had been cultivated in Salta and Jujuy since at least the mid-eighteenth century, but in limited quantities. The railroad connecting Jujuy and Tucumán was not started until 1882, when it was deemed necessary in order to capture potential Bolivian trade from Chile after the War of the Pacific (Guy 1973: 80). It was finished almost a decade later. The completion of the railroad had two repercussions. First, the production of sugar in the Norte (sugar zone of Salta and Jujuy) doubled in 1912, and by 1923 it totaled 40,000 metric tons, twice that of the previous year. This was 15 percent of the national production. Even so there was a need for greater output, as Argentina was still importing sugar at this time. From 1926 on, with the exception of 1942, the country was self-sufficient in sugar. The second consequence of the completion of the railroad seems to have been an increase in Bolivian migration to Argentina, especially to Jujuy, where the Bolivian population jumped from 3,779 in 1895 to 12,854 in 1914 (National Census). Some of the Bolivians came to work on the construction of the railroad. Others found work in agriculture, including the expanding plantations, although most of the seasonal workers at this time came from the peasant populations of the provinces of Jujuy, Catamarca, Santiago del Estero, and Salta.

During this period, Bolivia itself was undergoing change. Tin had become a major export and the private sector of the economy expanded rapidly, including some growth of light industry. But these changes did not affect the dire conditions in the rural areas. The building of roads and railroads provided easier access from villages to cities and increased individual mobility. Bolivian cities grew rapidly. La Paz had a population of 70,000 in 1900 but was a city of 115,000 twenty years later (Klein 1969: 59). Migrants moved to the cities or to Argentina to escape the poverty of being landless workers dependent on landowners or, in extreme cases, on tenant farmers (Heyduk 1974: 78; Buechler 1970: 40-42).

Despite an increase in Bolivian migrants in Argentina between 1895 and 1914, their proportion of the total immigrant population in Argentina changed only .1 percent because of the tremendous influx of European migrants during the same period. In 1914, migration to Argentina from neighboring Latin

American countries (Brazil, Bolivia, Chile, Paraguay, and Uruguay) accounted for only 9 percent of the total number of immigrants to Argentina. This proportion increased steadily during the following years as the scale of European migration decreased with the improvement of economic conditions in Europe and the growth of the labor pool in Argentina, in which mechanization of agriculture was a factor. With the beginning of World War I, international mobility decreased still further.

Between World War I and the Depression beginning in 1929, economic growth slowed in Argentina. Investment of foreign capital fell off drastically and the railroads were basically completed, no longer opening new areas to overseas markets. Despite the coming to power of the Radical Party, liberal economic policies were followed, which favored export of agricultural produce and import of industrial goods.

In 1930, as economic conditions deteriorated, President Hipólito Yrigoyen was overthrown by a conservative army coup. Exports continued to decline as the purchasing power of the European market fell. For the first time, after 1930, the agricultural sector found it advantageous to have industry grow in order to provide the necessities of the agricultural sector and a market for agricultural produce (Merkx 1968: 172). Import duties were raised, a bilateral trade agreement with England was established, and income and excise tax reforms were implemented. Laissez-faire policies were displaced by a policy of greater government intervention (Merkx 1968: 339). As a result, the small industrial sector grew rapidly during this period, expanding the job market in Buenos Aires. Between 1935 and 1946 there was a tremendous growth of the industrial labor force; the annual growth rate was almost 12 percent. By 1946 more than one million people were working in industry, mainly in the Buenos Aires area (Merkx 1968: 190).

The massive industrial boom in Buenos Aires, coupled with the inability of the agricultural sector to absorb labor, led to massive rural-urban migration after 1930, much of it to Buenos Aires. Between 1934 and 1943 an average of 85,000 new migrants arrived annually in greater Buenos Aires, approximately 72,000 coming from the interior. This process accelerated between 1943 and 1947 (Germani 1955: 74). Between 1936 and 1960 it is estimated that about 2,000,000 migrants from the interior became established in Buenos Aires (Mármora 1973: 68). The migrants from the interior became known as *cabecitas negras*[3] (little black heads), a derogatory term used by some elements of the host population. They could be distinguished from much of the population of primarily European origin by their physical appearance and their speech.

The impact of World War II was felt throughout the Argentine economy. First came the major decline of industrial imports as Europe and the United States focused their energies on the war effort. This helped Argentine industry, though in many cases the lack of key materials or equipment created a serious bottleneck in production. Meanwhile, agricultural exports were maintained throughout most of the period. In London foreign currency rapidly accumulated for Argentina, which led the agricultural elite to push for free trade. Conflict between the industrial elite and the agricultural elite intensified, with the conservative government supporting the latter (Merkx 1968: 192-198). In 1943, when economic growth slowed and election of arch conservative Robustiano Patrón Costas as president seemed probable, the unpopular conservative government was overthrown by the military. The military favored the industrial sector and pushed for its expansion.

When Juan Domingo Perón came to power with the small group of army officers in the coup of June 1943, he recognized the political potential of the working classes and utilized it to the advantage of all parties involved: "Major unions in the meat-packing and transportation fields became his disciplined followers, and membership increased rapidly as the government for the first time helped labor win concrete advantages. Through policies and programs which he continued as president, Perón became the savior of the *descamisados* or 'shirtless ones'[4]" (Scobie 1964a: 233).

Immediately upon taking office in 1946 Perón set in action policies of import substitution, nationalization of foreign firms, and industrial growth. During the first part of his presidency, Argentina enjoyed great prosperity and growth. It was a period of tremendous change. Foreign utilities and railroads were nationalized, national airlines and merchant fleets were established, major social legislation was passed, and labor became a powerful political force. The working man was one of the main beneficiaries of Perón's programs.

> For several years, at least until overwhelmed by the tide of inflation, the total increases in the working man's real wages ranged from 10 to 50 per cent. Labor's share of the national income rose from 45 per cent in 1945 to over 60 per cent by 1950. Workers began to enjoy unprecedented privileges. The factory laborer and his family received paid vacations and special excursions which permitted them to visit the beaches of Mar del Plata or the scenic beauties of Córdoba and Bariloche. Working hours became shorter while retirement and medical benefits increased. Ceilings were placed on food and transportation prices and the government began building low-cost housing projects. The working man could now own a locally made bicycle, radio, refrigerator, or washing machine. (Scobie 1964a: 233-234).

With the government controlling the press and radio as well as education, Peronista propaganda reached large segments of the populace neglected by previous regimes. The lower classes became politicized and for the first time were made to feel important. Perón and his wife, Eva Duarte (affectionately known as Evita) made constant appeals to the descamisados. A massive state welfare agency was organized by Evita; its charities were further publicity for Perón's concern for the lower classes.

Perón's favoring of industry over agriculture gave added impetus to the exodus from the interior to the coast and the cities, as did improved living standards offered in urban centers. The numbers of laborers and servants in the capital city and Rosario were augmented by the cabecitas negras, who vigorously supported Perón (Scobie 1964a: 234).

The massive rural-urban migration in Argentina was accompanied by another type of migration—migration from neighboring Latin American countries. Between 1914 and 1947, the number of Paraguayan migrants increased from 18,600 to 93,200; Chileans increased from 34,600 to 51,600; and Bolivians increased from 18,300 to 47,800. The number of Brazilians also increased, but the number of Uruguayans decreased (see table 1).

Migrants from neighboring countries began to constitute a higher and higher percentage of the total number of foreigners in Argentina, as shown in table 2. According to the 1947 census 13 percent of the migrants in Argentina were from neighboring countries, compared to 9 percent in 1914 (Recursos Humanos 1973: 6).

At the time of the 1947 census, almost 88 percent of the Bolivian migrants in Argentina were in the provinces of Salta and Jujuy (Recursos Humanos 1973: chart 7).[5] Many found work on tobacco farms and sugar plantations. In the period between 1923 and 1940, sugar production of the plantations of the Norte had climbed from 15 percent to 27 percent of the total national output. The 1940s was a period of considerable change in the sugar industry of Salta and Jujuy. Production fluctuated, falling in 1942 but rising again and holding during the rest of the decade. Some of the traditional seasonal labor was drawn to Buenos Aires by the burgeoning industries, which left the plantation increasingly in need of labor. During this period the Peronist government supported the development of unions on the plantations and strikes occurred as labor began to exercise its new muscle. Many plantations responded by sending labor recruiters to Bolivia to hire men without work permits, who as illegal immigrants could not turn to the government for help. Their recruitment served to weaken the union movement. In some cases Bolivians replaced Argentine labor that had moved south; in other cases they displaced Argentines by accepting lower wages. More and more, they found work, sometimes a series of jobs, year round in Argentina. A growing number eventually migrated to Buenos Aires.

Many Bolivians were willing to go to Argentina at this time because of the situation at home. Prior to the agrarian reform the departments of southern Bolivia were dominated by the haciendas. In payment for a plot of land on the

Table 1
Population from Neighboring Countries Settled in Argentina
1869-1964
(in thousands)

Country of Origin	1869	1895	1914	1947	1960	1964
Paraguay	3.3	14.6	18.6	93.2	216.0	271.6
Chile	10.9	20.6	34.6	51.6	99.1	124.2
Bolivia	6.2	7.4	18.3	47.8	89.6	121.3
Uruguay	15.1	48.6	88.7	73.6	72.5	64.4
Brazil	5.9	24.7	36.6	47.0	44.4	46.6
Total	41.4	115.9	196.8	313.2	521.6	628.1

Source: Elaborated by Marcenaro Boutell, using national censuses and his own estimations (cited in Panettieri 1960: 139).

Table 2
Percentage of Immigrants from Neighboring Countries
in the Total Number of Foreigners in Argentina

Year	Bolivians	Brazilians	Chileans	Paraguayans	Uruguayans	Total
1869	2.9	2.8	5.2	1.6	7.2	20
1895	0.7	2.5	2.0	1.5	4.8	11
1914	0.8	1.5	1.4	1.2	3.7	9
1947	2.0	2.0	2.1	3.8	3.0	13
1960	3.4	1.9	4.5	6.0	2.1	18
1970	—	—	—	—	—	—

Source: Mármora 1973: 70.

hacienda, *arrendatarios* (tenant renters) had to work a varying number of days for their *patrón* (employer), in some cases up to 150 days a year. Charles J. Erasmus (1969: 95-96) states that arrendatarios were afraid to leave one hacienda for another "with fewer obligations because their old patrón might do them bodily harm." Some of these men found greater freedom by moving to Argentina. Another group exploited by the hacienda system were the *arrimantes*. These men rented land from an arrendatario in exchange for performing most of the arrendatario's obligations to the patrón, plus working on the arrendatario's plot for free (Erasmus 1969: 2). Again it is not surprising that they would risk going to Argentina to do seasonal work.

As more and more Bolivians migrated to work on the plantations and on the developing tobacco farms during the late 1930s and early 1940s, the Argentine government was forced to reexamine its immigration regulations, which until that time had been directed at European immigrants. The government received further impetus from reports that Bolivians were competing with Argentines for jobs and that migrants without documents were being paid extremely low wages. In 1949, Decree 1.162 established punishment for those who gave work or aid to illegal immigrants. Although various decrees were passed during the next six years, the most important were 24.104 and 24.666. The former, passed in 1949, permitted employers to hire foreign workers for a period not exceeding a year; the latter, passed in the same year, was designed to help migrants obtain Argentine residence papers for a limited period (Villar 1972: 34-39). Although these laws were not enforced on plantations in the Northwest, they indicate an effort to deal with the increasingly important problem of migration from neighboring countries.

Between 1947 and 1960 the sugar industry grew intermittently. After a slight decline in production in the early 1950s, the plantations of the Norte experienced significant growth during the latter part of the decade, with production increasing almost 45 percent. Large numbers of laborers, many Bolivian, were used to clear and prepare the land during the postzafra season.

The tobacco farms in Salta and Jujuy were also important sources of employment for Bolivian migrants. In 1937 there was no record of tobacco cultivation in the province of Jujuy. Between 1937 and 1947, 3165.8 acres of tobacco were brought into production, equaling 5.7 percent of the national total. By 1960 the acreage planted in tobacco had increased to 115,236, representing almost 14 percent of the national total. Tobacco production began at an earlier date in the province of Salta, where 9.6 percent of the total national acreage of tobacco was planted. Over the next ten years this percentage grew to 15.4 percent, and by 1960 it was 23.9 percent. The periods of major tobacco expansion are important because tobacco production requires large numbers of seasonal laborers, many of whom came to the tobacco farms from Bolivia, either directly or after the Argentine sugar harvest.

Although the Bolivian revolution of 1952 and the subsequent agrarian reform brought about a major change, they did not bring increased prosperity to many peasants. According to Daniel Heyduk (1974: 78) "tenants gained in most cases only in the cancellation of their rent obligations." He goes on to point out that "subtenants and landless dependents were not affected by the reform and remained obligated to former tenants for the payment of rent. They also remained without secure possession of the land they worked." Furthermore, during the postreform period the cost of living rose drastically;

between 1955 and 1956, it increased by 132 percent (Thorn 1971: 186). The agrarian reform in Bolivia did not provide the credit, marketing, and transportation systems needed by many of the peasants. Over the next ten years small holdings were divided or sold off by many families, erosion and overutilization of marginal lands led to decreasing productivity, and population growth contributed to a process of proletarianization. Many of the peasants and laborers hoped to improve their lives by migrating to Argentina, at first seasonally to work in the sugar harvest in Salta and Jujuy and later permanently, moving from one harvest to another in different parts of the country.

Although Bolivia was struggling with economic problems during the 1950s, Argentina too had its problems. The decline in national production in 1949 and 1952 began a cycle of decline that was to plague Argentina every four years, thereafter occurring in 1956, 1959, 1962-1963, 1966, and 1969-1970 (Merkx 1968). After Perón was removed from office in the military coup of 1955, General Pedro Aramburu attempted to reestablish the economy by helping the agricultural sector. In 1957 Aramburu helped the plantations of the Norte by passing Decree 3.958, officially encouraging recruitment of Bolivian labor. This was followed by the Convenio Argentino-Boliviano of 1958, the first agreement between Bolivia and Argentina to deal with migration. It was intended to help implement the bracero program by giving the Bolivian migrant workers legal protection (Villar 1972: 43). The convenio stipulated that the Bolivian government would permit healthy men to leave the country to work in Argentina. Upon entering Argentina they would be given a physical examination; if a worker passed, he would receive an identification card that authorized him to work in Argentina for six months. Giving work to foreigners without proper documentation was declared illegal. Employment conditions and sanitation for the workers were to be controlled by the Ministry of Labor and the Ministry of Public Health and Social Assistance, respectively. The Bolivian consul was to help protect the braceros from irregularities in work contracts, and the Bolivian Ministry of Public Health was given the right to inspect work sites in Argentina. Finally, it was stipulated that Bolivian braceros would be able to return to Bolivia with articles of necessity worth up to five thousand Argentine pesos. Despite the importance of the agreement, many aspects were not enforced by either the Bolivian or the Argentine government. Its main effect was to facilitate the bracero migration for employers.

When the United States curtailed its trade with Cuba in 1960, after the Revolution, and began purchasing sugar from other sources, including Argentina, sugar production in the Norte expanded rapidly again and led to the recruitment of more Bolivian labor (Villar 1972: 143). The 1960 census reported 89,600 Bolivians in Argentina, an increase of 41,800 since the 1947 census. In the provinces of Salta and Jujuy the Bolivian migrant population fell to 76.9 percent of the total number of Bolivians living in Argentina; an increasing number were recorded in Mendoza and Buenos Aires, which suggests increased migratory penetration into the country.

In 1963 a second Convenio Argentino-Boliviano was signed, followed by *decretos de amistad* (friendship decrees) in 1964 and 1965, which helped large numbers of Bolivians obtain residence papers. The plantations were forced to hire only workers with documents, a requirement acceptable to them because by this time there was an overabundance of seasonal labor in the Northwest. This labor surplus, plus the increasing mechanization which put further constraints on the labor population, meant that wages could be kept low. Nevertheless many Bolivians stayed year round in Argentina as laborers, finding work in the growing tobacco production in Salta and Jujuy. Between 1960 and 1968 the tobacco acreage in Jujuy more than doubled, rising to 286,000 acres, or 20.9 percent of the national tobacco acreage. Tobacco production in Salta also increased over this period as the acreage planted rose from 19,707 acres to 31,020 acres. It was estimated that at this time 10,856 seasonal workers were necessary for the harvest period (Provincia de Salta 1969: 198).

Between 1960 and 1965 the production of the sugar plantations of the Norte rose 55 percent, totaling 33 percent of the national production, this despite the fact that the Tucumán sugar industry was also expanding rapidly. In 1965 overproduction caused a major sugar crisis in Argentina. Federal troops closed seven of Tucumán's most financially troubled mills in August 1966, reducing the number of mills to nineteen. Production quotas were allocated to each producer. In the Norte production dropped during 1966 and 1967 but recovered during the following years. By 1970 the Norte was producing 40 percent of the sugar in the country.

Despite the frustrations caused by the stop-go cycles of the economy, Argentina remained a relatively prosperous country with a large industrial labor force and middle class. The economy grew 3 percent annually between 1946 and 1966, but when population increase is considered, per capita increase amounted to only 1.5 percent (Merkx 1968: 310).

Although the cycles of inflation and recession caused Argentines considerable distress, Argentina continued to attract migrants from neighboring countries because of the job opportunities for low-income people. Until the mid-1940s immigrants from neighboring Latin American countries moved into regions and sectors of the economy that were expanding, but after this period the immigration was absorbed by regions and sectors which were not expanding: "Between 1950 and 1970 immigration was seen by certain economic sectors as a means of increasing the mass of unskilled workers, the losses of revenue are transferred to the workers. However, since the immigrants' incomes in their home countries were considerably inferior to those in Argentina, the wages offered were attractive for the immigrants but not the natives" (Carrón 1979: 487). According to one report, by 1969, 350,000 Chileans, 600,000 Paraguayans, 80,000 Brazilians, and 100,000 Uruguayans lived in Argentina (Rocheau, Perridón, Pedisic 1969: 18). This same report estimates that in 1969, 450,000 Bolivians lived in Argentina. But there are other estimates of the Bolivian population in Argentina in the late 1960s and early 1970s. P. Federico Aguiló and Luis Llano Saavedra (1968: 51-52) stated that in 1966 the Bolivians in Argentina totaled 212,833; in 1970 the technical secretary of the Argentine Catholic Commission on Immigration reported a figure of 600,000 Bolivians; and Frederic Hicks suggested a Bolivian population of 780,000 in Argentina. Less than 200,000, Hicks claimed (1968: 392-393), were migrants who worked in the zafra and then returned to Bolivia; another 100,000 looked for work in Argentina after the zafra.[6] Over 500,000 Bolivians lived in the *villas miserias* (slums) in the Argentine cities, especially Buenos Aires.[7]

The wide variation among these estimates suggests the difficulty of obtaining exact information on Bolivian migration to Argentina. According to a high-ranking official in the Office of Migration in charge of the five northwestern provinces, there were at least 70,000 Bolivians in the province of Salta in 1973, but the 1970 census recorded only 26,341 foreigners in the entire province.[8] When asked about the discrepancy between the two figures, the official said that for every Bolivian who enters Argentina legally, three enter illegally. Those entering illegally are not recorded as foreigners.[9]

While Argentina receives the vast majority of Bolivians who leave their homeland (approximately 70 percent in 1967), Bolivians do migrate to other countries. Table 3 shows the numbers and the percentages of Bolivians who in 1967 had migrated to Argentina, Chile, Peru, Brazil, and the United States.[10]

Table 3
Bolivian Emigration by Country, 1967

Country	Population	%
Argentina	212,833	70.0
Chile	53,992	17.8
Peru	12,303	4.0
Brazil	11,820	3.9
United States	6,220	2.0
Rest of Latin America	2,933	1.0
Europe	3,918	1.3
Total	304,019	100.0

Source: Aguiló and Saavedra (1968: 51).

Considering that the total population of Bolivia was approximately 4,350,000 at this time, the number of Bolivians living outside their homeland is particularly significant.

Today, as in earlier decades, Bolivians leave their homeland for a variety of reasons. Low pay, lack of resources and credit, limited access to land and irrigation, civil conflict, and limited employment opportunities combine to pressure people to look for new sources of income. Argentina, for many Bolivians, continues to be a land of opportunity. Many workers prefer to go to the Argentine zafra rather than to the zafra in Santa Cruz, Bolivia. Higher wages are one crucial reason. According to Hiber Conteris (1970: 53), in 1965 a worker earned 512 pesos in Argentina for each ton of cane "stripped, lopped, carried, stacked, and loaded." This was equivalent to 30,720 Bolivian pesos. William J. McEwen (1969: 23) also reports that Bolivians could earn more in six or seven months in Argentina than they could in the vineyards of their home community. Not only did they earn more working in the Argentine zafra, but they felt they received better medical care and housing and could buy better food than they could in the Bolivian zafra. In some Bolivian communities seasonal workers who return from Argentina may be called *campesinos civilizados,* because of their experiences abroad and because they have acquired luxuries such as radios, beds, and watches with their zafra earnings (McEwen 1969: 35-43). Though many Bolivians return home from Argentina, many others stay to become part of a labor pool drawn upon by both urban and rural Argentine employers for short periods at low wages.

3. Sugar Production and Seasonal Labor: Labor-Control Mechanisms

Along with sugar, the Europeans who colonized Latin America brought with them the institution of the plantation—a tool and product of earlier colonization efforts that trace as far back as the European colonies in Palestine following the First Crusade (Verlinden 1970). The establishment of plantations in the New World was based on a series of factors: capital, land, inexpensive labor, political support, and access to markets. In Latin America during the seventeenth and eighteenth centuries, technology, markets, and capital were provided by the European countries in order to "develop" plantation regions, particularly the tropical lowlands.

Plantations depend upon large numbers of laborers who can be paid low wages. Historically this has been accomplished by "disrupting indigenous societies or importing whole new populations" (Mandle 1972: 58). During the colonial period in Latin America the plantations established in the sparsely settled tropical lowlands imported slaves. In other regions nonmarket mechanisms were commonly used to create a labor force. Because plantations tended to take up as much land as possible regardless of capacity to cultivate it, no land remained for either the former inhabitants or the people brought in to work for the plantation to settle or cultivate (Beckford 1972: 34). In areas occupied by advanced aboriginal civilizations the plantations destroyed the pre-Spanish type of settlement and brought about a decrease in population density (Palerm 1959: 100-101). Much of the population was converted to permanent and temporary labor for the plantation.

As Latin American countries gained their independence, plantations in some areas have helped to maintain a type of internal colonialism, controlling vast tracts of land and dependent populations. Once established, the plantations' survival depends on continued monopoly of the land, an abundance of labor and control over it, a stable market, and the capability to adopt technological change whenever possible (Best 1973: 34).

When competing for land, plantations have a clear advantage over the small landholder in that they can draw on metropolitan-based branch banking systems, which are associated with the export-import system of economy. If the companies are foreign-owned, as many are, they may draw on parent companies for funds to finance expansion. When there is a market for the produce, land and labor can be rapidly drawn from the peasant sector by a series of mechanisms, some of which will be described for the Argentine case. The areas of plantation expansion are often in the best regions in terms of ecological conditions and access to good markets for commercial crops.

The ecological requirements of sugar cane limit its cultivation to tropical parts of the world and in many areas structure the organization of labor. Sugar cane thrives in hot, moist climates, although it can be grown within a relatively wide precipitation range (40 to 100 inches a year). Nevertheless, there are specific periods when moisture is crucial for optimal growth and prolonged dryness has a very deleterious effect. Once the cane has matured, the fields should be dry to facilitate harvesting. In many cases this makes it possible to burn the dead and fallen leaves, which makes it easier to cut the cane. In semimechanized harvests, the entire field is sometimes sprayed with a light dose of herbicide to kill off the leaves, and the field is set afire with a blow torch, leaving only the stalks to be cut, a process which can be done by machine but seldom is. Dry weather is needed during the harvest season also because an excess of moisture during this time dilutes the juice and encourages the sprouting of buds and the spread of disease.

The region in which cane can be grown successfully is restricted by frost. Any temperature below 27° F will kill the plant down to the ground. Furthermore, the plant will not grow unless the temperature is over 50° F. Of particular importance for optimal growth are warm nights in which the temperature is over 70° F. During the ripening season, a slight cooling facilitates the increase of sucrose instead of continued growth. The fact that both a drying and a cooling season are important in the accumulation of sucrose suggests that the optimal regions for growing cane are in the margins of the tropics and not within the equatorial belt (Courtenay 1965: 87).

Climate is an important factor influencing the number of harvests in different production areas. Of all the requirements for cane cultivation, the length of the harvest season is the most important ecological factor. Along with the types of technology available for cultivation and harvest, it structures the organization of work for thousands of people in the regions of cultivation. When the harvest ends and the mills are closed, only about a quarter of the labor force is retained to plant and cultivate the new cane crop. The period following the harvest is often termed the *dead season;* it is during this season that thousands of workers seek employment in other occupations.

The dead season has many social implications. The most important is that temporary workers on plantations must find a means of earning a living until the harvest period begins again. Dead-season occupational and migration patterns vary considerably, depending upon the economic, political, and social structure of the particular country and region. For example, in summarizing patterns found in the Caribbean, Hicks points out that on the smaller islands workers often sharecrop land owned by the plantation. The plantations thus maintain control of labor as well as land. On the larger islands of the Caribbean such as Puerto Rico and pre-revolutionary Cuba, a landless proletariat provided much of the labor, most of the workers having to take a series of short-term jobs to tide them over until the zafra began again. The revolutionary Cuban government has not changed the migration pattern. Instead it has organized an economy that concentrates much of the work in other economic sectors during the dead season and then releases laborers for the zafra (Hicks 1972: 79).

There are ecological areas where the zafra does not have to be seasonal. In Peru, high soil fertility, limited temperature fluctuations, and man's near control over water (the cane is irrigated as there is practically no rainfall) enable cane to be harvested ten months of the year. Under these conditions a permanent labor force is desirable from the standpoint of the plantation administration (Miller 1964: 21-22). This arrangement has resulted in the development of powerful workers' unions and considerable mechanization.

In another important sugar region in Latin America—the Cauca Valley of Colombia—ecological conditions make it possible to harvest sugar cane all year. But unlike the Peruvian situation, many of the cane growers do not harvest the cane year round and labor recruiters hire workers only on short-term contracts. The sugar growers do not want a permanent labor force because such a labor force facilitates unionization, which in turn could lead to strikes and possibly higher wages. With no union and little or no support from the Colombian government, workers cannot pressure for higher wages or any social security benefits (Knight 1972).

The Colombian situation described by Rolf Knight (1972) and Michael Taussig (1978) again points out the difficulty the temporary worker has in gaining control over his environment. Organization is one of the keys to gaining control and in most cases temporary workers find it extremely hard to organize. In many regions where sugar cane is grown, including Northwest Argentina, the cane harvest is seasonal for ecological reasons.[1] Such seasonal harvests impede labor organization as effectively as in Colombia, where the zafra is arbitrarily kept seasonal in order to prevent labor organization.

Labor-Control Mechanisms in the Norte[2]

The five plantations (*ingenios*) of Salta and Jujuy (San Isidro, San Martín de Tabacal, La Esperanza, La Mendieta, and Ledesma) were founded and developed by members of the regional oligarchy during the late nineteenth and early twentieth centuries. With the help of British capital and technology, they acquired vast tracts of sparsely settled land and access to river water for irrigation. The plantations became bases of political as well as economic power, which they used to guard their holdings and expand their markets. At election time the labor force was mobilized in order to send selected candidates to provincial legislatures (Rutledge 1977: 214-215). In addition, positions in the plantation administration were often given to members of the oligarchy, thereby strengthening class solidarity (Hollander 1976: 632). Plantation owners and their families not only dominated the governorships of the provinces of Salta and Jujuy, but also influenced national politics as national congressmen and political party leaders.

Labor was first recruited from the local Indian population that lived on the land taken over by the plantations. By gaining control of this land, much of which they left uncultivated, the plantation owners were able to force many of the Indians to work for the plantations in exchange for rights to small parcels of land. Black slaves were imported into Argentine sugar zones, but in insignificant numbers (Schleh 1921: 32).

As production increased more labor was needed, and the plantations began to import Indian labor from the Chaco. E. W. White (1888: 315) reports that by 1880 one plantation hired four hundred Mataco Indians from the Argentine Chaco and one hundred Chiriguanos from Bolivia. He goes on to say that the money the Indians received was insufficient and they were paid mainly in clothes and other necessities which had to be purchased at the company store. He characterizes the Indians as "children of the desert . . . great thieves and drunkards, who will not be tempted to settle by any [of] the most advantageous offers, but arrive at the commencement of the harvest mostly in gangs with a chief or *cacique* at the head of each, who although he does not work receives wages like the rest and acts as an overseer" (1882: 291).

By 1912, Pierre Denis (1922: 78) noted the serious scarcity of labor in Jujuy. He says, "the contractors who clear the ground . . . are obligated by terms of their contract to import their workers directly from the south, so they will not take away from the farming. There is no available labour, no free market, on the spot." Indian labor for the zafra was still important at this time.

> The recruiting agents . . . set out from Embarcación where the railway ends, and enter from the Chaco, from which each of them brings a troop of some hundreds of natives between March and June. The Chiriguanos of the north

leave their families in the Chaco and the men come alone. The Matacos immigrate in whole tribes. They camp under the shelter of the works, and are paid in maize, meat, and cigars. In October . . . they receive the remainder of the pay in money, and spend it in brandy, clothing, knives and firearms (Denis 1922: 78).

The advantage of Indian labor is clear. The Indians lived relatively nearby, many in the region where the plantations were established. Those brought from the Chaco were very poor and would work for little money, having no alternative source of income or trade. Trade items could be bought wholesale by the management and traded at retail value or higher. (Emilio Schleh [1921: 267] pointed out that the trade system made it possible to maintain labor costs below that of the Tucumán area.) Furthermore, the plantations did not have to spend money on housing for Indian laborers. The Tobas and Matacos built their own huts of bamboo and cane, forming villages of fifty to one hundred huts, each with its own chief. They had no furniture and cooked outside. When the huts became too dirty and bug-infested they were burned and new huts were built in a new location (Payne and Wilson 1904: 45). The Indians, few of whom spoke Spanish, were generally responsive to their cacique. There were no attempts to form labor unions or to try to articulate labor grievances to governmental authorities.

There were certain disadvantages to Indian labor, the most important being the difficulty of controlling the workers. The caciques were supposed to act as brokers between the plantation management and the Indians, but their role became modified somewhat for they tended to filter management information and at times were not the effective taskmasters management desired. One plantation maintained an army of forty soldiers to keep the Indians in line. William Payne and Charles Wilson claim that about forty Indians had been killed shortly before their arrival in 1902. They also wrote that the Indians fought among themselves with long knives and bows and arrows. Unable to adequately control Indian looting and fighting, management sought another source of labor.[3]

A larger, manageable work force became more important as the market for sugar increased, and the plantations turned to Argentine peasants as a source of labor. The major areas of labor recruitment were the Quebrada de Humahuaca, the highland Jujuy departments bordering Bolivia (such as Santa Victoria), the Calchaquí Valleys in Salta, the valley of Santa María in Catamarca, as well as some highland regions of Santiago del Estero. These highland regions are characterized by cold and dry winters, which coincide with the zafra period. Areas such as Santa María were already supplying labor for cane growers in Tucumán (Herrán 1976). In the early twentieth century Denis reports labor recruiters from the two sugar regions competing with each other and dividing the labor from Santa María (Denis 1922: 76).

Like the Indians, the peasants had little experience with organized labor and were not expected to initiate labor protest. Besides that, hiring peasants had other benefits. In contrast to the Indians, they were agriculturalists, which made them more efficient in cutting and hauling cane. Furthermore, since they spoke Spanish, the cacique broker was no longer necessary and company employees could directly run the harvest activities. Also the peasants were not as unruly as the Indians and fought less among themselves.

The labor recruiter, *contratista,* became the arm of the plantations in the highlands. Often wealthy peasants or storekeepers, they used their position to greatly enhance their personal wealth and political power (Herrán 1976: 8). With the support of the plantations some were elected to the provincial legislature. In the 1930s contratistas were paid 15 pesos for each peon recruited (in contrast, the seasonal workers were paid 2.50 pesos per ton of sugar cane—approximately what one man could cut and load in a day [Solari 1940: 18]). The contratistas who owned stores sold goods to workers on advanced credit to be paid at the end of the harvest. After paying prices inflated by as much as 50 percent, plus interest, many workers left the zafra without any money and in debt to the contratista. This debt could be paid off only by returning to the zafra the following year.

During this period there were numerous reports of worker discontent with the conditions on the plantations and the system of payment, and labor became increasingly difficult to recruit (Bisio and Forni 1976). Since the plantations' labor requirements were growing in response to an expanding market for sugar, the plantations turned to other nonmarket mechanisms to ensure a supply of labor. They purchased or rented highland haciendas with resident Indian peasant communities.[4] Traditionally, families living in the communities either rented the land or paid for access to the land in the form of goods and services. Once the plantation owners bought the haciendas, the peasants had to pay their rent by having one member of their family work six months on the plantation. In this way the plantations gained access to labor which they could keep under rigid control. Seasonal workers from this period reported being whipped for working too slowly and told of families being thrown off land they had farmed for generations when they were unable to provide workers.

In one particularly well-documented case in 1923, the owners of a plantation rented a vast hacienda in Santa Victoria. They then required all of the able-bodied men to work on the plantation during the harvest season. The consequences for the local economy were devastating. Lack of manpower reduced the area cultivated, and the little income earned in the zafra was partly allocated to buying industrial goods which replaced local products such as pottery, baskets, and blankets. This process led to a state of dependent poverty in the area

(Reboratti 1974: 495).

In 1927 the owners of the same plantation purchased another 300,000 hectare hacienda located in the Calchaquí Valleys. They began charging the hacienda peasants for the use of the land, as well as requiring them to continue to work fifteen days a year for the hacienda. Moreover, the peasants had to sell their produce to the hacienda instead of to merchants, as they had formerly done. Most importantly, the men were required to go to the plantation to work in the zafra, with only the old and sick excused. At the end of the zafra the cost of the workers' transportation between the hacienda and plantation, in addition to rent and debts at the store, were discounted from their earnings (Gatti 1975: 32).

During this period pressure against the plantations began to mount. Juan Antonio Solari gave a report on the conditions of exploitation to the Argentine legislature in 1932, published in 1937 as *Trabajadores del Norte Argentino.* His book, *Parias Argentinos: Explotación y miseria de los trabajadores en el norte del país,* was published in 1940, and that same year the Salta legislature asked for an investigation of the Salta ingenios.

At this time a series of new laws was passed which had a direct impact on the plantations. The most significant new legislation (Ley 12.921) was passed in 1943, after the military government came to power, and became known as the "Estatuto del Peón" (Statute of the Worker). Several sections of this law were directed specifically at the sugar plantations. They mandated higher wages and better work conditions in the field and factory, reduced the power of the contratistas, regulated prices at company stores, and required plantations to provide free and improved housing and medical care. Yet the plantations benefited from sections that allowed them to withhold 30 percent of the workers' salaries (interest free) until the end of the harvest and to punish insubordination.

The legislation reflects a significant political shift in Argentina. During the period of Perón's presidency that followed, the plantations were under constant pressure to improve conditions. New housing was built and hospitals were established. Work hours and conditions improved. Laborers who had worked before this period point to the significant improvement in their treatment by contratistas and administrative personnel.

In the highlands the new legislation freed peasants of the obligation of going to the plantations. Growing agitation led to confiscation of many of the highland haciendas and the promise of land reform, but most peasants still have not received title to the land. In Jujuy the province holds title to many of the haciendas, and in fact the government never seriously considered breaking up the plantations and colonizing the lowlands (Rutledge 1975a: 59).

During this period the first unions were formed. Factory workers and permanent fieldworkers were included but not the canecutters. In 1945, a major strike occurred in the largest ingenio of the Norte when the company failed to pay the traditional 10 percent bonus at the end of the harvest. Considerable amounts of property were destroyed. Another major strike followed in 1949, accompanied by small strikes on other plantations. Three years later the plight of the seasonal workers was further brought to public attention. In La Esperanza troops fired upon seasonal workers who were protesting low wages and the high prices charged by company stores. Four workers were killed and a large number wounded. After a federal review the plantation was ordered to lower prices and increase wages (Rutledge 1977: 219).

The plantations tried to control the growing discontent and early labor organization in several ways. Workers from the same village were housed in different work camps separated by miles of cane. The separation tended to limit organization by fragmenting friendship and kin groupings, temporarily isolating workers in the new environment. Police enforced rules against large gatherings, and outsiders were kept off plantation lands. Nevertheless, pressure built.

It was at this point that plantations began to turn to Bolivia as a source of labor, although some Bolivians had always been employed on the plantations. An important wave of Bolivians came to Argentina as deserters from the Bolivian army during the Chaco War of 1932-1935. But it was in the 1940s that recruiters were sent to Bolivia to hire labor. They lured the workers with flowery descriptions that were totally at odds with the stunningly harsh reality that awaited them on the plantation. One such description promised "high salaries for six hours of work, healthy and comfortable rooms, plenty of inexpensive food almost given away at the stores, good clothes and medical aid" (Solari 1940: 43). The actual conditions on the plantation were anything but good. In fact, the workers were "given unservable food, the clothes were rags acquired at auctions in Buenos Aires, they were obligated to work fifteen to eighteen hours straight, and saddest of all, the Bolivian worker was paid a salary much less than the proportional salary paid an Argentine" (Solari 1940: 44).

The advantage of Bolivian labor for the plantations was threefold. First, Bolivians were eager to work long, hard hours for what amounted to a low wage in Argentina but was relatively rewarding when converted to Bolivian pesos; they were undemanding, accepting heavier and longer work loads with less complaint (even in 1971, plantation administrations pointed this out as an important difference between Argentine and Bolivian workers). Second, the Argentine government was not as concerned about the welfare of the Bolivian worker as of the native worker. Closely related to this advantage is the third one, namely that the Bolivian worker usually did not have documents and thus had no legal rights in Argentina. The sugar companies in Jujuy and Salta had the upper hand to such a degree that they effectively stopped provincial authorities from enforcing labor laws. Any laborer who created a disturbance or made an effort to organize or to strike could be reported to the authorities and thrown out of the country. Furthermore, the workers could not take their grievances to government labor-regulating agencies that had been created in the last decade. More important than the influence of plantation power over these agencies was the fact that the grievances of illegal Bolivian labor were not their concern.

This is not to say that the conditions of workers continued to deteriorate through the 1940s. In fact they did not, because Perón came to power in 1943. During the Perón era, which lasted until 1955, the plantation unions were formally recognized and had government support. Migrant laborers had representatives on the union boards. Housing for migrant labor improved, wages rose, and legislation gave the workers fringe benefits, such as powdered milk for their children and extra pay for children in school. Hours also improved. It was during this period that Argentina witnessed massive migration of its peasants from the interior provinces of Catamarca, Santiago del Estero, Salta, and Jujuy to Buenos Aires in search of work in the booming Argentine capital. This movement drew off surplus labor from the region that normally provided part of the plantations' labor pool. As a result the ingenios turned to Bolivia for more of their labor. Many Bolivians also were drawn to the big cities of Argentina at this time and worked temporarily at the zafra to earn capital for moving further south.

Once the economic boom peaked, jobs became scarce in metropolitan Argentina. By the time Perón was removed from power the problem of unemployment was again felt in all parts of Argentina. By this time the ingenios were thoroughly dependent on Bolivian labor for the harvest. Not only did this labor come seasonally from Bolivia, but it also included a large number of Bolivians who lived in Argentina more or less permanently. During the postzafra period some worked part of the year in a city, but most worked harvesting other seasonal crops, such as tobacco in Jujuy and Salta, grapes and vegetables in Mendoza and San Juan, apples in Río Negro, and vegetables in Mar del Plata.

As unemployment became a problem in Argentina, unions began to protest the employment of Bolivians, especially Bolivians without documents. Meanwhile, concern developed in Bolivia over the treatment of Bolivians in Argentina. A Committee Pro-Bracero formed to protest to the Bolivian government the treatment of workers on Argentine plantations. In 1966 the ingenios began enforcing the law requiring work permits for all prospective zafreros. Many Bolivians did not return to Argentina, feeling the cost of obtaining documents was too high.

While governmental pressure and bad publicity were important factors in the ingenios' decision to require work permits, other factors were probably more important. By this time Bolivians were receiving the same pay as Argentines.

If the ingenios' labor pool had been decreasing, Bolivians without documents still would have been advantageous. Instead, underemployment and continuing Bolivian migration into Argentina increased the size of the labor pool. In 1970 the ingenios could control their workers simply by offering work in an area of high underemployment. The growth of the labor pool from which the plantations now recruit is indicated by the great ease with which recruiters can find workers.

Although it has been advantageous for the plantations' owners to hire Bolivian labor, the administrators are not always complimentary when talking about the Bolivians. *Siete Días,* a major Argentine magazine, quoted an important administrator for one of the plantations in the Norte as saying, "I am going to be categorical; what is important here is that the Bolivians leave. We are in Argentina, and we have a moral obligation to give work to the men of this land . . . . [The Bolivians] are a plague, bad workers, and hard-hearted drunks" (November 2-8, 1970: 27).

Although this attitude exists, most contratistas I interviewed felt that the Bolivian is a better worker than the Argentine. One contratista confided to me that "90 percent of the Argentines hired read and write. They cause more trouble." Another pointed out that the Bolivians who have lived in Argentina or who had been coming to the zafra many years are more *vivo* (clever and aware). Others claim that the workers from Catamarca frequently take Saturdays and Sundays off and drink most of the time. The Bolivians, they suggest, come to Argentina to earn money and will work from sunrise to sunset every day of the week. Many Argentine zafreros themselves feel that the Bolivians make better workers than they do; as one told me, "We Argentines say that the Bolivians are born in the cane fields." Most Bolivians I interviewed about the subject proudly agreed with the evaluation that they are *guapos para el trabajo* (well suited for the work) and cited the frequent fights and bad working habits of the Argentines.

The change in labor recruitment patterns is an ongoing process. All the major plantations of the Norte are mechanizing the harvest. This is deemed necessary, not because it increases production per unit of land, but because there is a fear that workers' demands for higher wages and better living conditions could be successful, forcing the cost of production above what it would cost to mechanize the harvest. By mechanizing, the managements hope to eliminate their dependence on seasonal labor and further decrease the seasonal workers' bargaining position. Of course, skilled personnel are required to run and service the machines, but they are not recruited from the manual-harvest labor pool. So far there has been no protest against the mechanization, although many seasonal workers are aware of its implications. The reason the union has not protested is that it is run by permanent employees who could benefit from the mechanization.

In the long run mechanization might be beneficial to the workers if it leads to recognition of the serious employment problem of the region and to the development of new sources of work for the seasonal workers—employment that would be year round, pay well, and eliminate the grueling work required by the zafra. Or the loss of jobs could lead to the development of class consciousness, mobilization of the workers, and revolution resulting in a redistribution of resources and the end of capitalism in Argentina and Bolivia. There has been little to indicate that either of these scenarios will take place in Argentina, given the actions and development policy of the Argentine government. Mechanization has only aggravated a serious employment problem for those who can least afford it and has given plantation management increased power over the labor force.

4. Recruiters, Canecutters, and the Work Camp

As the cold winds from the Antarctic sweep up into Argentina with the beginning of winter, the sugar cane ripens on the vast plantations of the North. The length of the harvest season for sugar cane is closely regulated by the climate of the region, which in turn dictates the rhythm of human activity in the sugar zone by drawing mass seasonal migrations of workers, merchants, truckers, and vendors at the time of the harvest and rejecting them when it is over.

The workers' world is not bounded by the work camp, and most canecutters are not "plantation oriented" as they have homes in villages, towns, cities, or farms where they may have relatives or immediate family. Yet for some families the plantation is the only place the members of the family meet. More important, information about postzafra work is shared and discussed among people with differing postzafra experiences, both in Argentina and Bolivia, but confronted by a common problem: earning enough to support themselves and their families year round. The efforts of workers and their families to bring order to their work lives in an employment structure fraught with limited opportunities, unpredictability, and potential deception are reflected in the strategies developed in the work camps. The work-camp ethnography, then, is a backdrop for the drama of decisions and the struggle for subsistence bounded by the constraints of capitalism which are being examined in this book. The postzafra strategies, their differences and similarities as well as their interrelationships, is the subject of chapter 6.

The Labor Recruiters

Labor recruiters play a vital role wherever seasonal workers are needed by agricultural interests. In Peru and Central America they are commonly known as *enganchadores*, in Northwest Brazil as *empreiteiros*, and in Guatemala as *habilitadores*. In Argentina they are derogatorily called *negreros*, as well as contratistas. By late March or early April administrators of sugar plantations in Salta and Jujuy know how many zafreros they will need for the harvest beginning in early June. The contratistas are sent for and told the number of men to hire.

As mentioned earlier, at one time the contratistas had to work long and hard to fulfill the companies' labor needs. But in 1970, owing to the reserve of employable agricultural labor in Northwest Argentina comprised of Bolivian migrants and underemployed or unemployed Argentine workers, they were assigned quotas of men to hire. In urban areas, advertisements giving the contratista's home address are placed in newspapers, and men seeking work go to his home to sign up. In rural areas of Bolivia and Argentina the contratista still has to look up his old workers at their homes, but he no longer has to go to great lengths to sell prospective workers on the jobs he is offering. Zafra employment is now a tradition in many areas of high underemployment and unemployment.

With the rise of unemployment in the Northwest and the ever-increasing supply of potential seasonal workers, the contratista's importance to the plantation administration has diminished. This is reflected in the change in pay. The contratista had always been extremely well paid for his efforts. In the mid-1960s, for example, he was paid 2 pesos for every man he signed up; in addition, for each ton of cane cut, stripped, deheaded, carried, piled, and loaded by the men he employed, the contratista received 1 percent of their earnings. If a team finished one and a half tons of cane in a day, the contratista earned 6.03 pesos; when multiplied by an average of 135 work days, he earned 814 pesos a season for each recruit or team leader. If he recruited 1000 team leaders he earned 814,050 pesos a season, which was then equivalent to US $4,000 and a substantial figure in Argentina at the time (Antezana 1969: 95). Some contratistas annually vacationed in Mar del Plata, the popular summer resort south of Buenos Aires. Others accumulated vast holdings. For example, one powerful contratista who has been with the company for many years owns several stores in Libertador, a house in Salta, and a farm in Yuto, all of which were acquired before the new pay scale. Furthermore all of his children have gone on to get university degrees.

In 1971 Ingenio del Norte[1] reduced the contratistas' pay, putting them on a monthly salary ranging from 50,000 and 80,000 pesos. The company administration figured that labor was so abundant that the contratistas were no longer worth the income they had been earning. Although the contratistas complained bitterly to one another, they seldom complained to other people because they suspected there might be some resentment about their past earnings. Despite their grumbling, not one of the contratistas quit. It was, for most, the only job they knew, and it still paid relatively well.

Although their influence with the administrators has decreased, the contratistas still perform a vital role. Since plantation jobs are scarce in relation to the demand, the company can afford to be more selective than earlier in choosing its workers. This task is passed on to the contratista, along with some general hiring guidelines formulated by the head of the personnel office. Only workers with three consecutive years of experience with the company are to be hired. Since workers with large numbers of children are entitled to family pay bonuses they are discouraged from signing up. Men over forty years of age are not to be hired, as opposed to the previous cut-off at fifty years. Finally, unproductive workers or troublemakers are not welcome.

With the labor pool increasing and employment opportunities decreasing, migrant workers have become more and more dependent on the contratistas to reserve an employment opportunity for them. Commonly, bribes of a few thousand pesos, a day's income, are paid to the contratista by prospective laborers in order to guarantee employment, although this practice is not universal. One recruiter told me he turned away over fifty men, many of whom offered a small bribe in the hope of getting a job.

On some plantations in Northwest Argentina, the contratista only recruits the men and then returns to his job in his home community—as the druggist in a small town, a truck driver in Salta, or whatever. On the other plantations, Ingenio del Norte for one, the contratista remains on the plantation with the workers he has hired, coordinating their work. In this case he serves as a power broker between the administration and the temporary workers, and as such he is a key person in the zafreros' life during the zafra season.

A power broker "specifically wields power at each of two levels, and his power in one level depends on his operation at the other level. He controls one domain only by virtue of having access to derivative power from a larger domain" (Adams 1970: 321). The contratista has control over job slots allocated to him by the plantation administration, therefore he has power over the workers who want to fill those slots. On the other hand, the contratista knows how to find zafreros who will work long, hard hours and not cause trouble for the administration. Thus, the contratista has some power over the administration, although this power is considerably diminished when labor is abundant. As a broker the contratista has traditionally mediated between workers and the administration. Complaints about work conditions, medical care, and pay irregularities are usually taken to him instead of to the union. This is particularly true during periods when the union is weak.

As Richard Adams (1970: 324) pointed out, a power broker does not usually change his position within the total structure by virtue of his activities as a broker. Since his power in each level depends upon maintaining his control over resources in both areas, he generally cannot move into a new position without losing control over one or both resources.(As a result, contratistas like Don Pedro[2] of Ingenio del Norte seldom take other jobs in the company. It is also partly for this reason that contratistas may work for only one company for years, which means that some workers have a dependable person to turn to for work during the zafra period.

When dealing with the workers, the contratista is paternalistic, often referring to them as *hijos* (sons). He is blunt with the workers and takes little back talk. On the other hand, contratistas are generally wary of the workers, a feeling which indicates that the worker has some power in the relationship, limited though it may be. Contratista Don Rubén carries a loaded pistol in the glove compartment of his pickup. He says you never know what will happen, that a contratista can have many enemies. I have seen a contratista who lived on the lote with his men refuse to break up a fight but instead send for the police, who could not arrive for twenty minutes at the earliest. He pointed out that one can never tell what the men will do, especially when they have been drinking, and it is better to use force when dealing with them than to try to exert authority with nothing to back it up.

Don Pedro is a straight, sinewy man of medium height who talks positively and directly to you, using his long fingers to make his point. He drives back and forth from the lote in his new Ford pickup. Now fifty years old, having worked twenty-five of those years as a contratista for the same plantation, as had his father before him, he is an established figure in the region. Like other contratistas he expresses sympathy for the workers, when asked, and claims to abhor the work conditions and the pay scale. But, also like the others, he is a strong supporter of company policy. I have never heard of a contratista actually risking his job to side with a worker against the company; nor have I heard of one willing to initiate any effort to change the living conditions on the work camps. The contratista's job is too dependent on maintaining close personalistic ties with the plantation administrators and supporting their policies. Sympathy for the plight of the workers, if it ever really existed, is turned into callousness by the hard realities of self-preservation.

During periods when political parties were active, plantation owners in Jujuy and Salta were major political figures, wielding almost caudillo-like power. Being the largest employers in their regions, they expected to get the votes of their workers—and expected the contratista to help this come about. I was told about one contratista who was a member of the Radical Party and worked for a plantation owner who was a prominent member of the Conservative Party. When his political affiliation became known he was fired, but was promptly hired by a rival plantation run by people more sympathetic with his political leanings.

In 1970 the contratistas claimed that workers were still interested in their

political opinions. A more accurate appraisal could indicate a worker's reluctance to fall into disfavor with his contratista by supporting the "wrong" can-
didate. A contratista can make life difficult for a worker he dislikes, even if he
hires him, and most workers keep their political feelings to themselves, seldom
making any effort to discuss political subjects with the contratista.[3]

In general, the workers are humble when talking with the contratista, taking
off their hats in his presence and speaking in low, subservient voices. Some
workers, viewing the contratista as an extension of plantation bureaucracy, resent his authority. But most regard him as a combination patron/broker and
are resentful if he fails to be interested in their affairs. A "good contratista"
should be understanding, helpful, and available in times of need; he should stay
on the plantation with his workers instead of driving about in a truck or spending days in Salta or Jujuy. If a zafrero is hurt at work, he wants to feel certain
that his contratista will help him get indemnity from the company. If a worker
can prove he was underpaid, he wants to know that his contratista will support
him by asking for proper pay. When a worker thinks his contratista is an unre-
liable, ineffective broker, he will look for another contratista for the following
year.

Contratistas still play an active credit-merchandizing role. Zafreros who
have been working for the same contratista for a number of years can usually
go to him for a loan during the postzafra season. During this period, most
workers who sign up for the zafra can also get credit advances from the company store through the contratista. Everything from bicycles to tennis shoes is
purchased with this credit, even though the items are usually 25 to 30 percent
more expensive than in local stores. The workers pick up the items at the contratista's home; for his service, the company pays the contratista 10 percent of
the retail price. Vertical ties with the contratistas have other values for the
zafrero. A contratista often hires workers for postzafra jobs on the plantation.
His work crews, which plant and cultivate the cane, usually number less than
two hundred men; for some zafreros, access to this work through the contratista is crucial.

As may be expected, many zafreros ask contratistas to be *compadres* (god-
parents) of their children. One contratista claimed he had between five and
six hundred *ahijados de bautismo* (godchildren of baptism), most of whom he
did not know by face or name. He has another two hundred ahijados of first
communion and was even less sure how often he became a compadre of marriage.
Although he says that theoretically the compadre should be a second father to
the child, he suggests that all he has ever done is to get work for his godchild's
parent. Another important contratista refuses to be the compadre of any of
his workers, claiming it is "too much responsibility." In fact, he does not want
to commit himself to them.

Crucial to the contratistas' success are the *mayordomos*, who are directly responsible to them and appointed by them. Usually each contratista has three or four mayordomos, depending on the number of workers he has hired. The rule of thumb is one mayordomo for every hundred workers. The mayordomo has usually worked as a zafrero for a number of years and knows the work well. In addition, he must be able to write and do some arithmetic because he keeps track of the work assignments and tonnage of each worker under him. In many cases mayordomos are skilled artisans, such as tailors or cobblers, who came to Argentina in order to earn money to set up their shops. These are highly competitive professions in Northwest Argentina, and some were grateful for steady work on the plantation during the zafra, especially if they did not have to actually cut and load cane.

In general, the mayordomo does not earn as much as the zafreros during the zafra. In 1970 he earned 1,090 pesos a day. His work starts when the contratista begins recruiting; in most cases the mayordomo knows where workers live, and he plays a major role in the contracting. The mayordomos enjoy a special relationship with the contratista and are inclined to drink beer and spend leisure time with him more than with the zafreros. The mayordomo also helps the contratista function as a broker, and at times may become a broker between the workers and the contratista. As we shall see, the unitary nature of the plantation domain is one important cause of the exploitation of the workers by the administration, the contratista, and the mayordomos.

Canecutters: The Move to the Zafra

In 1970 approximately 16,892 zafreros were hired on the six major plantations of Jujuy and Salta and about 5,250 zafreros worked on the forty smaller private farms that produce cane which is milled on one of the five large ingenios. The head contratista for Ingenio del Norte estimated that the plantation hired about 6,500 canecutters in 1970. When family members were included, the temporary population of the plantation swelled to about 13,800 people. It is difficult to estimate how many of these zafreros came from Bolivia and how many were Bolivian but living permanently in Argentina. Until 1967 Ingenio del Norte brought in over 8,000 Bolivians every year. Then a law was passed restricting Bolivian zafreros to 30 percent of the labor force, and these had to have documents. According to the head contratista, in 1970 Ingenio del Norte hired 500 men from the department of Tarija, 300 from Chuquisaca, 1000 from Potosí, and 20 from Santa Cruz. None was hired from Oruro and Cochambama, as had been the case earlier. Another contratista was skeptical of these numbers, saying that only he and two other contratistas who worked for the ingenio hired Argentines, and all of them hired more Bolivians than Argentines. The numbers, he suggested, represented Bolivians who were in Bolivia *before* the zafra; Bolivians living in Argentina prior to the harvest were included as Argentines. For the 1971 harvest, Ingenio del Norte reported to the National Government Office of Migration for the five northwestern provinces (located in the city of Salta) that it was hiring 2,192 Bolivians, of whom only 543 needed temporary work permits, which suggests that the others had taken out residence papers in Argentina. The Migration Office, however, did not check these figures. The other ingenios of the Norte did not bother to send the office their figures on the number of Bolivians being hired and did not request temporary work permits.

The Argentine workers come mostly from the Quebrada de Humahuaca in Jujuy, the region of Cafayate and the Calchaquí Valleys in Salta, and from Santa María, Belén Colalao del Valle and Amaicha del Valle in Catamarca. Other Argentines are recruited from the tobacco areas of Perico in Jujuy and Cerrillos in Salta, as well as from the towns and cities of Jujuy and Salta.

The following ethnographic description of the train trip the zafreros take to a plantation in the Ramal conveys part of the sacrifice and disruption that the seasonal move to the zafra necessitates. It also raises the question of what role the zafra plays in the migrants' lives and why they are willing to submit themselves to its inconvenience and hardship.

By June the sugar cane in the Ramal stands tall and verdant and a feeling of expectation fills the towns of the valley. Within a few days thousands of zafreros will descend upon the region to cut and load the cane needed to send millions of dollars worth of machinery into action. The administration and staff of Ingenio del Norte have returned from their vacations and are carefully watching the preparations for the harvest. The arrival of the zafreros is anticipated by the merchants in nearby towns, who buy new stock and jack up prices a bit. Other people arrive seeking work in the mills or looking for the contratistas who hire trucks and drivers to work for the factory. Vendors arriving from out of town take up lodging in the nonplantation towns nearby. Everyone is waiting for the *expresos* (express trains).

Further north, at a much higher altitude, others also wait for the expresos. The area around the railroad tracks is jammed with masses of people huddled together in their blankets, trying to keep warm. The outer walls of the company recruiting offices are lined with people swathed in bright blankets, the only color in the bleak windswept outpost of La Quiaca, located on the Argentine-Bolivian border. High in a chain of the Andes, La Quiaca is the starting point for the expreso, literally an express but actually a sluggish wood- or coal-burning train chartered by the company. It will make many long stops as it picks up zafreros en route to the plantations.

Many workers have traveled as long as two days to be at the station for the scheduled departure, and they may have to wait there another two or three days before the train actually leaves. Having little money, the families camp in whatever protected spot they can find if they are not fortunate enough to find room inside the large company shed. Once the trains have arrived there is a mad rush for the wooden seats, and late arrivals often have to ride on the floor or in the baggage cars. Some even ride on the protective railing outside. Fernando Antezana (1969: 86), writing about the same trip in the early 1960s, found that the companies used "simple cattle trains into which [the workers] are all squeezed and must remain enclosed, without stops, till they reach their destination." Although conditions have improved, even today most trains lack light, and the bathrooms are horribly dirty, with smells that permeate the entire car.

Just preparing for the journey is a difficult matter, for many arrangements must be made. For some the zafra separates the family for five to seven months. If the man feels he can manage without the help of his wife in the canefields she may stay behind with the young children, who suffer the most from the rigors of zafra life. Or an older daughter or relative may stay behind anyway, to guard the house, no matter how modest. There are numerous stories of people leaving their houses vacant and returning to find them stripped of everything including the tin roof slats.

Packing is done carefully. Material possessions are few, and if a man is leaving half of his family behind, decisions must be made about bedding, cooking utensils, and other goods which have to be shared. Usually clothing and kitchen wares are stuffed into several big bags made from old blankets or gunny sacks. Some people have old suitcases in which they carry their crucial documents and most important possessions, such as the elegant velvet fiesta skirts worn by the women on rare trips to town. Men like to take their bicycles, if they are fortunate enough to own them. When the whole family goes, a mattress or two may be rolled up and included in the load. Some people bring a couple of chickens (tying their legs together and wedging them in among the other belongings) and occasionally a dog. Since food staples bought at the lote stores are more expensive than in Bolivia, most families try to bring one or two month's supply of staples such as potatoes and dried corn, often home grown.

Getting to the train station with so much luggage is an especially difficult task for those who live in isolated rural areas. Workers must often use their last bit of cash and sometimes sell household items to help rent a truck. Those who live in towns closer to the station have an easier job, but it is a time of uncertainty nonetheless—there is always the fear that one of the few material possessions will be lost or stolen. In addition to a free ticket to the plantation, the company allows each worker thirty kilos of luggage free of charge; anything in excess costs twenty pesos per kilo.

For each family the zafra is an uprooting that swiftly moves them into a world over which they have little control. Anticipation mixes with anxiety. The men hope the harvest will be good—the cane tall, thick, and heavy. If the cane is good and they are given *cortada libre*, or allowed to cut as much cane as they want, they feel they can earn a decent wage. But they also worry about the family. José, for example, was aware of the ugly cycle that the zafra perpetuated.

My father had a big family and I had to work in the harvest. Sometimes it was tomatoes, at other times, tobacco. At times we went to Mendoza to pick grapes and other fruits. But we always returned to the zafra. We all worked. Of all work the zafra is the worst, but pays the best. So we returned every year, and I could never go to school. Now my oldest child helps me in the field. He's little, but strong and fast. He may be strong enough to load this year, but he will not get much schooling.

There are other concerns. For the last three years Miguel had taken his family to the zafra, and they had always gotten sick. He wished he could leave them in the highlands, but he had no relatives there. Since his wife had to help him in the fields, she could not stay behind with the children. Although his fears were great, there was nothing Miguel could do. He had to go to the harvest. During the zafra his three-year-old daughter became violently ill and died in the ingenio hospital.

Many men like Julio look forward to the day they will no longer have to work in the zafra. He told me he was not going to work as a zafrero much longer:

Bastards, they don't pay us for our work. It's dangerous. Last year on a cold rainy day I was loading a *zora* [cane wagon] and slipped on the wet step and fell, ripping my leg on the ladder.[4] I went on working because I couldn't let anyone else load my cane and earn my money. The next day my leg was so sore I couldn't walk. The *enfermero* [male nurse paid by the company] on the lote sent me to the hospital. I had to stay there two weeks, and couldn't work for two weeks after that. When my wife tried to collect the accident pay, the company said no—I hadn't told the mayordomo when I was hurt. The mayordomo said it was too bad but he couldn't help, and the contratista said he would like to help but could not. Finally my wife, crying and pleading for the sake of our children, got the contratista to talk to the administration and we were paid. Not as much as we would have earned but at least enough to pay for food. I started working again when my leg was still bad because we needed money. Another month passed before I could work well. Two months lost! The company cares about the cane, not the workers.

Although the men look forward to their last zafra, they are not without excitement when the zafra begins each year. Many told me the best days of the zafra are the first and the last. Some people, mostly men without children, claim to feel restless in May. Their thoughts are oriented toward returning to the plantation. They are tired of their work, and the zafra offers a change of pace and a chance to renew friendships and see family. It is common for those who work in a city or farm to stop work a few days in advance to pack and get ready for the zafra. Damián claimed he needed to drink some wine before the zafra, because once it began he could not afford to get drunk. You had to get up too early in the morning and could not work effectively with a hangover. Moreover, the bosses do not want you to have wine and can fire you after three warnings.

By the time the train arrives at the plantation everyone is tired. The huge open area near the sugar mill, called the *cancha*, is full of people milling around. The train is quickly unloaded, and the men go off to have their documents checked. Here and there women unpack some of their possessions and start small fires to cook some food. Many of the people from other expresos that arrived during the night are still waiting to have their documents processed and to pass the health examinations. Some plantations inoculate zafreros against smallpox and tuberculosis when they first arrive. Apparently several years ago Ingenio del Norte had the enfermeros dust everyone from head to toe with DDT. Although the workers did not know it was bad for them, they disliked being treated like animals. Many became bitter and said they would not come back if it were done again. It was not.

By late afternoon everyone has been checked in and tractors arrive pulling flat-bed wagons. Each is careful to board a wagon going to the lote to which he has been assigned. Baggage and people are crammed on—little kids with runny noses and grimy faces, tired men and women about to arrive at what will be home for the next five or six months. The most immediate concern is with living arrangements. The first arrivals can choose their *piezas* (rooms), which is a big advantage. Some rooms are shaded by trees, while others bake all day in the hot sun; some are close to water spigots, others are far away and the women have to make many trips to haul water. Many zafreros like to return to the same lote year after year. This affords some sense of security as the enfermero, *sereno* (watchman), and mayordomo are usually the same as the year before and one's friends are there as well. Each lote has its advantages and disadvantages. While ours was isolated from town and had no transportation or electricity, it had a nice grove of trees and was less crowded than some of the other lotes, which meant it was more tranquil and less filthy.

The Work Camp

Physical Environment. Separated from other settlements by miles of green cane fields crisscrossed with irrigation ditches and dusty roads, the rows of *galpones* (housing units) with their corresponding kitchen huts, the ramshackle latrines set at the perimeter, the clumps of trees, and the inevitable soccer field gave the lote its basic outline. During the day the willows growing on the banks of the irrigation ditches are draped with brightly colored clothes drying in the hot sun. Firewood carried on the shoulder from uncleared forests usually at least two kilometers away is stacked next to the kitchen huts and the occasional dome-shaped clay oven used two or three times a week for baking bread.

Some of the largest lotes house up to fifteen hundred men plus their families, while the smaller ones may have as few as three hundred men plus families. Except for the small percentage of families remaining year round to tend the irrigation systems, most lotes are occupied only four or five months of the year. More than ten years ago, when large numbers of workers were required to plow, plant the cane, and cultivate the fields, the lotes had much larger permanent populations. Today some stand almost completely empty during the off-season.

In many respects the lote is a squalid and barren environment, providing shelter in its crudest form. Communal latrines are used only occasionally. In the afternoon, wind blows dust into the piezas and kitchen huts and activates the pervasive smell of human excrement that clings with the heat and flies to everything. On many lotes, especially those housing only temporary workers, the irrigation ditches provide the only water for bathing and washing clothes. At times, when the pump breaks down, they provide drinking water as well.[5] Because the zafreros do not own land on the lote and all the arable land is planted in cane, there are no gardens and few people have animals except for an occasional chicken or dog. Furthermore, there are no physical adornments around any of the piezas, such as flower pots, plants, or fences, except those owned by the few permanent workers. There is neither time, energy, nor motivation for fixing up one's quarters, which will be home for six months at the most.

Usually all of the buildings on a lote are constructed out of the same material giving the lote a homogeneous look. The newer housing units are made of brick, with rough brick floors, corrugated metal roofs, and screenless windows; the more common, older units are made of adobe, with dirt floors, thatch roofs, and no windows. In the brick units each room measures three meters by three meters. Here a family of four or five may live, but at times more than one family are put together—one of the most resented aspects of zafra life. Not uncommonly a bachelor is housed with a married couple. At other times a family may take in a *cuarta*—a helper who receives one-fourth of the zafrero's wages and who may or may not be related to the family. Sometimes several men share a room, paying a neighbor to prepare their meals. The rooms are dark and cluttered with a confusion of clothes and other miscellaneous belongings that can be hung from nails or flung on ropes which stretch across the room. Most of the floor space is taken up by makeshift beds of bamboo stalks, ancient ones of metal, or cots, and occasionally a homemade table and cheap folding chair. Many lotes have no electricity, and kerosene lamps are a luxury, owned only by the most fortunate, such as the sereno and mayordomo.

Each lote has a small store, usually company-owned or leased from the company. Many have a *carnicería* (butcher shop) and are also visited daily by vendors selling meat from unrefrigerated pickup trucks. Every day additional vendors arrive with bread, fresh fruit, and vegetables, as well as coca leaves and clothing. On some lotes, especially those with a sizeable permanent population, there is a small building or room designated by the union as a club for the workers where men can play cards or have a soft drink. Many lotes, however, are without this facility. Each lote does have its own chapel—often no more than an empty room where the image of its patron saint is kept—as well as an office used by the resident male or female nurse to treat zafrero patients. If a worker is sick enough to require hospitalization he is taken to the company hospital on the ingenio. Finally, some lotes have grammar schools; children in work camps without schools are taken in company trucks to the nearest school.

Social Interaction. In many ways the lote differs from the traditional village. The workers' lack of control over their physical environment is manifest in the monotonous, bleak appearance of the lote. This lack of control is also reflected in lote social relations, the most striking feature of which is the absence of any real sense of community, despite common work and living conditions. Sharing between unrelated families seldom occurs, and compadres are rarely selected from lote acquaintances. Although people tend to return to the same lote year after year, the nuclear family, and in some cases the extended family or close friends from the same village, remain the primary source of friendship and support. Despite the sharing of information and happenstance discussion, individuals or families without friends from previous experiences cannot easily establish enduring friendships on the lote; and they do not necessarily want them—alliances with other workers are seen as having little value. The temporary nature of the group, the long work hours, the individual's lack of control over the physical and work environment, the heterogeneous origins of the workers, plus the lack of traditions and "community" events on the lote, combine to inhibit the development of horizontal ties among workers. The nearly atomistic family life styles on the lote are a product of these factors. For a family moving from one work camp to another throughout the year, development and maintenance of social ties is very difficult.

Lack of privacy is one of the salient conditions of lote life affecting interpersonal relations. The workers complain bitterly about the crowded, cramped living quarters. As mentioned before, it is not uncommon for two families (sometimes strangers) to share a room and the same cooking hut. Conflicts most frequently grow out of squabbles between the children, which often lead to full-fledged fights between the different sets of parents. Pedro shudders at the thought: "All we did was fight and argue, mostly because the children fought. It was terrible." Even if a family has the pieza to itself, neighbors are always close by. The thin walls separating the different rooms of the galpone do not filter sounds, and a discussion or argument in one room is heard readily in the next. The work day itself provides little escape from the others who live on the lote; everyone goes to work in the back of the same trucks, works in the same fields, and returns in the same trucks. On hot nights meals are taken out in front of the rooms, which makes eating a public event.

Another factor affecting interpersonal relations is the vigorous work schedule, which permits few social events. Only two fiestas are officially sanctioned by the company. The first blesses the lote for a successful zafra season. A priest is brought in to give a short Mass and to lead a procession as the chapel Virgin is paraded around the lote. The second fiesta occurs when the zafreros have finished the last section of cane in the area allotted to their lote. They celebrate the end of months of hard work and, they hope, take-home pay for the workers. According to some veterans, these fiestas are not as good as they used to be. These days there is no *vida* (life), they complain; the fiestas are haphazard and lack enthusiasm.

The company prohibits all other fiestas until the end of the zafra and also prohibits drinking, even though this rule is sometimes ignored, especially by Argentine zafreros. In general, the Bolivian zafreros have come to the zafra for one thing only: money. After working all day in the fields the workers have little energy left for carousing. There may be an occasional birthday party, usually restricted to the host's friends, but zafreros are often wary of attending, saying they have to get up too early the next morning and do not want to become involved with people who are drunk. Another type of ceremony is the *velorio* (a twenty-four hour vigil following a death, before the body is removed for burial at the company cemetery). Here again, attendance is usually limited to acquaintances of the family.

Boredom often settles over the lote. There is the boredom of doing the same work, day in and day out, with little to break the monotony. On the other hand, when there is no work to be done, the boredom becomes more intense. Waiting for the cane wagons is a waste of the men's time, but they can talk and rest after having worked. On days when the work ends early, however, men suddenly find there is nothing to do. Except for lotes which house a large population of permanent workers, there are no permanent gathering places—

no cafes, plazas, big market places, or churches. Some lotes at least have bus service to the nearest town once or twice a day, and a few located on the main highway are served by frequently scheduled public transportation. Many, however, offer no transportation; the people must hitch a ride on a company truck (officially prohibited) or go by foot or bicycle, which usually requires more time and energy than they have. The dullest waiting period occurs after the zafra is over and before the men are paid. During this time, which often lasts up to ten days, boredom mingles with impatience and apprehension as the men and families wait to move, not sure of finding new work. Drinking begins, to celebrate the end of the zafra, and continues because there is nothing else to do.

The only day that may break the monotony of a long work week is Sunday, although not always, especially toward the end of the zafra when the company is anxious to finish the harvest. On Sundays the men work only in the morning, returning to the lote in the afternoon to relax. The big Sunday entertainment is soccer matches organized by the contratista's office between all-star teams from various lotes. These games are well attended by men and boys, but the women, except for young unmarried girls, usually remain at home.

The other event that zafreros can participate in is the *feria*. Every fifteen days after the workers receive their *quincenal*, a portion of their wages, a small market develops alongside the road at the edge of the lote. The company pays quincenales to different lotes on different days, so the merchants manage to schedule stops at the lote which has received the quincenal most recently. Many merchants live in nearby towns and arrive in their shiny pickups equipped with kerosene lanterns and cots. The cots are set up and the wares spread out on top of them. At night the feria glows magically next to the dark lote—an enchanted world bustling with activity and excitement that offers a brief diversion from the monotony of lote life. The company prohibits the merchants from selling any alcohol, but some manage to do it anyway. Many sell clothing, sunglasses, soft drinks kept cool in huge ice buckets, trinkets, and staples such as oil, flour, and corn. Occasionally a truck with inexpensive furniture will arrive. Prices are higher than in town, but usually the zafreros, especially those living on the very isolated lotes, have neither the time nor energy to travel to town, and the vendors prey on their temptation. Some lote women take advantage of the occasion to set up small tables offering homemade delicacies such as highly spiced *empanadas* and *humitas* which cook festively over small fires. The feria always ends early because the workers have to rise at four o'clock the next morning.

Although life in the lote is bleak compared to that in a village, or even barrio or *villa* (low-income neighborhood), the fact that almost all men have work, though temporary, creates a unique atmosphere. It shows in the men's swagger at the day's end, their canvas chaps stained by cane juice, their brown muscular chests exposed through unbuttoned shirts, their hats tipped back jauntily on their heads. They have just finished a long, hard day of work; a peaceful exhaustion settles over them and the work camp. The lote moves to a daily rhythm which all families share. As long as the cane is good, the quotas are adequate, and the family is healthy, there is a feeling of purpose that contrasts sharply with the air of work insecurity that seems to hang like a cloud over many *villas de emergencia* (slums).

Health. Because the livelihood of the migrant workers depends on their physical strength and endurance, health is a constant concern. In general, the lote population is a select group since the zafra operates its own kind of selectivity process. One sees few cripples. Men too old, sick, or apathetic to work are rarely present.[6] The women too must be strong to survive the rigors of the zafra, the frequent pregnancies, and multiple moves. At the same time the very nature of the work and the living conditions the families are forced to endure generate a multitude of health problems. In addition to new ailments contracted on the plantations many workers arrive at the zafra with potential health problems that are aggravated by long hours of hard physical work in the hot lowlands. Babies and young children are particularly susceptible to infectious disease.

Most workers and their families view the Ramal as an unhealthy region and fear the consequences of moving to the plantations. Many attend Mass before leaving for the plantations and make promises to the Saints to assure the safe return of their families after a successful harvest. That they consider themselves involved in wage labor in an unhealthy environment is also reflected in the belief of some workers that the devil resides in the bowels of the sugar mill; in exchange for higher productivity people can sell their souls to the devil. Death of children at the plantation is often attributed to parents' greed and the devil.[7]

A variety of factors on the plantations influence the health of the workers and their families. Accidents occur with alarming regularity. Hidden under cane leaves as their mothers work in the fields, babies are sometimes run over by trucks or tractors hauling the cane from the fields. Men may be badly cut with machetes or seriously hurt when they fall off ladders as they are loading up to 140 pounds of sugar cane.

Exposure to a variety of pesticides is a major threat to migrant-worker health, yet little has been done to regulate the use of pesticides. Until recently workers arriving at most of the plantations were dusted with DDT by company officials as part of the health inspection. DDT was also used in the work camps to control flies. Herbicides are used to dry out the cane leaves for burning prior to the mechanized harvest and young cane is sprayed with pesticides to control weeds and pests. People working in neighboring fields are periodically sprayed by the planes or caught in the spray drifting in the wind. Workers report stinging eyes, vomiting, weakness, and severe rashes after being exposed to the spray.[8]

Malaria was once a major problem in the region, and though greatly curtailed it has not yet been eliminated. Unprotected by mosquito netting or screens at night, workers and their families are vulnerable to the disease. Crowded housing increases the probability that other diseases will spread. "Hospital de Milagro" in a nearby Salta ingenio reported tuberculosis as the most common problem of its Bolivian patients (Cornejo 1973: 13), and migrants are exposed to tuberculosis in the villas and cities as well as in the plantations. Hordes of flies, spawned in garbage and human waste, hover ready to blanket any food left uncovered.

Small children and babies are the most common victims on the plantations. In the work camp described here twelve children under the age of five died during one zafra season. The principal cause was dysentery, which resulted in serious dehydration. There are many potential causes of dysentery, but on the work camps the principal sources can be traced to the water supply. Although some work camps have water piped from wells, it is not purified in any way. In others the drinking water is taken from the same irrigation ditches where people wash their clothes and bathe. More important, many of the ditches pass very close to the inundated outhouses which encircle the work camp. While no studies have been made, the water could well be a major source of contamination, leading to acute cases of parasites and amoebas. Doctors at the major clinic at Ingenio del Norte found that 95 percent of the population was sick with parasites.[9]

Babies and young children do not have to be exposed to the water if they are breastfeeding. Yet the company, in conjunction with government child-care programs, gives all children free powdered milk. The milk mixed with contaminated water becomes a direct cause of health problems. Some parents boil the water, but lack of refrigeration often leads to feeding milk that is slightly spoiled, another cause of diarrhea. Because many women must work in the harvest helping their husbands, their babies are taken to the fields and covered with leaves. Under the intense sun they become dehydrated, especially if they already have diarrhea, and some die directly from exposure. Others, given water from the irrigation ditches, develop even greater parasitic infestation.

5. Working in the Fields, the Union, and Postharvest Planning

Daily activities are largely determined by the needs of the sugar mills which process the cane. If the mills are running, cane is needed and all capable men are expected to be in the fields working. If one or more of the three cane-chewing monsters breaks down, the zafreros' work allotments are curtailed to considerably below what they need to make their time on the plantation worth their while.

The chain of command that connects the demands of the mill to the machetes of the zafreros begins with the supervisor of the mill and ends with the contratistas or mayordomos in charge of work crews, who assign the rows of sugar cane to be cut daily by each crew. Early in the season when the weather is cool and the men are enthusiastic about the money they expect to earn, many hope they will be given cortada libre, permission to cut, trim, and load as much cane as possible in a long day's work. During this period with cortada libre, some men may load three or four tons of cane a day and feel that it is a good season. In 1970 men restricted to one ton earned about 1,090 pesos daily in contrast to a possible maximum of 5,400 pesos during a day of cortada libre. Men complain bitterly when they are limited in the beginning of the season. However, towards the end, when the work has become monotonous, the biting gnats unmerciful, and the temperature sweltering, zafreros hope to finish most of their work by noon. Nevertheless, the company frequently requires the men to stay in the fields all day as they push to meet their deadline for ending the harvest.

Many variables affect how much money the zafreros will earn. These can be divided into two categories: environmental/ecological factors over which the zafrero has no control and personal factors for which the zafrero is at least partly responsible. The first category includes the following variables: (1) the weather—extreme heat and rain slow the work; (2) the quality of the cane—size, weight, and straightness of the stalk are the most important variables as short, light cane takes just as much time to cut and trim but yields far less in terms of earnings; (3) the topography of the terrain—hilliness and rocks are handicaps; (4) the size of the production quota allotted by the government to the particular plantation that year, which in turn is determined by export agreements and internal demand; and (5) the needs of the ingenio—the breakdown of the mill or other machinery restricts the quantity of cane needed.

Variables in the second category require more lengthy discussion, and include the following: (1) the worker's relationship with the mayordomo; (2) the skill and health of the zafrero plus that of the others in his *yuto* (work team); and (3) the amount of assistance the zafrero receives from his family or hired helper. The first variable critically affects a zafrero's earning ability as it is the mayordomo who assigns the rows which each team will cut, trim, and load. As indicated above, there is considerable variation between rows, and one worker may earn much more or much less than another for the same amount of cutting, hauling and loading. The mayordomo often has his favorite workers, whom he assigns the best rows of cane. Also, he may spread the word among a few workers that for a small fee he will assign them superior rows. If the company needs additional cane the mayordomo often assigns the extra rows to his favorite workers, expecting part of the earnings to be paid back to him. New workers, especially those who sign their employment card with a fingerprint, are particularly in danger of being exploited. A mayordomo may offer to raise the worker's tonnage figure (which in reality he cannot do, since he has no control whatsoever over the weighing process) in exchange for money. Friends may try to warn the novice about the mayordomo, but at the same time they fear antagonizing the mayordomo, who has such a direct influence on their wages and who out of spite could assign them few rows or a section of poor cane.

The second variable, concerning health and skill, needs no further explanation but is related to the final variable. Assistance in the fields is crucial to the zafrero's success on the plantation. Although women do not cut or load cane they often work long hours in the fields topping and trimming the cane stalks— a considerable aid in boosting the zafrero's productivity during a time of cortada libre. The women are not paid for the labor except through the increased productivity of their spouse. When the mills are working slowly due to repairs, the women are expendable from the company's point of view, and they earn nothing for their time on the plantation. Labor laws prohibit children under eighteen from working in the harvest as certified workers. But individual workers can take on sons and daughters, or even hire another man who could not get a job on the plantation to work for him. Again, when the company needs large amounts of cane and allows workers to cut all they can, men who have older children or who hire others to help them can increase their earnings considerably.[1] When a zafrero hires a boy outside his nuclear family or an older man not employed by the company, he usually pays him one-fourth of what he earns with his help. This is referred to as the cuarta system, which some feel is more common among Bolivians than Argentines.

The cuarta system is a product of a capitalist economy which has generated a labor surplus. It is also a response to the minimum-age law. Although many parents of young children do not want them to become zafreros, by the time a boy is fifteen, he is usually considered old enough to work in the fields.[2] Zafreros often view the cuarta system as a stage in a boy's life when he can begin to earn some money and learn about zafra work.

The cuarta system may be a vehicle for the exploitation of one worker by another worker. A Bolivian man without documents may go to Argentina as cuarta for a zafrero with documents and a job. He shares the zafrero's room and food, working with him in the fields. When there is cortada libre, which depending on the year and the lote may be much of the harvest, the zafrero can earn a considerable sum of money from the labor of a male cuarta. Although the cuarta could leave the zafra with 25,000 pesos, his patrón may earn 75,000 pesos from his labor. In some cases zafreros hire four or five men as cuartas and bribe the mayordomo for additional row allotments, thus doubling or tripling their income. Although manipulation of the cuarta system to this degree is uncommon, people are aware of it and may even talk about trying it in future years. I know of several cases where men have hired relatives as cuartas; one man hired his own father and took 75 percent of his earnings. In other cases the patrón, upon receiving his final payment, including the money the cuarta(s) earned in his name, catches the quickest bus or train away from the plantation, leaving his cuarta(s) penniless. The union is supposed to be an arbiter in cases where the cuarta and patrón disagree about a payment, but squabbles are usually settled before they are taken to the union.

Although the company is officially opposed to the cuarta system, they do nothing to control it. In fact, the cuarta system works to their advantage since they can often obtain a man's work without having to pay a man's wages as well as the additional pay required by law, such as *salario familiar* and *escolaridad*—payments shared by the company and government for each child of an employee and for each child attending school. The plantations are the major beneficiaries of the cuarta system.

Attitude towards the Company. The seasonal workers are willing to work in the zafra, enduring the physically exhausting work under a hot sun, the unpleasant living conditions, and the biting insects, because they are paid regularly, receive most of the bonuses required by national law, and can earn more at the zafra than in any other type of work available to them during that period. They feel underpaid, considering the difficulty of the work and the long hours, and speculate about the profits made by the company. But after the zafra many will work for employers who will neither pay them on time nor pay even the low minimum wage, much less the government-required bonuses. Thus, for comparative reasons, many workers do not resent the company as much as one might expect.

Since the owners of the plantation live most of the time in Buenos Aires, the workers are never in contact with them and do not see the wealth of their private lives. The workers seem to have little interest or knowledge about who owns the plantation or the other plantations in the Ramal. The plantation is a world to itself, with its own ecology of work and payment. This is not to say that Bolivian zafreros feel the plantation system of land ownership is just, but since it is in Argentina, many are more awed by the vast agricultural wealth than envious. Several mentioned that it would be better to nationalize a plantation of this size but at the same time felt that nationalization would lead to the elimination of the Bolivian worker, which they did not want.

The zafreros' knowledge about upper-level administration employees who lived on the plantation is very limited. For example, Eduardo, who has worked at the Ingenio del Norte many years, explained the plantation organization by beginning with the administrator who he felt was part owner and then skipping down past the "guys who drive trucks around" to the *jefe de área* (area chief) who was in charge of his particular lote. Although some workers knew more than Eduardo, most do not care—there is money to earn and they are not affected by the changes in the plantation bureaucracy.

For the workers the major figure representing the administration is the contratista. As stated earlier, a "good" contratista who shows interest in his workers is highly respected by them. Some workers feel it is particularly advantageous to establish compadre relations with a contratista. Complaints about contratistas stem more from their failure to be interested in the workers than from the fact that they make money off them. In fact, none of the workers I interviewed knew how much the contratista earned. As long as zafreros are assigned enough cane and get paid, they feel the contratista is doing his job. The conditions of the zafra most resented by the workers—crowded living conditions, lack of schools on certain work camps, medical problems, and mechanization—are not considered to be the contratista's fault. These are issues which zafreros consider to be the domain of the union, which is supposed to be working on these problems for the workers.

Zafreros are aware of the differences in pay, living conditions, and difficulty of work on the plantation. They feel that their work is dirty, hot, and *muy sacrificado* (grueling). They feel cheated by the company when it weighs their cane and humiliated by their lack of recourse. At the same time they are proud of their ability to do a task requiring great physical strength, coordination, and endurance and are aware that others higher in the plantation hierarchy cannot do the work. They do not question, however, the fact that others hold higher paying positions. They attribute their zafrero status to a lack of education, acknowledging they had had to work instead of attend school. It is interesting to note how lack of education is blamed for their structurally low position, instead of the structure being blamed for their lack of education.

What effect does the zafrero's relative lack of power have on him while he is at the plantation? We have already seen his vulnerability to various forms of exploitation. This, in turn, leads to his distrust of other people at the zafra. On the lote the zafrero is usually reserved and quiet, shying away from people he does not know. As stated earlier, alliances with other workers, except one's own family, are felt to have little value. This distrust and reticence is one of the factors inhibiting worker solidarity and action against the administration.

Lack of protest stems from several other causes. Although there is a feeling of protest pent up inside many of the workers, lacking support even from one another, they are afraid to express it. Their jobs and lives are too precarious for protest. They are aware that talking back to men higher in the company hierarchy can only lead to trouble. Although friends may complain bitterly to each other about union leaders, mayordomos, or contratistas, direct complaints or protest are rare. When a union representative made an infrequent visit to the lote to tell the workers to go on strike, a crowd gathered to listen. Several times during the talk, a worker yelled, "What about our money? Why us?" The union speaker stopped the talk and asked who had spoken. No one responded. Nor did anyone else raise a question from then on, despite the fact that many workers admitted later that they disagreed with the union speaker. In another situation, a group of men were waiting outside the enfermero's office to be treated. One of the men yelled, *Apure!* (Hurry!), and a little later there was another loud complaint. The enfermero came out of his office and asked who was yelling. No one answered, nor did anyone again complain about the long wait.

Another factor inhibiting protest is that leaders do not evolve on the lote. One reason for this is the company's selectivity in hiring: troublemakers, those who speak out, are weeded out each year, and all workers are aware they can lose their jobs. Also leaders do not emerge because there are few situations in which an individual can act as leader, nor is the four-to-five-month duration of the zafra enough time for successful leadership to develop, especially considering the arduous work conditions that leave workers hungry and tired at the end of a long day. Finally, as we shall see in the following section, workers (especially seasonal workers) are given little support by the one body that could help them and foster leadership: the union.

By following the rules of distrust, nonalliance, and silence, a worker can manage to accomplish his main goal in coming to the zafra: earning money.

The regular pattern of daily life and the certainty of pay temporarily rule out the ambiguity and uncertainty usual in the migrant's life.

The Union and the Seasonal Worker

On sugar plantations the basic organizing unit through which workers can confront management with demands for higher wages and improved working conditions is the union (Mintz 1956; Padilla 1956; Miller 1964; Knight 1972). Unions, however, vary considerably in their ability to successfully challenge plantation administrations and in their methods of confrontation. Conflict resolution often depends upon the respective support the unions and plantation management can gain from the major source of power in the country: the national government. This may vary considerably over time.

Support of workers by the national government also varies as do the strategies of union officials in soliciting the support. For Puerto Rico, Sidney W. Mintz and Elena Seda Padilla showed how a political party could be the dominant source of articulation for workers on one plantation, while on another the union was more important (Mintz 1956, Padilla 1956). In Argentina at the time of the study, political parties were weak and ineffective. On the plantation the union was the most important institution for articulating worker needs to the national level.

The earlier described labor-control mechanisms which helped plantation owners combat the formation of unions and salary demands were employed with the tacit approval of the government. They reduced the political and economic base of the workers, particularly seasonal workers, and in so doing mitigated their potential political input from their home regions. Only with the increase of derivative power from the national government did unions become strong. When this power was reduced, the union was not destroyed, but the administration was in a position to develop another labor-control mechanism: division of the workers by means of unequal distribution of benefits from the company.

The union at Ingenio del Norte was formed in 1943, rather late considering that the ingenio was started in 1884. Until the beginning of unionization the company administration enjoyed a relatively free hand in labor relations. By bringing in Bolivian seasonal workers to harvest the sugar cane they managed to hold down production costs, gaining an increasing share of the sugar market from their rivals in the region of Tucumán. The incentive for union organization possibly came from Tucumán, whose unionized growers hoped to force up the cost of production in the competing province. Another possibility is that organizers came from the urban unions which were beginning to receive support from the minister of labor, Juan Perón.

The longest labor strike in the plantation's history occurred in 1945, touched off by the company's decision not to pay the customary 10 percent bonus at the end of the harvest. The strike became violent: windows were broken and oxen slaughtered. Government troops were called in to protect plantation property. Although the strike lasted a full month, no seasonal workers participated. Very few belonged to the union; furthermore, all the seasonal workers had already packed their belongings and moved on to other jobs.

The Perón years were golden years for the union and a rough period for the plantation administration and owners. The union officials pushed through demands for higher wages, medical facilities, better housing, and shorter working hours for both seasonal and permanent personnel. Workers could no longer be fired or evicted from company housing with only twenty-four-hours' notice; nor could men be whipped for breaking rules. At this point the union was very strong, receiving a large amount of derivative power from the national government. It supported the changes which benefited both permanent and seasonal workers. During the Peronist period, seasonal workers for the first time were admitted to union membership, with representatives on the union boards.

With the removal of Perón from office in 1955, there was a dramatic reversal as the union's access to derivative power from the national level was greatly curtailed. Without governmental support and mediation the weakened union could no longer expect to win in confrontations with the plantation. Although a strike could cripple the plantation, the loss of income was harder on the workers, especially the seasonal workers who were highly dependent on the zafra income and had few, if any, alternative sources of employment during this period. The union could not financially support striking workers even for a short time: as a result workers were reluctant to go on strike. Because of its reduced power the union could make only minimal demands, thus becoming ineffective as the voice of the workers, particularly the seasonal workers. Generally when needs were unique to seasonal workers they were ignored by the union leaders in favor of the needs of permanent workers.

Today many of the individualistic labor grievances of zafreros are presented to the company labor office by one of two routes. The seasonal worker either tries to get the mayordomo or the contratista to help him articulate his problem or he goes to the union for help. Usually he attempts the former first. In labor cases particular to Ingenio del Norte, upon which the company and the union cannot reach an agreement, the Secretaría del Trabajo de la Provincia (State Secretary of Labor), appointed by the governor of the province, acts as the arbitrator.

Both the union and the management belong to organizations which give them access to higher levels of articulation. The union of Ingenio del Norte is a member of the Federación Azucarera Regional (FAR–Regional Sugar Federation), which includes unions of the other plantations in the province, and often joins with labor representatives of the ingenios of the other northern province on issues specific to the Norte.

Until 1965 the union of Ingenio del Norte was a member of the Confederación General de Trabajadores (CGT–General Federation of Workers), the largest Argentine labor organization. In 1965 the crisis in the Argentine sugar industry led to the shutdown of seven big sugar mills in Tucumán by the end of 1966. The competition for the limited production quotas between the sugar interests of Tucumán and those of the Norte became intense. Government support of the Tucumán cane industry was sought by three Tucumán labor unions: Federación Obrera Trabajadores de la Industria Azucarera (FOTIA–Federation of Sugar Industry Laborers), which was founded in 1944 and today includes fifty-four unions; Federación de Empleados de la Industria Azucarera (FEIA–Federation of Sugar Industry Employees); and Federación de Obreros del Surco de la Industria Azucarera y Agropecuarias de Tucumán (FOSIAAT–Federation of Field Workers of the Sugar Industry and Farm Workers of Tucumán). When the CGT threw its support to the Tucumán sector, union members in Salta and Jujuy felt that this was at the expense of the workers in their provinces and they dropped out of CGT.[3]

The interests of Ingenio del Norte's owners are represented on a regional level by Centro Azucarero Regional del Norte (CARN–Regional Sugar Cane Center of the North). In the Norte there are other growers' associations. The independent cane growers of Salta and Jujuy are divided into the Unión de Cañeros Independientes de Jujuy y Salta (Independent Cane Growers' Union of Jujuy and Salta), the Cañeros Unidos del Norte (United Cane Growers of the North), and a group of six growers who belong to neither group. All of these groups belong to CARN, which coordinates efforts to obtain larger sugar quotas for the Salta-Jujuy sugar zone. Through the Cámera Gremial de Productores Azucareros, the national sugar producers' association, CARN works with the cooperatives and with the Tucumán growers' associations: Unión Cañeros Independientes de Tucumán (UCIT–Union of Independent Cane Growers of Tucumán); Centro de Agricultores Cañeros de Tucumán (CACTU–Center for Cane Growing Agriculturists of Tucumán); and Compañía Nacional Azucarera (CONASA–National Sugar Company). Together they work to increase sugar prices and production quotas and to hold down labor costs. For prices and quotas, the arbitrating arm of the government is the Secretaría de Industria y Comercio de la Nación (National Secretary of Industry and Commerce) and the Dirección Nacional de Azúcar (National Office of Sugar Management). Issues such as minimum wages for workers in the sugar industry are decided at the national level through the Paritaria Nacional, which is under the guidance of the Ministry of Labor and includes representatives of the unions, the independent cane growers, and the ingenios.

Seasonal workers at Ingenio del Norte have little input into the union affairs, and the articulation of their needs to levels higher than that of the local union is rare. Seasonal workers benefit little from their union membership because of the limited power of the union and their own lack of influence in union decisions. Despite explicit statements by union leaders affirming their interest in the welfare of the seasonal worker, there is little communication between the zafreros and the union personnel. Part of this is due to the formal structure of the union. Article 15 of the union bylaws explains: "The temporary worker will enjoy all of the rights established during his period of work, but he *cannot* occupy any union office" (Sindicato de Obreros y Empleados de Azúcar 1964: 13 [my translation]). Union officials justify this discrimination by saying, correctly, that it is more difficult for the company to fire a permanent worker than a temporary worker. Nevertheless, the bylaw keeps seasonal workers from becoming officers or delegates in the union, leaving those positions open for permanent workers, who tend to serve their own interests. The union officials have comfortable office jobs with considerable prestige and power in relation to the other workers. They can get along better with the administration if they organize only those programs for the temporary workers that they are sure the administration will accept.

The permanent workers would not have such strong control over the union if the seasonal workers could vote in the union elections; but they cannot. Both the union elections and the major union meetings are held after the zafra has ended. No union meetings are scheduled during the zafra. One union official mentioned the fear that extending voter rights to seasonal workers would possibly put the union in the hands of foreigners, in this case Bolivians, who compose over 70 percent of the seasonal work force. While seasonal workers are barred from holding office, there is also a clause prohibiting permanent workers who are Bolivian from gaining control of the union. Article 15 of the union bylaws states that the board of officers must be made up of at least half Argentines plus one. This is justified on the grounds that Argentines are more difficult to fire and have a better knowledge of union activities; furthermore, the residence requirements are intended to maintain stability among the officers. In total the laws effectively prohibit the possibility of having a majority of Bolivian officeholders, who might be more inclined to integrate the seasonal workers into the union activities.

This is not to say that the seasonal workers have been forgotten by the union. On the contrary, when controlled they are a source of power for the union because they pay dues and make up a large union constituency. Given the opportunity and government support, the union officials would work for the seasonal workers. For example, during an interview at the Ingenio del Norte union office, an official took out an envelope of pictures concealed under a pile of paper in the bottom drawer of his desk. With strict instructions not to tell anyone, he said the pictures of the temporary workers' housing were being sent directly to the president of the country by a personal friend. When asked if he thought something would come of it, he said he thought so, as the president was a "friend of the workers," a strangely optimistic appraisal of the situation. In this case the union was attempting to gain some derivative power from the central government for use in its confrontation with the plantation owners and administration. Union officials felt the government was increasingly interested in supporting labor. A further reason for the action was that because of its neglect of the seasonal workers the union was losing control of part of its constituency—some seasonal workers had indicated they would not join the next strike unless they received more immediate tangible benefits from their participation.

In 1970 the plantation hired over 6,500 seasonal workers while permanent workers numbered around 2,900. The company extracts 350 pesos a month from each worker's pay check to cover union dues; this is equivalent to a quarter day of work. With the zafra lasting more than five months, seasonal workers provide more than half of the union's income for the year, yet they do not participate in the decision-making process of the union. Not needing the votes of the seasonal workers, yet having complete access to their union dues, the union officers are unresponsive to the problems of the seasonal workers.

Workers occasionally attempt to circumvent the union in an effort to get help on individual grievances. Argentine laborers may go directly to the Dirección del Trabajo (Department of Labor), a provincial agency entrusted with enforcing labor laws and regulations. Bolivian workers may go to the Bolivian consul who, depending upon his evaluation of the case, may hire a lawyer and take the case to the Dirección del Trabajo, which in turn deals directly with the plantation labor office. The Dirección has the power to evoke penalties and enforce decisions. In the late 1960s seasonal workers on the plantation seldom attempted to go to the Bolivian consul or the Dirección del Trabajo because of the costs of travel and time as well as their limited expectations of help.

Although union officials justify the automatic extraction of dues by claiming that it is the only way to insure universal payment, as well as saving large amounts of time, the zafrero sees it as an involuntary payment for an intangible service. Some zafreros feel that if the union had to come to collect money, the officials would have to talk with the workers and possibly do something for them. As it is, they do not even bother to go to the lotes to explain to the seasonal workers what services the union offers or to ask for suggestions. Generally they visit the work camps only to announce a strike and to elicit support. As one zafrero put it, "When they want a strike, they tell us not to work, that workers must stay together to get what they want. After the strike we never see them again. They use us and our money."

How do the zafreros account for the union's lack of activity on their behalf? Most seem to feel that the union is *comprado* (paid off) by the administration. They see the union and the administration as working together, jointly collecting union fees, and located close to one another in the company town, distant from the work camps. Furthermore, they cite a strong resemblance in the treatment they receive from union and administration officials alike. Some suggest that the union officials' interests are the same as those of the administration: to keep things the way they are. There is also a strong feeling that the union, when it does act, favors the permanent workers, particularly the skilled workers such as tractor drivers or mill personnel. They point to the union's eager acceptance of mechanization of the harvest, which is displacing seasonal workers from their jobs but promises higher pay to permanent employees. Some zafreros were particularly disturbed when the company reduced the maximum hiring age from fifty years to forty years, leaving some who had worked in the zafra the longest without work. The union did not protest.

Seasonal workers would like the union's help in certain areas where unions traditionally offer aid, such as helping workers get *jubilación* (retirement pay) and indemnity for injuries. As it is, zafreros feel the union gives little assistance. When a seasonal worker has a problem—for example, in receiving indemnity for a work injury—he first goes to his mayordomo or possibly to the contratista who is in charge of the work force. Usually this person will try to help the worker without putting any pressure on the administration. If this fails but the worker still feels he has been dealt with unfairly, he will weigh the time and the humiliation of going to the union against the possible gains. Generally, the seasonal worker will decide to drop the issue.

When the zafrero does go to the union office, he often does so hat in hand, humbly asking for information or service. Relatively long waits are not uncommon once he has arrived at the office. By itself the trip from the work camp to the office, located near the sugar mill and administration building, may take up to an hour, if transportation connections can be made. In some cases only one bus a day connects the work camp and the mill town; in others no transportation is available. When the union official does talk to the zafrero, more often than not he is brusque and patronizing, which the zafrero resents. Uncomfortable in the union offices and suspicious of its officials, many zafreros vow that they will visit the union as seldom as possible.

There are many areas in which the seasonal workers would welcome union support. Zafreros often feel cheated by the company when the cane is weighed. They wish the union would supervise the weighing procedure but claim it is unwilling to help. According to the union, government inspectors began coming to Ingenio del Norte in 1954 and have come ever since; in 1970 however, there had been no inspection, yet union officials seemed unconcerned. Many zafreros on Ingenio del Norte complain about the living quarters, in which two or three families are often packed into a single room. Many houses are run down and squalid as well, which aggravates the overcrowding. The union has repeatedly failed to make an issue out of the housing problem of the temporary workers. This may be such a touchy issue with the administration that union officials are afraid to push the subject and have waited to approach it differently, as we mentioned earlier.

Zafreros dislike and distrust the doctors at the company hospital, fearing that students are being brought from Buenos Aires to practice on them and their children. The union, they feel, is unresponsive to their fears. Many zafreros consider the problem of schooling unsolved, despite union claims of improving education on the plantation. Some lotes do not have schools near enough to be easily accessible by the company trucks. During the Perón era schools were built on many of the isolated lotes, but apparently today some of the schools are closed down from time to time, much to the distress of the parents. Sometimes children have to walk several miles to the nearest school. On other lotes children are turned away from overcrowded schools. The general feeling is that the union does little to better the situation. Of course the union cannot be blamed for all the educational problems that stem from the disruptive migratory existence of many of the children.

The resentment against the union and its officials runs very high. Partly this attitude may reflect the active role of *sindicatos* (unions) in Bolivia (see, for example, Heath 1973, and Heath, Erasmus, and Buechler 1969). Most of the workers expect the company to be exploitative but recognize that little can be done about this if the union is ineffective, especially considering the orientation of the Argentine government at the time. Because of their lack of power and their dependence on zafra income, the workers are in no position to protest. They are forced to finish their work, take their pay, and move on to another job.

Although permanent workers make up the most influential constituency of the union, the zafreros do not resent them individually. Seasonal workers generally have little social or work contact with the permanent workers on the plantation. The zafreros regard the unskilled permanent workers who work in the fields as being much like themselves: "They are like us, unimportant in either the union or the company." Some of the permanent fieldworkers had worked originally as zafreros. Although some seasonal workers would like permanent work, many others consider enduring the long, steaming summer as too much of a sacrifice for permanent employment. The skilled permanent workers were seldom seen, although the zafreros knew they were more important in the union.[4] In 1969 both permanent and seasonal workers went on strike for a day. As a result the union did get a long overdue wage increase, but much to the surprise and resentment of the seasonal workers, it did not take effect until after the harvest. While part of this resentment was directed towards permanent workers, most of it was focused on the union as an organization.

The Bolivian and Argentine seasonal workers often, but not always, live in separate quarters. They seldom mingle socially but share a distaste for the union. The Bolivians seem to feel more hopelessly disenfranchised and power-less, but as foreigners in Argentina they are careful not to protest too loudly within earshot of either union or company officials. The Argentine zafreros are freer with their criticism and generally tend to blame the government as well as the union for part of the problem. Some even said they felt that they were be-ing treated as "Bolivians" or foreigners by the union.

The Work Camp and Postharvest Planning

No discussion of the lote environment would be complete without mention-ing its relationship to migrant adaptation and its important role in the strategiz-ing process. What at first appears to be nothing more than a collection of run-down buildings used to house temporary workers is in fact the physical form for a dynamic locality of human exchange and planning that crucially affects decisions about postzafra activities.

Life in the lote is more than work and rest. For some families who during the postzafra season migrate nomadically throughout Argentina, in search of employment, the lote serves as a type of home base, helping them cope with feelings of isolation, loneliness, and insecurity by offering regular companion-ship in familiar, if less than desirable, living quarters. For nuclear and extended families who split up after the zafra, the lote may provide a place to reunite with family members who have more or less settled in Argentina. Juan, for ex-ample, lives and works on a tobacco farm in Salta during the postzafra period but joins his brother's family every year on a lote at Ingenio del Norte. Al-though he has not been back to his home community in Bolivia since he left over twenty years ago because of matrimonial problems, by returning to the lote every year Juan reestablishes ties with his family and home community.

The New Arrivals: Preadaptation on the Plantation.. For new migrants, the beginning of the zafra and life on the lote represent a very different encounter. Unlike Juan, few are rejoining friends and relatives but on the contrary may be leaving them for a new, potentially threatening experience. The zafra is some-times used by the Bolivian agricultural worker as a first step into Argentina;[5] he may sign up for the zafra feeling that the work is secure and that he can learn about other work opportunities while working on the plantation. Martín came to the zafra for the first time in 1970. Eighteen and unable to find work in his hometown of Culpina in the department of Chuquisaca, Bolivia, he decided to work as a cuarta for one of the men from his village. While at the plantation he began to consider searching for work in Argentina after the zafra. But he was nervous about traveling in Argentina; he did not have proper work papers and was unsure of how to get them. Several of the more experienced workers told him he was a fool not to have papers, citing numerous examples of men badly exploited because they lacked documents. Despite the warnings, Martín was not convinced, saying it was too costly and time-consuming to take out papers. Finally his friends approached him from another angle. They told him places to avoid as he searched for work, Tucumán for one. "They don't like Bolivians there," he was told. "Take a truck to Perico. Stay at Hostería San Martín. It's inexpensive. There will be an old *paisano* [countryman] by the name of Don Jaime. Don Jaime will get you work on a farm. You will not earn as much there as you would at other farms, but they usually pay the workers, even those without papers." Martín soon began to learn what to do and what not to do—where to get a "safe job," where to stay, how to travel, where not to go, what to expect from the police, and where they check the buses that connect the plantation and the highland towns. As he spent more time on the lote lote he learned about more jobs and more places to stay. Most important, he made friends he could travel with, men who had made the trip before and had contacts in other parts. At the end of the zafra Martín had enough money to travel in Argentina and went with two boys his age to a farm in Mendoza. When he returned to the lote the next year he had seen the world and had a new confidence—it was his turn to give advice. But he still had to learn: his last job had ended too early, leaving him unemployed for three weeks before the zafra began.

At the lote Bolivians not only learn about work conditions and job openings, but they also have an opportunity to live for four to five months with other Bolivians while being exposed to a new culture and having work contact with Argentines. During this period they are in a good position to ask questions about labor laws, salaries, prices, availability of foods, national holidays, union activities, politics, and national-level soccer teams. Obviously, not all of this information is uniformly important for successful adaptation in other regions of Argentina; nor will the migrants necessarily be isolated from their countrymen when they leave the zafra. Nevertheless, the companionship of large numbers of Bolivians and the gradual exposure to Argentina is an important aid in the adaptation process. In some cases temporary migration evolves into permanent migration. Of course, the tremendous power of the company over the zafreros and the isolation of the lotes filters and colors the new cultural milieu.

Critical Concerns. As the zafra moves to a close, people become restless. The administration's target date for ending the harvest is rarely announced to the workers, but rumors circulate throughout the lote during the final weeks of the zafra. This is not idle gossip, but is crucial to many men and their families because with the end of the zafra thousands will be suddenly unemployed. Workers view the end of the zafra with mixed feelings. It means possibly escaping the ever-increasing heat of the impending summer, the swarms of flies and biting insects, and the crowded rooms; and for some it means returning home to work their own land and plant their own crops. For many others, though, it is the beginning of a period of uncertainty. They need to find work that will tide them over until the zafra begins again. Housing immediately becomes a problem. Families without relatives or friends with whom they can stay, and without employment on farms which provide housing, must begin to use up their zafra earnings for shelter. Strategies which have been discussed during the long zafra must now be activated or forgotten until another year. Families may divide up, individual members going separate paths in search of work. Friends may decide to travel together after sharing information and advice. Information is essential for making these decisions. Although the migrants' evaluation of the job market and work conditions depends upon their past experiences and the information they can accumulate throughout the zafra, it is not until the last weeks of the harvest that specific information is available about job conditions in traditional work areas.

Information Needs for Postzafra Decisions. On a general level workers trying to decide where to seek postzafra employment usually consider the type of work, the length of the work season, the reputation of the employer, the cost of transportation between the region and the sugar zone, the wages, and how all of these affect earnings. Of course, few decisions are ever made based on *complete* information. Nevertheless, the search to learn about work situations is of crucial importance.

One of the critical pieces of information guiding a worker's postzafra choice is the reputation of the employer. For some workers a "good" patrón is someone who pays the established wage and that on a regular basis. In many cases these two requirements are not fulfilled, especially for Bolivians without documents. Workers caught in this situation have little recourse. Help for Bolivians is not likely to come from the two major rural worker unions in Salta and Jujuy: Federación Unica de Sindicatos de Trabajo de Campo Agropecuario (FUSTCA—Federation of Farm Workers' Unions) and Federación Argentina de Trabajadores Rurales y Estibadores (FATRE—Argentine Federation of Rural Workers and Stevedores). These unions feel that the Bolivians' acceptance of substandard pay undercuts wages in Argentina. Furthermore, many farms lack unions altogether. The rural union organizers have had difficulty establishing unions on many farms due to the high employment in rural areas and the strong vertical ties workers often try to maintain with their patrón in order to protect their employment. In the rich Santa Rosa region of Salta, FUSTCA organizers were thrown off several farms by the workers. Wages had recently been raised to the minimum wage required by law and were much better than on other farms in the area. The workers did not want to lose their positions. Unlike the large plantations concerned with public image and located close to main highways, many of the farms hiring temporary workers are relatively isolated and not subject to public scrutiny. "Good" patrones are particularly adept at persuading their workers not to join a union. Workers with families are concerned about reliable payments, but they are equally concerned with the patrón's dependability in providing work during future postzafra seasons and with his ability and willingness to help his workers when they have a problem, especially medical.

Some zafreros feel that really "good" employers do not exist. Julio put it most succinctly: "A patrón may be good when it helps him to be good, but he may be bad when he wants to be. There is nothing we can do." This observation seems to concur with the point made by both Ernest Feder (1971: 401) and Peter Singelmann (1971: 141), that in many cases the patrón can assume a role of being good when it benefits his case but is generally free to reverse himself at his convenience. The "good" patrón generates a series of dependencies with workers which allow for a form of manipulation.

Of course, zafreros must consider many other variables besides the quality of their prospective employers. They are interested in specific types of information about farms: living conditions (they do not want to share rooms with other families), location of stores and the prices charged for food, availability of credit, proximity of schools, size of fields to be harvested, quality of the crops, length of the workday, isolation of the farm, transportation connections with other locations, proximity to farms which may have other crops that could be harvested at a later date, medical help, and sometimes availability of garden plots. Obviously not all of these are given the same weight, but together they indicate that workers often seek a wide variety of information about a region or a particular farm in order to maximize security and to minimize risk during the postzafra period.

Ignacio, eighteen and single, in considering the basic work possibilities, first thought about returning to Bolivia after the zafra: he could live with his father and family; his neighbors might need some temporary help planting, but he would probably work for his parents; however, his two younger brothers could now do most of the work he once did. If he could get a job in the tobacco harvest in Jujuy he could earn about 800 pesos a day, but would have to pay about 300 pesos a day for meals. He thought it would be interesting to go to Mendoza, but the round trip itself would cost him over 5,000 pesos. He knew of others who had only 8,000 or 10,000 pesos after they returned from working all season in Mendoza in various harvests.

For a young single man the opportunity to travel and see Argentina outweighs the risk of not finding sufficient work and the unpredictable problems such as bad patrones, poor crops, or illnesses. For older men with large families, including children who must pay travel fares but who may not be able to earn much, the trip imposes a greater risk. This risk is considerably less if the children are old enough to take advantage of higher pay scales that may be offered and if the sources of work are relatively secure. Information about the quality of the crop in the area is still crucial. For example, a dry growing season and early frost may badly damage fruit crops in Río Negro, as they did in 1971. When this happens, many workers feel the trip is not worth the effort. On the other hand, some may have made previous arrangements with the patrón to return for the harvest and by not returning may risk their relatively secure source of work.

Sources of Information. Workers on different lotes may not receive identical information. An individual's access to job information is often determined by an important difference existing between lotes on the same plantation. Workers from certain lotes may finish harvesting the cane in their specific work area as much as a month earlier than workers from other lotes finish their harvests. This is most common when one work area has many hectares of new sugar cane which cannot be harvested that year, rather than cane that is over a year old. When this happens, the company often transports the workers to another section, sometimes as much as fifteen miles away, to help harvest. But other times the men are paid and free to leave if they desire. If the timing is right they may get a jump on the job market; however, if it is too early many of the traditional seasonal jobs will not have started yet and they could lose a month's work on the plantation. Thus, the condition of the cane in a lote's work area may affect a worker's availability for postzafra work, as well as his earnings at the plantation. Although many men would like to leave the zafra early to scout for employment opportunities ahead of the crowd, the company will not pay in full the workers who leave early without permission—and permission is difficult to obtain.

Another variable affecting a worker's access to information is the relative isolation of his particular lote. Lotes located miles off the main road with infrequent or nonexistent bus connections to local towns do not receive as much information as lotes on main transportation routes. Nevertheless, some sources of information are available to all lotes. Many of the vendors who visit the lotes live in Salta or Jujuy during the postzafra period and maintain close ties with wholesale vendors and friends in these areas; some work as part-time contratistas for small construction jobs. Although their information about the job market is usually limited to a small geographic area, they are always willing to venture opinions. Truck drivers who haul cane stop and talk on the lote, often giving out information about big construction jobs where they hope to get a job with their truck. Other sources of information are visitors who come to the lote and family or friends who may leave the lote to check on nearby job possibilities.

Mail is not delivered to most lotes, and few zafreros write letters to find out about employment opportunities. Newspapers are not considered an important source of information, since jobs advertised will either be gone before the men are able to leave the plantation or require qualifications the zafreros do not have. Occasionally a newspaper article provides information about environmental conditions, such as a freeze in Río Negro, the popular apple region in southern Argentina.

Mayordomos and other plantation personnel are continually asked whether the company will be hiring men after the zafra to clear new areas, plant cane, or cultivate. In 1971, 153 workers from a lote of 322 men signed up to work for the plantation during the summer. Some felt this was a good job as it required minimal moving and was relatively secure. Others did not want to stay on the plantation to face the intense 110 degree heat and felt they could earn more money on other jobs.

Occasionally contratistas from other companies arrive at the lote looking for workers for postzafra periods, especially if they need large numbers of people. Although many workers are wary of them, feeling that if the jobs were good they could fill them without coming, the contratistas manage to sign up workers unwilling to take the trouble of looking for a job, with the risk of not finding one. In 1970, a contratista came to Ingenio del Norte to contract workers for a company that hand-sprayed herbicides and insecticides for cane growers in Tucumán. He had once worked in the ingenio as a mayordomo and knew many of the workers. Some workers felt it was strange that he should come to Ingenio del Norte to recruit workers when Tucumán had one of the highest rates of unemployment in all of Argentina. He flattered those who were curious by telling them no one could work like the Bolivians, that the Tucumanos were much slower and lazier. Promises of good food, high wages, eight-hour work days, and possible permanent work were too much to resist. In a matter of hours, over sixty workers from two lotes signed up. The following year, the lote throbbed with news about the contratista's swindle. In Tucumán, the Bolivian workers were kept separate and isolated from the unionized Argentine workers; they were paid much less than they had been promised and had to work longer hours; the housing was bad and the food atrocious. People were very bitter, pointing out that this was what happens to foreigners.

Not all of the information regarding the job market is available on the lotes. One strategy a worker may use to increase his knowledge is to move to a town in one of the traditional seasonal-work areas and then find out about exact work sites. Ciudad Perico, located in the middle of one of the most productive tobacco belts and easily accessible by bus from Ingenio del Norte, has traditionally been an important stopover for families after the zafra. Towns like Perico serve as a locality where information is refined and where workers come for more specific information. For example, workers may go to Perico knowing that there are prospects for a good tobacco harvest. They may have the names of several farms near Perico and know generally when the harvest begins and ends in the region. In Perico they will get more exact information about the crop, the number of farms hiring labor, and other jobs that might be available before and after the harvest. Some of their leads may be cancelled out immediately; for example, a farm where a worker had hoped to find employment may have filled its quota of workers. Other communities in Jujuy which have similar functions as Perico, though to a lesser degree, are San Pedro, the city of Jujuy, and Fraile Pintado. In Salta, Güemes, the city of Salta, Cerrillos, and Santa Rosa de la Frontera are also centers where zafreros seek employment and employment news.

Some trips in search of work may involve stops at many different locations instead of only one work area. In 1968, for example, Santiago went looking for work with a friend who had made the trip before. On a Tucumán farm they found work harvesting garlic and onions from November until January and were paid 680 pesos a day. In February they moved to Comodoro Rivadavia (southern Argentina) and worked harvesting peaches for the same daily wage. When the harvest ended they moved to Mendoza to look for work. At their rooming house they saw a notice for grape harvesters, and soon afterward they were employed. They were paid 21 pesos a basket and could do forty to fifty a day. The harvest lasted about a month; it was then time to return to the zafra. Santiago felt that they had been lucky that year as they had not encountered a bad patrón, having turned down work with several who might have been unsatisfactory.

In discussing information and its application to the choice of postzafra work, it is important to stress that the worker and his family cannot usually pick and choose among a number of possibilities. They are constricted by their lack of resources and their socioeconomic position within the capitalist political economy. The opportunity to make a choice brings a burden—that of minimizing risk and maximizing security in an effort to survive. Furthermore, although the largest number of alternative courses of action are available during the postzafra season, there are only limited opportunities for the worker to break away from his migrant status. In general, all of the alternatives during the postzafra period are short-term and supported by the worker's knowledge that he can again return to the zafra.

At one time or another during the year almost all of the workers are forced to face unemployment. When the worker or family has no place to live during these periods, the ambiguity, insecurity, and frustration become particularly great. Yet few families seem to accept their situation with apathy. Their response is far from disorganized, as some studies of migrant workers suggest (see, for example, Friedland and Nelkin 1971: 1). In order to cope with the obstacles imposed by the socioeconomic structure, strategies evolve: apolitical and individualistic strategies in which the individual, family, and even the extended family attempt to maximize certain controls over aspects of their lives and eliminate some of the risk involved. Information about their environment is crucial for these decisions—and much of this information is gathered at the lote.

6. The Multiple Faces of the Labor Reserve

While working on the plantations the laborers share a similar position in relation to the means of production. In addition they experience the same work and living conditions. Yet at the end of the zafra when the men and their families disperse to diverse parts of Bolivia and Argentina, they earn a living in many different ways. The vast majority of families seek postzafra jobs to sustain themselves until the following sugar harvest, and they are part of a labor reserve that cuts across rural-urban boundaries. The subsistence activities and associated migration patterns are different than most patterns of seasonal migration reported in the social-science literature, namely, population movements of semiproletarianized peasants living in highland communities who seasonally work in the lowlands. This was once the dominant pattern in the Norte, but today a growing number of laborers are drawn from a pool of landless workers who during the year move between jobs in different localities.

This chapter examines the different patterns of labor migration presently associated with the sugar harvest. The patterns are responses to the constraints limiting individual and family options. In an effort to cope with these constraints people make decisions defining needs, resources, and tactics for solving critical problems. The patterns reflect the different faces, or dimensions, of the labor reserve drawn upon by the plantations. Development of class consciousness and collective action is limited by the individualistic nature of the responses, which are made to cope with immediate and pressing problems and which ultimately serve to perpetuate the labor reserve.

I distinguish four major migration patterns. The patterns are intended not to differentiate between classes in the Marxian sense but rather to show variations in the lives and work of those in the labor reserve. The patterns differ in terms of control of work opportunity, residence security, resources available, and the social organization developed to cope with the problems. Families or individuals may pursue a particular pattern for limited periods, often correlating with stages in the family cycle. Transitions are usually associated with shifting concerns, changing constraints and opportunities, and new strategies.[1] Although patterns involve great spatial mobility, they also indicate the limits of social mobility for individual families and the social class as a whole.

Rural Semiproletarian Pattern

Every year hundreds of families leave their small farms in the Andean regions of Northwest Argentina and Bolivia to work in the zafra. During the previous summer months they have stayed on their farms raising vegetables, grain, and possibly a few cattle or sheep. But winter in many of these regions is either too cold or too dry for agriculture. Their low incomes force many of these peasants to come to the Ramal to work in the zafra during the winter months.

The rural semiproletarian pattern allows the families to remain in their villages, farming their own land during part of the year. Because of this, their demands and desires are directed towards their home area rather than towards improving the conditions of work away from home. Without the income from the zafra, many more would be forced to migrate to the city or to become part of the year-round labor force. Of course, while the plantations provide seasonal work, which functions to maintain a labor reserve, they also control the best agricultural land, receive credit and price supports, and technical inputs from the government. The peasants are left with small pieces of highland valley land or larger sections of arid, steep, mountainous terrain, unable to get credit and encountering problems storing or transporting the produce.

Thirty years ago most of the Bolivians who came to work on the plantations were semiproletarians, but by the early 1970s the percentage of semiproletarians was considerably lower (although still significant). In a random sample taken on the plantations of the Norte in 1971, Juan Villar (1974: 77) found that 24 percent of the workers planned to return to Bolivia after the zafra; in a random sample I took on the work camp, 30 percent planned to return to Bolivia, and almost all of these planned to work on family farms they or their parents owned. Although some Bolivians with access to family land remained in Argentina after the zafra, the vast majority returned to Bolivia to work the land during the post-zafra season. Of the workers who remained in Argentina after the zafra, almost 80 percent did not own or have access to land in Bolivia.[2]

There are two major spatial variations in the rural semiproletarian pattern. Men migrate to the zafra with or without their families and directly after it return to the family farm in Bolivia or Argentina. Another pattern includes work on a tobacco or vegetable farm either before or after the zafra. This second pattern usually reflects a stage in the man's life cycle when he is young, single, and does not have land of his own but lives and works on his parents' farm.

A rural semiproletarian may participate in different patterns of migration during his life. When a boy is very young he often travels with his parents to the zafra, usually going to the field to play in the cut cane leaves. By the time he is ten or eleven his parents usually begin to teach him to work in the fields. Of course, he may attend school, but he often is considered strong enough to help the family by this age. At about fifteen he may be hired as a cuarta, often by someone from his extended family. The boy usually lives with the zafrero unless his own family lives on the same lote, and he is expected to work almost full time in the fields, helping with cutting, stripping leaves, and topping the cane. If he is strong enough he will also help with loading. Sometimes on weekends he is dismissed from work in the field to cut and haul firewood for cooking. Occasionally girls are hired as helpers. Their primary job is to prepare meals, especially if the zafrero is single, but they may also help trim cane leaves in the fields.

Until a boy is old enough to work as a helper he will return with his family to his *pago* (homeland), where he helps plant, cultivate, and harvest the crops. After the age of fifteen, it is common for him to travel in Argentina with several older companions, usually close relatives, in search of postzafra work. The Bolivians say a boy is going to *rodear el mundo* (see the world) when he is ready to leave the camp. It is a big adventure and is greatly anticipated. Some will find work on tobacco farms in the provinces of Salta or Jujuy, taking advantage of the proximity to the provincial capitals to explore the cities, where, if fortunate, they can stay with friends or relatives. Many hope to go south, lured by the exciting stories of Buenos Aires and possible work opportunities. Their trip south is usually direct, at least until they arrive in Rosario. Few want to stop in Tucumán, for Tucumanos have a reputation among Bolivians of being hostile to them. This probably stems from the high unemployment in the area that followed the closing of the sugar mills. Córdoba is rarely mentioned as a place of work. The glittering city is Buenos Aires. If the boys do not have relatives in Buenos Aires, and if they cannot find work quickly, they often move on to Mar del Plata, where contratistas hire workers for the vegetable and fruit harvests. Others may go to Mendoza, the favorite Argentine region of many Bolivians. Ample work on the farms, a refreshing climate, and the generally friendly attitude of the Mendozino patrones are often cited in conversations between workers. The high cost of transportation and time lost in traveling make the experience of rodeando el mundo temporary and reserved for young single men.

Until he marries, a boy may continue to work in Argentina after the zafra if his help is not needed on the family farm. Once married he may receive rights to some farm land, or try to buy land near his home community. The zafra income and postzafra earnings are important in this acquisition. On the other hand, the family may be forced to move to Argentina to seek employment.

To supplement my ethnographic material on rural semiproletarians, I gave a short questionnaire at the plantation to a sample of fifty rural semiproletarians from near the village of San Lorenzo, Bolivia. Located about fifteen kilometers from the colonial town of Tarija, San Lorenzo enjoys a milder temperature than many of the other Andean regions where zafreros live, but its dry winter prohibits agriculture without irrigation. Working in the zafra is relatively new for San Lorenzo inhabitants, in contrast to residents from such areas as Río San Juan, Tupiza, and Chaco Pampa.

Few San Lorenzo men who now work in the zafra had fathers who were zafreros. There was a period after the agrarian reform when many families had enough irrigated land. With inheritances and sales, however, landholdings became smaller, and in about 1961 some of the men started looking for new sources of work to supplement their farming income. The zafra proved to be one source. At this time the conversion rate of the Argentine peso to the Bolivian peso was particularly advantageous for the zafrero returning to Bolivia. In 1963, for example, a man could get 88 Bolivian pesos to the Argentine peso. Although this exchange fell to 25 Bolivian pesos per Argentine peso in 1970, many men still find the zafra worth the travel and the hard work. In fact the zafra provided more than 50 percent of the annual income of the men in the sample.

In the San Lorenzo sample, the mean age of the workers was 30 years, with a range from 20 years to 52 years. The mean level of education was 1.4 years of school, and the range was from no school'ng to 6 years of school. The high average number of years worked in the zafra—11.5 years—does not really reflect the zafra experience of the group in general; a small nucleus of workers had worked 15 to 20 years, but most of the workers had less than 7 years of zafra work experience.

Ninety percent of the men paid others to work on their land while they were at the zafra in Argentina. The work consisted of preparing the ground for planting and caring for the animals, usually sheep but also some cows and burros. The usual payment for a *jornal* (a day of labor) was 300 pesos, much less than a day's earnings at the zafra. Often the money was paid to family members, most commonly the man's parents or in-laws. Siblings also worked for one another, usually on a pay basis.

Sixty percent of the men felt they would be forced to move to Argentina at some time in the future. They cited insufficient landholdings and lack of irrigation water as their two major problems. They felt that they did not have enough land to feed their families or to justify returning to Bolivia to cultivate, and few felt they would be able to buy more land. They wanted to move because they felt there were more work opportunities in Argentina than in Bolivia. Of the 60 percent, all but three wanted to stay in the Northwest. Perico was the most popular choice as a place to live and work, followed by Ledesma-Libertador, Jujuy, and Salta. The three men who did not want to stay in the North-west wanted to go to Mendoza. None had relatives in Mendoza, but all had worked there before, liked the area, and knew there were jobs. None of the workers expressed a desire to go directly to any of the major Argentine cities.

As the above data suggest, the semiproletarian pattern is not a stable condi-tion for families over many generations.[3] As Alain de Janvry (n.d.: 143) points out, there are a series of contradictions in contrived functional dualism. Pea-sants are forced by poverty to overwork small landholdings, which threatens the ecological base and lowers yields. This generates a vicious downward spiral. E-qually important, poverty forces families to develop every productive resource. Family size often increases, especially if wage labor is available. Children can take household jobs and so free parents to earn incomes outside of the house-hold. They also provide security for parents in old age and poor health. When children move away to Argentina or other regions at an increasingly younger age, parents want to have other children at home to work. Those who move away often provide important additional income by sending remittances. All of these factors combine to make large families advantageous to parents. Yet all of the children cannot remain semiproletarians. Landholdings are fragment-ed if inheritance is passed to each child; in other cases the land is left to the first or last child. In either case the process generates families whose land is inadequate for subsistence production. Some of these families become landless workers seeking employment in both the countryside and urban centers.

Rural Mobile Proletarian Pattern

Landless agricultural workers without a particular farm where they can de-pend on finding postzafra employment face a particularly difficult time. These are rural mobile proletarians.[4] The postzafra travel may take the men and their families to many different jobs of short duration, usually in the country but oc-casionally in the mines or in towns or cities. The towns and cities are most of-ten in the Northwest, but the men sometimes go as far as Buenos Aires. Some also return to towns in Bolivia.

Individuals or families may remain highly mobile for varying lengths of time. For example, we have already seen how some young men from peasant or rural semiproletarian families spend a period of time exploring Argentina working at a variety of jobs, later returning to their family farm. For others the pattern of holding multiple rural jobs over a short number of postzafra seasons may be a transition stage before they become established on farms as permanent employ-ees or move into another pattern. But for many, establishing a predictable base of work and residence is very difficult. At times a job may last longer than usu-al, but generally there is little opportunity to establish a secure base to return to after the zafra.

Many factors make it difficult for Bolivian workers to gain permanent employment in either the city or the countryside. During the late 1940s and the early 1950s less postzafra agricultural work was available in Salta and Jujuy than exists today. Tobacco was just becoming an important crop. Vegetables now grown for the Buenos Aires market were not cultivated for sale in the Buenos Aires market then. With the development of commercial production of tobacco and vegetables, the need for seasonal labor to harvest the crops grew dramatically. The increased market for seasonal labor generally coincided with the end of the zafra. This labor market seems to have quickly absorbed both Bolivians who had not found "permanent" work in Argentina after the zafra and those who had been working year around on farms in the region.

During the following ten years mechanization had a profound impact on the labor situation of the region, particularly on the plantations where many zafreros had traditionally found postzafra work. Formerly, plowing had been done with mules, oxen had pulled the seedcane wagons, and all cultivation had been done by hand. Today giant caterpillar tractors pull huge plows, tractors are used for much of the cultivation, airplanes spray herbicides and insecticides, and tractors or trucks haul all of the seedcane. Hundreds of people have been replaced, either because they did not have the skills to handle the jobs and the companies were unwilling to train them or because there was no work. The same process is taking place on farms all over the Northwest, although to a lesser degree. Workers who have been laid off have had to seek work harvesting seasonal crops or move to the city. Although some have found work on new farms as the agricultural sector expanded, the number of new full-time job openings is comparatively small.

Only in the late 1960s did mechanization of the sugar harvest become an important factor in terms of the labor market, although previously tractors and trucks sped up the process of moving the crops from the fields to the processing or storage sheds. On some plantations today the cane is sprayed with a defoliant and burned to eliminate manual topping and trimming of the leaves, and several of the plantations are experimenting with machines which cut and load the sugar cane. Ingenio del Norte officials found the machines so successful they planned to buy eleven of them before the 1973 harvest. Each machine, when working properly and with a coordinated wagon exchange, is expected to replace 350 men.[5] Another plantation in the Ramal has already mechanized its harvest, cutting the number of zafreros needed from 3,000 to under 500. But no one thinks that the sugar harvest can be mechanized completely. Heavy equipment cannot be used after rains and often tends to break down. Furthermore, the fields must be free of rocks and have a smooth contour, which is not always feasible.

On the smaller farms, where most of the vegetables and tobacco are grown, mechanization of the harvest is not taking place. Nevertheless, both temporary and full-time labor find their employment insecure. Market fluctuations, which in turn affect the acreage allocated to particular crops, have enormous effect on the labor markets. A reduction in tobacco prices, for example, has led some growers in Salta and Jujuy to reduce their acreage planted in tobacco. In other regions in Salta some farmers are replacing cultivated fields with cattle, one of the oldest forms of land use in the area. Since cattle require fewer laborers, men are dismissed.

Ironically, another factor hurting many laborers is the indemnity law, which states that a permanent worker must be paid a special indemnity if he is laid off. Many employers get around the law by laying off their workers a few days short of the time when they would achieve permanent worker status. This practice affects many workers besides the so-called unskilled.

When the above forces are coupled with the steady flow of Bolivians into the region the result is a large labor force of mobile workers which is immensely useful to agricultural producers. The growers have access to large numbers of potential workers who with considerable difficulty maintain themselves at a subsistence level by seeking temporary work in many different activities, workers who cannot find permanent work, which would remove them from the labor-force reserve on which the harvests depend. When labor is needed, the available supply of workers is large, which helps growers to keep wages low. Yet wages are not allowed to slip to a level so low that the workers cannot maintain themselves and their families with the seasonal work.

Many families in the rural mobile proletarian patterns—and in the rural shuttle proletarian patterns described later—work in the tobacco harvest; the difference is that workers in the former group are not employed for the entire post-zafra season and therefore must make multiple moves in search of work. Access to work soon after the zafra ends is crucial for many rural mobile proletarians. The timing for planting tobacco seedbeds, transplanting, and harvesting vary within each area, but some generalizations can be made. In the Perico area, the most productive tobacco zone in Jujuy, seedbeds of Virginia tobacco can be planted starting mid-June to early July, transplanted around the middle of September, and the first leaves harvested in November. Seedbeds for Burley tobacco can be planted starting in mid-July, transplanted mid-to-late September, and harvested beginning mid-December. At the time of the study, the zafra ended in late September, but the end of the zafra varies depending upon the plantation, work camp, and year. Although some workers may get work transplanting and cultivating, most are forced to use up part of their zafra earnings while waiting for their employment as harvesters on tobacco farms. (Usually those who find work on fruit or vegetable farms in the area also must wait to be employed.)

After the tobacco harvest many are left unemployed and have to seek work and shelter in another area. Some are able to get temporary work in tobacco harvests in Salta, but many return to Bolivia or go further south in Argentina to Mendoza, Río Negro, or Mar del Plata to work in other harvests. Still others may look for work in towns or cities.

In a survey of Bolivian workers on tobacco farms in the province of Salta, Juan Villar (1975: 40) found that 34 percent of the Bolivian laborers also worked in the sugar harvest during the year of the study. His material shows several migration routes not associated with the sugar harvest, including circular migration between Bolivia and the tobacco farms, between vegetable farms in Salta and Mendoza and the tobacco farms in Salta. Villar found that 21 percent of the workers did not have papers, that the daily wage was little over a third of what is earned on the plantations, and that very few farms paid the required fringe benefits of bonuses for workers with children, retirement payments, or accident indemnity. Eighteen percent of the workers, most of whom were paid once a month, reported late payments (Villar 1975: 67-69). The findings of Villar's study, coupled with workers' reports of crowded housing, poor water, and expensive food, help document the exploited and precarious position of the seasonal worker on most tobacco farms.

In Salta, in the Valle de Lerma, the seedbeds for Virginia tobacco are not planted until July, the transplanting does not occur until mid-September, and the harvest does not start until the middle of December. Seedbeds for Burley tobacco are planted mid-August, transplanted mid-to-late October, and the harvest begins the end of December. Those workers who have signed up with Salta fincas may get work transplanting and cultivating before the harvest, if they are lucky, but many have to wait to work until the harvest begins. If the harvest ends in March or early April, the worker is again left without lodging and work, until the zafra starts. Many leave for other areas. Those who do not, scramble for the odd jobs that may be available in the region, jobs ranging from clearing land to weeding. Some are able to join ongoing harvests on vegetable farms in the area; a few get jobs in the cultivation and early harvest of Criollo tobacco in parts of Salta such as Cerrillos, La Merced, Chicano, and La Viña the few months prior to the zafra. As a group the rural mobile proletarians are seminomadic, migrating to different farms with the changing of the seasons and the ripening of the crops. Unsure of where they will obtain their next job, the zafra is their only dependable source of employment. Insecure, at the mercy of the foremen and farm owners, and constantly migrating, the state of the rural mobile proletarians is extremely difficult.

Single women find it very difficult to get jobs during this period. Often women who arrive with their families must wait until the beginning of the tobacco harvest before they are hired. On large farms, some women earn money cooking meals for men without families. This may be very time-consuming as they may have to travel regularly to the nearest market for supplies. It is the uncertainty of employment for the women and children as well as the men which makes the rural mobile patterns so difficult for the family. With a labor surplus, women are given the lowest-paying jobs, are the last to be hired for many jobs, and the first to be dismissed.

Tobacco farms vary in terms of size and isolation, but most share certain characteristics. The temporary workers are given living quarters, usually a room in a shed near the drying stoves. Medical facilities are often located miles away from the finca. Schools are rarely within walking distance and transportation is seldom provided, but few workers complain since school-age children can earn money during the harvest period poling the tobacco leaves and possibly sorting leaves when older. Furthermore, most children are demoralized by the constant changing of schools during the year and fall hopelessly behind in their studies. This, of course, is a factor in reproducing the labor reserve.

Because of the scarcity of work many workers consider it important to develop a filial relationship with a "good" patrón. In so doing a worker enters into a clientage relationship—a relationship in which each party receives something specific from the other. In general, it is the worker who selects the patrón, and as we shall see later in this chapter, the workers have specific criteria that guide their decision. Nevertheless, the worker's options are limited; in fact he is deciding how to cope with a system which will exploit him no matter who his patrón may be.

The state Labor Regulatory Board, the government agency in charge of enforcing labor laws, has made few investigations of the problems facing temporary workers, and employers are rarely fined for violations. Few workers go to the Dirección, feeling it would side with the employer. Bolivians in particular feel intimidated and suggest that the Dirección supports the Argentine employer over the Bolivian laborer and that bribes are common. Even more important, Bolivian laborers without work permits would be deported.

The worker in this situation has to cope with the institutional realities. As already noted, he attempts to choose between patrones and to establish a strong relationship with his employer. In the view of some workers a successful result of this strategy would be being hired each year immediately following the zafra to transplant tobacco seedlings, cultivate the fields, and work in the harvest—all on the same finca. After the harvest a worker might even stay on the finca doing odd jobs like cutting weeds, loading firewood, or plowing a field to be planted with another crop. The family may leave possessions in a finca storage room and expect them to be there when they return the following season from the zafra. Workers with large families and consequently high transportation costs, who need a relatively steady income in addition to their zafra earnings, especially covet this situation. If they could achieve it, they would move into the rural shuttle pattern. However, entering into this type of arrangement is difficult because the tobacco harvests require many more workers than the other activities such as cultivation and planting. Other strategies must be developed to cope with the situation.

Rural Shuttle Proletarian Pattern

In the rural shuttle proletarian pattern are landless laborers who return year after year to work on the same farm during the postzafra period. The Bolivian migrant who establishes this arrangement with a mayordomo or the owner has the security of knowing that he will have work soon after the zafra. At the same time the owner or mayordomo knows he can rely on a worker of proven quality when he needs seasonal help. It is uncommon for a young single man to settle into such an arrangement because it curtails his mobility to search for more lucrative jobs. On the other hand, once a man has a large family which he has to feed and house, predictable security is more important than flexibility. At the same time he becomes more vulnerable to exploitation.

Perhaps the most common movement pattern is between the tobacco regions of Salta and Jujuy and the sugar zones of the same provinces. Each farm has its own core of permanent workers but hires seasonal workers, including women and children to plant, cultivate, and harvest the tobacco. After the Virginia or Burley tobacco harvest, further work can be provided, possibly in the transplanting and cultivation of the Criollo tobacco if the finca is in Salta, but more commonly in general farm activities left untended during the harvest. When the zafra begins in early June a family is often given permission to store some of its few belongings at the farm. While still inconvenient for the migrant and his family, the pattern offers greater security than the rural mobile proletarian pattern. Needless to say, however, the farm and plantation owners are the real beneficiaries of the arrangement.

Adolfo has a family of eight children. At fifty-one he has a rough life of hard physical work. He is proud that he has been able to keep his family fed, but there have been many difficult periods when there was no work and the family had no money. Once they had to sell the few possessions they owned, such as his prized watch, some Catamarcan blankets, and a bicycle. They never again had enough money to buy them back. When Adolfo was younger and his family smaller, they traveled a great deal for work. Traveling was not enjoyable. They traveled in the back of trucks or third-class on the train; it was tiring and the children were always crying. But there was no alternative. They had to go where there was work which paid well. During two postzafra periods when his wife was ill and could not travel far, Adolfo worked for Don Carlos in Jujuy.

Don Carlos was what Adolfo called a "good" patrón: he usually paid the workers on schedule and paid almost the minimum wage. He also allowed four of the children to work during the tobacco harvest poling the leaves. The family had a room to itself and was allowed to have a small garden in back of the drying sheds. When Don Carlos suggested that Adolfo and his family return the following year early enough to help with the preparation of the tobacco, the family had to weigh the advantages and disadvantages. The pay prior to the harvest would be very low and only Adolfo would be employed but they would save on travel and lodging costs and would not have to worry about where they would find work next. Furthermore, Adolfo would not be able to continue working in the zafra many more years. The work was too much for a man his age. Perhaps eventually he would be hired year around on the finca. Searching for security the family decided to accept Don Carlos's offer and prayed it would work out.

Although in many cases the nuclear family is the decision-making unit in highly mobile situations such as in rural mobile and rural shuttle patterns, it is common for members of extended families or people from the same village to want jobs on the same farms during the postzafra season. They feel that by traveling, working, and living with relatives or friends from the same village they can avoid conflicts with people they do not know. Problems between workers often end with dismissal from the job. Equally important, the companionship of friends and family is important on isolated farms. Owners of farms, especially those in areas where there is labor agitation, are careful not to hire people from the same village or family. In this way they feel they are able to retard the development of unions and worker protest.

Rural-Urban Proletarian Pattern

Workers in the rural-urban proletarian pattern return to towns or cities after the zafra. Their choice of a city such as Salta or Jujuy may be based on its proximity to areas where they have access to rural work which they plan to continue or on the fact that they have relatives or friends in the city. In either case it may be part of a strategy of eventually abandoning rural work. The rural-urban proletarian pattern may be a transition stage between the rural proletarian patterns described and the permanent move to urban life or it may prove to be long term and the final break with the zafra may never occur. Analysis and description of the rural-urban pattern is developed in greater detail in the remaining chapters.

Interrelationships of Proletarian Patterns

The description of the different proletarian patterns gives a static picture of the kinds of migration associated with the zafra. It does not include the whole range of variations, nor does it show how or why people may move through a variety of patterns, trying many strategies over a period of years. Families or individuals may move from one pattern to another in a general sequence. The most common patterns are diagrammed in figure 1. For example, some small independent peasant producers are forced to work in the zafra as a means of maintaining the operation of their farm, thus moving temporarily into the rural semiproletarian pattern, possibly the first step in proletarianization. Division of holdings through inheritance, declining production due to overworked soil, bad markets, or other factors may contribute to dependence on zafra earnings. Children of families that have been trying to eke out a living on fragmented landholdings may not have access to land and may remain in Argentina after the zafra to seek temporary work on fincas. Doing so, they could develop a rural mobile pattern. Or they may be able to establish ties quickly with a finca and seasonally migrate between the finca and the plantation. Or they might find "permanent" work on a finca or plantation. However, because establishing dependable, long-term agreements is difficult, often requiring considerable experimentation by both the patrón and the worker, the rural mobile proletariat stage is often a prolonged period. In any case, many families opt to remain in the countryside instead of moving directly to the city.

Of course, not all of the rural proletarians working in the zafra start as peasants or rural semiproletarians. Many are sons of farm laborers in Bolivia; others come from small Bolivian towns; still others have grown up traveling and working with their families in the fields as the parents developed one migration pattern or another.

Among the workers there seems to be general agreement about the advantages and disadvantages of different types of postzafra migration patterns. The rural shuttle pattern is viewed as a more secure alternative than the rural mobile pattern because it eliminates the time, money, and some of the risk involved in finding work after the zafra. Often young, single men can temporarily afford the risk of traveling great distances and taking multiple jobs during the year, but as they marry and have children, which usually happens during their early twenties, they lose their flexibility. At first they may feel that the rural shuttle pattern (if they can find a postzafra job) has some advantages—they can continue to work in the zafra, with its relatively high earnings, and reduce the risk during the postzafra period. But many families are unable to develop a secure postzafra job and thus are forced to remain in the rural mobile pattern for extended periods of time, in some cases a lifetime.

Most families in the rural shuttle pattern tend to view their situation as transitional, or at least hope it is. Aside from the semiannual moves, their major

Figure 1: Major Interrelationships of General Proletarian Migration Patterns Linking Urbanization with the Zafra in Northwest Argentina

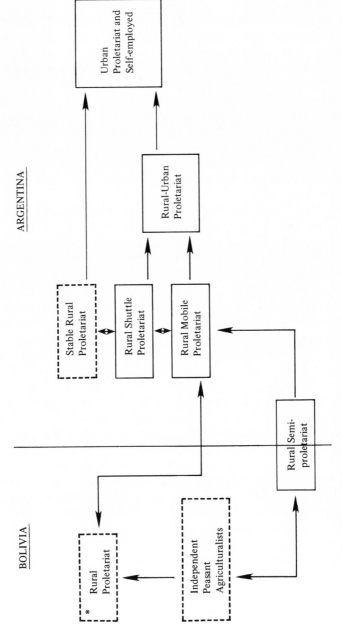

* Dotted lines represent categories not included in focus of the study.

problem is that they are at the mercy of the patrón on the postzafra farm, often accepting low pay and poor living conditions in exchange for postzafra security. Seldom do they receive the worker benefits required by law, such as monthly allowances and milk for their children. In a sample of twenty-one heads of households in the rural shuttle pattern who were asked about their future plans, all but five suggested that although they earned more at the zafra than they would as permanent workers on a farm, they hoped eventually to find stable rural work on a plantation or farm, abandoning zafra work entirely. There was a strong preference for full-time employment in Argentina on a large farm or plantation where unions exist and where government labor laws are followed. Most agreed that it would be best to have their own land to farm, but only five in the sample had the option. All five planned some day to work their fathers' land in Bolivia.

Rural semiproletarians try to stay in their village and avoid the zafra altogether. In many cases this is not possible, for reasons already mentioned. As we have seen, in the sample of fifty rural semiproletarians, those who were planning to move to Argentina were planning to do rural work during the postzafra season, though several were considering moving to the city of Salta or Jujuy. Like many other rural workers, they felt more comfortable working as laborers on farms or plantations than with the prospect of moving to the city, but they considered the cities of Northwest Argentina an alternative option if they are unlucky in the countryside.

Although this section has examined the different movement patterns of zafreros, it should be clear that the men and their families have more similarities than differences. For all of the workers and their families, regardless of their postzafra work or living situation, the year has at least two major breaks when they must abruptly change their activities. The first break comes when they pack their belongings and migrate to the zafra to take up life on the work camps; the second, when they leave the zafra. Furthermore, in a sense they are all trapped by their socioeconomic position. They are part of a surplus labor pool. Lacking political support that could legislate laws on their behalf and implement already existing legislation, they have had to cope in atomistic ways. The low wages they receive for most of their labor plus the rapidly rising cost of living have functioned to make their scramble costly in terms of the future. Capital cannot be accumulated or credit obtained. Education and possible job skills for themselves and their children are forsaken for a minimal but vital income. The result is a perpetuation and aggravation of an already difficult situation. The children of most zafreros (many born in Argentina and thus Argentine citizens), with the same lack of opportunity and preparation as their parents, will have to face even more severe employment problems as agriculture is mechanized.

7. Urbanization and Seasonal Migration

As suddenly as the men are paid, the plantation work camps empty and the bustle of human activity is replaced by the steady rustle of growing cane at the lote's edge. Single men and families have left, traveling in many directions hoping they will find jobs, hoping their health and strength will allow them to make the most of the little fate has given them, and that their children will somehow get enough schooling to pass on to another grade. One annual migrant current is in the direction of the city of Salta. Some of these families are returning to a place they have lived in for a considerable time; others enter it as a new world.

The remainder of the book focuses on Bolivians who moved to the city of Salta after the zafra. The move is perceived by them either as only one of many stops or as part of a strategy for long-term stability. Although the migrants vary in age, experience, family size, number of contacts in Salta, and ties to home communities, they share common problems of making a living in a situation of precarious employment.

The following examination of the process of urbanization explores which urban resources the migrants view as important while they remain dependent, at least seasonally, on rural work. This approach will provide insight into important aspects of the urban environment. The examination also points to a critical dimension that the city and countryside hold in common for the low-income migrant, yet one that is often neglected in the literature: by moving to the city many migrants do not in fact shift from one form of socioeconomic structure to another, but remain part of a labor reserve that traverses rural-urban borders, as does the capitalist mode of production.

The City of Salta

The city of Salta (population 180,696) is the capital of the Salta province

and is the largest city in Salta and Jujuy. A major trade center during the colonial period, Salta's importance in Argentina has greatly diminished with the
growth and development of distant Buenos Aires and the littoral region of the
country. In contrast to cities in well-known studies of urbanization (Monterrey,
Mexico City, Lima, Rio de Janeiro, and Buenos Aires), Salta is neither large nor
important industrially—a fact which is reflected in the clear air and scarcity of
permanent work for low-income residents.[1]

The Valle de Lerma where the city is nestled has perhaps the most delightful climate in Argentina. Summer days are warm but not uncomfortable, and
nights are cool. Although winter weather is sometimes raw, it is not uncommon
for midday temperatures to reach into the 70s as the sun warms the city. The
rich and varied agricultural regions surrounding Salta, including the sugar zone
already described, contribute to the thriving commercial activity in the city.
Modern buses that link Salta to the outlying regions give rural workers easy access to the city and urban residents access to the countryside.

The hills surrounding the city of Salta turn green when summer rains begin
in November. When the rains stop, the hills gradually turn brown, the unpaved
streets in the villas (low-income neighborhoods without pavement) on the outskirts of the city become dusty, and the holes that were filled with water during
the rains dry up and crack. The downtown area of Salta is compact, and like
many Latin American cities much of the commercial activity centers around
the beautiful and well-manicured plaza. Banks, stationery stores, pharmacies,
clothing and jewelry stores, small department stores, movie theaters, cafés and
restaurants, tourist shops, and a motorcycle store surround the plaza, along
with the magnificent cathedral and the arched government buildings of the colonial era. Three major hotels, built to take advantage of the tourist trade, have
joined the beautiful colonial buildings but fail to blend in, standing out like
creatures of another era. The streets leading from the plaza are narrow, and the
one-way traffic moves slowly past the confusion of neon signs jutting out from
the stores. Sidewalks are too narrow to accommodate the flow of pedestrians,
which constantly spills into the street wherever there is a break in the fence of
bicycles lining the curb. Rattling buses squeal their brakes as they turn out of
the flow of traffic to let off shoppers and pick up burdened passengers.

Within twenty minutes most of the buses will have arrived at the unpaved
sections of town (40 percent of the streets in Salta are unpaved). During the
dry season every disembarking passenger is cloaked in a column of dust as the
bus roars off, restoring once again the silence of a nearly bucolic environment.
Few cars or motorcycles disturb the peace in the villas; instead the streets hold
bicycle riders, pedestrians, and barking dogs. Often the busiest places are the
water spigots on the corners, where women or children draw water to take to
their homes. It is in these villas on the outskirts of the town that many of the

families that labor in the sugar and tobacco harvests reside.

History. The city of Salta was founded in 1582 by Don Hernando de Lerma, then the governor and *capitán general* of Tucumán province. Once the control of land was taken from the Indians, *encomenderos* were placed in charge of the Indians and given extensive landholdings. During the 16th century a significant part of the Indian population was sent off to the Potosí silver mines (located in what is now Bolivia), thereby depopulating the region (Hollander 1976: 117). Salta became an important town on the route connecting the mines of Alto Perú and the agricultural regions of Córdoba and Tucumán. The huge mule sales which took place annually in Salta during this early period drew vendors and buyers from all parts of the viceroyalty. Up to fifty thousand mules were sold at the fair and taken to the highlands of Peru (Denis 1922: 51). Salta was also the center of an agricultural region which produced cattle, rice, and cotton. The city exported oxcarts, rough fabrics, and alcohol.

At this time Buenos Aires (founded in 1580) was but a small town, and Northwest Argentina had over two-thirds of the Argentine population (Zorraquin 1959, as cited in Laks 1971: 22). But Portuguese and British penetration forced the Spanish to decentralize their control, giving Buenos Aires and Montevideo the same trade rights held by other Spanish ports. Buenos Aires quickly became the port through which exports and imports passed to and from Europe. Along with other colonial cities of the interior, Salta began to lose its privileged position.

Independence was the crowning blow to Salta's position as a major trade center. Although some Salteños may have been aware of the possible threat that independence posed to Salta's economic position, the men of the province, led by the gauchos, played an important role in the Wars of Independence (1810-1814) and became known as the "shield of Argentina." Led by the gaucho general Martín Güemes, the Salteños kept the Spanish troops occupied in the Northwest while General José de San Martín prepared in Mendoza to cross the Andes in his march to defeat the Spanish (Haigh 1968). Salta confronted a difficult situation at the end of the wars. "Not only had trade been suspended and markets extinguished or reduced but much havoc had been wrought amongst the live-stock, the produce upon which Salta was absolutely dependent" (Wrigley 1916: 124). Salta lost its markets in Upper Peru (which became Bolivia) and was no longer a central component of the trade network linking Lima and the ports on the Río de la Plata.

With the introduction of free trade and the support of foreign interests, especially British, Buenos Aires grew rapidly. The export of agricultural produce led to increased concentration of landholdings, and the importation of foreign manufactured goods replaced manufactured produce from the interior. Buenos Aires evolved as the primate urban center in Argentina, with a predominant concentration of industry and supporting commercial activities (Frank 1972: 13). In the process it came to dominate the development of the interior, including Salta and the rest of the Northwest. The organization of transportation systems, primarily the railroads, further increased the dominance of Buenos Aires by connecting it with all areas of Argentina while leaving major urban centers without direct access to one another. The railroads were built by foreign companies to bring agricultural produce to Buenos Aires for shipment overseas and to distribute imports through Buenos Aires to the interior.

The changes in the economic pattern corresponded with changes in the patterns of population growth. The littoral region of Argentina experienced the largest population growth, helped substantially by foreign immigration. The provinces of Buenos Aires, Santa Fe, and Entre Ríos received 87 percent of the total of foreign born, according to the 1869 census (Lattes 1973: 8). The Salta province, however, neither drew large numbers of migrants nor generated new sources of production. "Sunk in a subsistence economy and without land attractive to immigrants, the province stagnated" (Laks 1971: 36). Yet the province never became totally depressed economically, primarily due to its rich and varied agricultural regions. Particularly important was the export of beef to the nitrate mines of northern Chile beginning in the 1840s until 1921 (Hollander 1976: 173).

While the Salta economy was not strong enough to attract a significant number of European migrants, in none of the six censuses taken from 1869 to 1970 did the province show a net population loss (see table 4). In all censuses the city of Salta grew faster than the province, and has continued to grow increasingly fast.

Table 4
Populations of the City of Salta and
the Province of Salta

	1869	1895	1914	1947	1960	1970
City of Salta	16,877	20,361	33,636	76,552	123,172	182,770
Province of Salta	88,933	118,015	142,796	329,826	412,854	511,744

Source: National Census of Population. Figures for the city of Salta include the neighboring suburb-village of San Lorenzo.

Social Consequences of Colonial Heritage: Rural Seasonal Work and the Regional Center. Today the mark of the past is visible in the colonial architecture that graces many of the buildings opening onto the beautiful central plaza. But the colonial heritage is also clearly etched on the social fabric of the town and the province. "By the outbreak of the wars of independence, the core lineages that would dominate the city and province of Salta throughout the 19th century and to the present day were already established" (Hollander 1976: 119). Closely linked by kinship with the oligarchy in other provinces, the Salta families exerted national political influence until the rise of Perón.

Because of the economic importance of Salta during the early colonial period, it was natural that a wealthy and powerful upper class developed. As would be expected, this early elite controlled much of the land of the province, which left most of the population with few resources and little land. This situation remains basically unchanged for the elite "still own almost all of the great farms and estancias of the province, the sugar plantations and mills" (David 1963: 108). The consequences of this system of land tenure have been well articulated in the CIDA (Comité Interamericano de Desarrollo Agrícola) report of 1965. Salta shares many of the same problems of the other Northwest provinces:

> The tenure problems of the Northwest are more profound, more difficult to solve than those of any other part of the country. In no other region is the tenure structure less adapted to the needs of a developing, commercial economy or to a political democracy. Agriculture is the major, usually sole, source of employment. Economically worthwhile land is held by relatively few families. Its exploitation is predominantly along traditional lines, continuing in the shadow of the encomienda established by the early Spanish conquerors. Three quarters of the farm labor force are hired workers or operators of minifundios who must hire out in order to earn more than subsistence incomes. With several marked exceptions, the quality of technology and investment by the large owners are low, although these same operators have easy access to good technical advice and sources of capital. Large seasonal immigrations of farm workers create further social problems. (CIDA 1965: 50)

As figure 2 indicates, seasonal labor migration, proletarianization, and urbanization are consequences of the factors which developed and continue to maintain the unequal distribution of resources and power.

Unequal access to good agricultural lands, unequal distribution of income, population growth leading to increased cultivation and parcelization of marginal lands, coupled with a poorly developed agricultural infrastructure, forced many peasants to look for other sources of income (see fig. 2). Some moved to cities in search of employment; others found work as seasonal agricultural

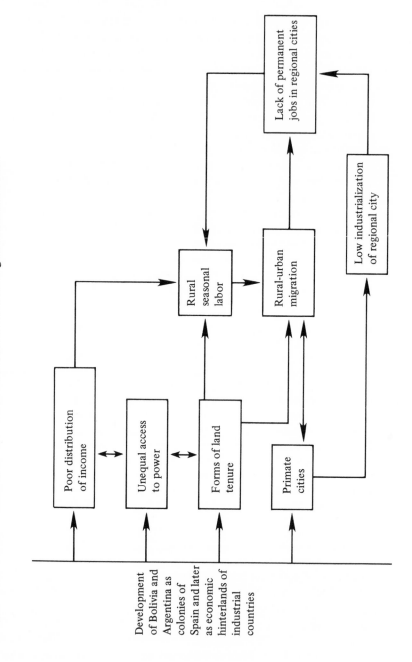

Figure 2: Factors in Development: Rural Seasonal Labor and Regional Urbanization

laborers. At the same time, individuals or groups with large amounts of land that could be exploited for commercial production, with capital to develop part of the land and with political power to gain price supports and other types of protective legislation, needed seasonal labor to harvest their produce. The development of large-scale capitalist agriculture benefited from and perpetuated the underdevelopment of regions which provided the seasonal labor. The basic components of this process continue to influence the course of development in the contemporary era.

From the colonial period on, the laboring population in Salta was poorly paid and often lived a precarious existence. Lacking good land and permanent rural work in the hinterland, many of the workers migrated, at least temporarily, to the regional center, which had a diversity of economic activities. Yet the regional center was often no panacea for the migrant. Cities such as Salta grew, not because of the concentration of jobs in the industrial sector, but because of the harsh rural conditions and because of their location in agricultural regions (Laks 1971: 31). Industrialization evolved in the center of power, the primate city of Buenos Aires. For the unskilled migrant, reliable and regular employment in the regional city was, and still is, difficult to obtain. As a result, many were and still are forced to take seasonal rural work periodically or to move on to Buenos Aires or other centers of production.

In the period between 1947 and 1960 the Northwest as a whole lost population, despite an increase of the foreign population (see table 5). During this

Table 5
Net Migratory Balance, 1947-1960
(In Thousands)

Province	Argentine Population	Foreign Population	Total
Catamarca	− 25.2	0.1	− 25.1
Jujuy	− 10.5	16.0	5.5
La Rioja	− 19.1	− 0.3	− 19.4
Salta	− 0.8	14.1	13.3
Santiago del Estero	−111.8	− 3.9	−115.7
Tucumán	− 22.6	− 6.0	− 28.6
The Northwest	−190.0	20.0	−170.5

Source: National Census of Population 1960, as cited in Consejo Federal de Inversiones 1967.

time Salta and Jujuy were the only Northwest provinces that did not experience a net population loss due to migration. The increase in the foreign population of the Northwest, which was predominantly Bolivian, was far and away highest in the provinces of Salta and Jujuy. Significantly, not only did the province of Salta have the lowest rate of out-migration, but its total growth was much higher than any other province in the Northwest.

Employment in Salta

Today the province of Salta is not a highly industrialized center. On the international level, produce comes from the United States, Western Europe, and Japan in exchange for raw agricultural and mineral products from Salta. Some companies, mines, and plantations in the area belong to foreign owners. But more important, Salta is a hinterland for Buenos Aires.

Table 6 shows the division of the economically active population in the province of Salta and the relatively small percentage employed in industry. Agricul-

Table 6
Distribution of the Economically Active
in the Province of Salta

Economic Sector	Personnel	Percentage
Agriculture and Cattle	43,089	29.4
Mining	2,556	1.3
Industry	26,415	18.2
Construction	8,549	5.8
Electricity	1,252	0.9
Commerce	12,846	8.8
Services	29,456	20.2
Transportation	9,382	6.4
Unspecified	12,774	8.7
Total	146,316	100.0

Source: National Census of 1960.

ture, on the other hand, is of great importance in the province of Salta as a source of employment. Figures for 1960 show 41,992 persons working in agriculture (excluding cattle-raising), of which 13,977 were permanent, 12,694 were temporary, 6,368 were producers, and 8,953 were family producers (Oficina Regional del Consejo Nacional de Desarrollo 1965). For the 1966-1967 period, 25 percent of the tobacco, 13 percent of the sugar, 9.6 percent of the tomatoes, 58.6 percent of the garbanzo beans, 18 percent of the grapefruit, 8.9 percent of the oranges, 8.2 percent of the lemons, 64 percent of the beans, and 54.6 percent of the cumin in Argentina were produced in the province of Salta. A range of other produce, including grapes, chickens, potatoes, corn, rice, onions, olives, tangerines, and garlic were also raised (Secretaría del Estado de la Producción de la Provincia de Salta y Dirección Provincial de Estadística 1970).

According to the 1964 National Economic Census, 73 percent of the workers in the city of Salta were employed in the commerce and service sector and only 27 percent in the industrial sector. In a nonindustrial city like Salta there is a large labor pool of unskilled workers from which employers fill a limited number of jobs (usually short-term). This abundance of labor allows them to pay low wages, often lower than those paid in rural areas during harvests. When the specific job is finished, the workers must again look for employment.

While at the time of the research there had been no study of unemployment, economists in Salta estimated unemployment at about 8 percent. Unemployment figures for other cities in Argentina were available, although official employment figures always leave much to be desired. In Tucumán, a neighboring province with admittedly the most aggravated unemployment situation in Argentina, government figures for unemployment were 11.7 percent. Other estimates ran as high as 15 percent (*El Tribuno*, Salta 6/25/71: 10).

The Decision to Try Urban Life

We have seen that many of the processes responsible for shaping the urban character of Salta also influenced the development of agricultural production and land tenure patterns of the hinterland, where large numbers of seasonal workers are used and thus a labor reserve is needed. Because Salta lacks a major industrial sector it could be argued that a labor reserve does not play an important role in the city. Yet the availability of cheap and often temporary labor in the city not only makes it possible for employers (nonindustrial as well as industrial) to pay lower wages but also reduces the cost of the service sector for the consumer, at the expense of the laborer. For these reasons the workers in the labor reserve play an important role in the capitalist urban economy too.

For unskilled workers, a city with a highly unstable opportunity structure holds special problems. Yet migrants may continue to go there because of other resources the city may offer and the migrants' bleak alternatives elsewhere. As becomes clear in the following pages, the social adaptations that best insure access to resources, given the constraints and limitations, are not possible for everyone, and a variety of "adaptive" tactics have to be made to survive. But what all of these migrants that we interviewed have in common is work in the zafra—the families live in Salta for part of the year but continue to work in the countryside during the harvest.

Bolivian families view work on the plantations as an important resource because it is annually available and its pay dependable. Once they have learned the work, which many do as children, they know what will be expected of them and know the conditions under which they will have to labor. For many, the postzafra season is the time of year that carries the greatest risk but also offers the possibility of establishing another way of life. Although postzafra jobs vary considerably, few offer a real break from the low-paying, short-term employment that makes the zafra seem an improvement by comparison. As families grow, multiple moves become less desirable and the uncertainty of not knowing where the next job will be found creates increasing anxiety. In these cases, security is not found in multiple moves during the postzafra period, but by obtaining employment of greater duration in either the countryside or the city.

Most families at the zafra are reluctant to move to the city. The temptations of urban life are usually overshadowed by fear of potential urban problems, and if rural work is available many workers consider it a better alternative. Jorge, father of four, felt that there was little he could do in the city. He knew agricultural work and did his job well but was uncertain of his ability to find and hold urban work. Furthermore, he worried about the high price of food and lodging, fearing that these expenses would not be balanced by a higher income. Like many zafreros with growing families, Jorge was attempting to maximize security, and with good reason. The potential returns on risk were too low, and the price of failure too high.

This reluctance to move to the city is seldom mentioned in the social-science literature. Most studies of urbanization in Latin America have found a wide variety of reasons people have moved to the city. While these reasons are often complex and multifaceted, the majority of studies suggest that the move to the city is more a first choice among options than a last resort. Positive features of the city stand out as appealing to the workers in terms of "economic incentives, desire to educate children, need for medical care and fascination with the city" (M. Whiteford 1976: 14). In this study, however, the Bolivian migrants of rural origin who were interviewed seldom made the city their first choice, especially if they did not have family already there. Instead, the city for many (even landless rural workers) was a last resort.

Some workers choose the city because they hope to break away from seasonal rural work, including the zafra, but have given up on finding steady rural employment. This desire for greater stability stems from deteriorating health or age or from anxiety about the health and education of a growing family. Although farms occasionally have relatively stable jobs available, the city with its density of jobs offers the hope of relatively stable employment in a variety of short-term jobs even if a long-term job is not available. (This is discussed in greater detail in chap. 9.)

Another group of workers, who have no family in a village or town, turn to the city only after losing their rural jobs and finding no other work available in traditional rural work areas. They may discover they can make a living in the city during the postzafra season, or they may continue to seek rural work, combining it with urban work at times. Twenty-one out of the sample of forty zafreros went to the city when they were unable to find rural employment.[2] Men lost jobs for a variety of reasons: the end of the harvest, sudden loss of the crop, interpersonal problems with a mayordomo or another worker, union involvement, or even political beliefs. With no other place to turn for lodging or employment, they moved to the city to look for work. Most of these migrants had previously been contemplating moving to the city. Having discovered that they could find work in the city, many returned the following year after the zafra, hoping to establish themselves some day. Although there were none in the sample, I was told about men who had also come to the city and worked during a postzafra season but had never returned, finding the urban experience much more difficult than life in the country.

Jorge and his family had decided to work in the tobacco harvest in Jujuy after the zafra. They found work on a farm. Five days after the harvest began, a hail storm devastated the area, ruining much of an abundant crop, and the families that had signed up for the tobacco harvest were forced out of work. Yet at that time of year no alternative sources of rural work were available locally. Although Jorge's patrón was willing to let laid-off workers stay at the finca for a short time, he did not want them to stay long. Some of Jorge's friends returned to Bolivia to live with relatives until the zafra began again, but Jorge had no close family ties there. He had no place to turn except to a brother who lived in Salta. Feeling that work was not as seasonal in the city and that they could stay temporarily with his brother, Jorge and his wife decided to go to Salta.

Not all the migrants view the city as a last resort. Some young men, either single or with small families, may "experiment" by going to the city for a short period to see if they can find jobs and to ascertain the cost of urban living. Usually this is done between the end of the zafra and the beginning of the tobacco harvest. With their zafra earnings they are able to explore a new environment which they feel may have jobs with greater security in the long run. If unsuccessful, they know that they can return to the zafra within a matter of months. Since they have not been forced to the city, they may not be as dependent on relatives or friends for aid, as are many of the migrants who are not able to choose their time for migration. Another group of workers go to the city out of choice, not necessity. Starting with the first year in the zafra, these workers use the zafra income to establish themselves in an Argentine city. Usually they have special urban skills.[3] Of the families interviewed, this pattern of urban migration was much more common among those no longer working in the zafra than among those who still do.

The Appeal of Salta. Why do migrants move to Salta, especially considering the nature of the employment-opportunity structure? First, no cities in Argentina have a reputation among Bolivian migrants for abundant job opportunities. Some places have the opposite, such as Tucumán, where the closing of various sugar ingenios had helped to send unemployment skyrocketing. Although some of the men interviewed have friends or relatives who had moved to Buenos Aires and acknowledged that there is work to be found in the city, most feel the trip to the capital is too expensive and arduous for a large family. The consensus is that if one moves to Buenos Aires it is best to go alone first, get a good job, and then have the family follow. Even then, many feel the living conditions in the squalid villas miseria will be a bad influence on their children.[4] Higher wages, greater range of jobs, and, for the younger men without families, the excitement of the big city are the primary drawing cards of Buenos Aires. Mendoza, like Jujuy and Salta, has the advantage of being close to rich agricultural zones which need seasonal agricultural labor, and as a result there is the possibility of seasonal work in the countryside if the move to the city is unsuccessful.

The city of Salta offers additional advantages. It is close to the sugar zone, thus decreasing travel costs between the urban residence and the zafra. Like Jujuy, Salta's proximity to Bolivia may offer some psychological insurance to the migrant. The migrants in my study, however, seldom took advantage of this, averaging less than one visit to Bolivia every two years.

Another attribute of Salta is the temperate climate. Highland Bolivians dislike the sweltering summer heat of the sugar zone and feel that Salta's climate is healthier. Furthermore, winters in Salta are warmer than in Mendoza or Buenos Aires—an important consideration for the migrant living in a temporary construction on his urban lot.

Because Salta is relatively small, people with low incomes can buy land in the villas on the outskirts of the city and still be relatively close to the center of town. Here many of them build their own homes and plant vegetable gardens, which helps hold down the cost of living in the city. In Buenos Aires the same family would have to live in the vastly overcrowded villas miseria. In contrast, few of the Salta villas are overcrowded, even if individual units are usually cramped. Although there is some variation from one villa to another, Salta is growing outward without the large-scale squatter invasions or the teeming inner-city slums that characterize some large cities in Latin America (Mangin 1967). There are 32 squatter settlements (*villas de emergencia*) classified by the city government, but most are very small and tightly regulated by the city government. According to a municipal study, the "squatments" house 2,348 people; only 102 of these are reported to be foreigners (Municipalidad de Salta 1970).[5]

Salta lacks industry but has an active commercial sector which generates employment opportunities. Jobs, usually short-term in nature, do become available. Population growth alone has stimulated construction of new buildings and houses, which creates a demand for labor and materials. In contrast to the countryside, where workers have few options in terms of employer or type of work near their homes, in Salta a variety of jobs become periodically available within easy commuting distance for the worker. This reduces the amount of time and money spent on transportation, both in going to and from the job site and during the search for employment.

Finding Help in Adjusting to the City. New migrants to the city are usually confronted by a blur of activities and systems—from transportation through hiring practices—which are difficult to understand and utilize. Getting housing, a job, or just moving about the city can be a complicated task for even the most sophisticated new arrival. For people unaccustomed to city life it can be an unpleasant and possibly an expensive experience.

Only 40 percent of the Bolivian migrants in the sample had friends or relatives who could help them with lodging or in getting jobs. Frequently the migrants had been temporary rural workers since early childhood and did not come from communities where they had many friends and relatives. According to the migrants the absence of friends or relatives upon their arrival in the city did make their initial adjustment more difficult. After several postzafra seasons many still feel isolated and have not developed strong ties. Partly this is due to the disruption of returning to the zafra.

Even when a migrant arrives in Salta knowing he has a relative or friend living in the city from whom he hopes to get temporary lodging and help, it is not always easy for him to know how to make contact—just finding the family or individual may be arduous if one does not know exactly where they live. The villas seldom have carefully marked street names or house numbers and in some neighborhoods people do not know one another and cannot help with directions. In others they will not help the new arrival. Individuals who have money may use radio spots and newspaper ads to locate their friends or relatives, but even they are often unsuccessful in their quest.

Although it may be mutually assumed that shelter will be provided for the new migrant and his family, often this is not possible because of the crowded conditions in which many of the residents live. For example, of the nineteen zafreros in the sample who have their own homes, only four have more than two rooms. Alonso has a wife and four children. They have a one-room house of rough brick with a dirt floor in which the whole family lives, and the two beds take up most of the space. Cooking and other activities take place outside in a protected alcove. Alonso considers himself lucky to have protection from the cold winds of the Salta winter, but he does not have room for another family in his home. Like many, he is in no position to give shelter to a new migrant, even though he might want to help.

There are exceptions, however. Two of the migrants in the sample are particularly affluent compared to their fellow workers. They own houses with six and seven rooms respectively, with tile floors, electricity, running water, and glass windows. It is interesting to note here that these families are easy to find, living in well-marked houses and well-known to their neighbors. They have a constant flow of relatives and friends coming from Bolivia to visit, some of whom plan to settle in Salta. As this example illustrates, when the contact family has resources and room, it can be depended upon for temporary help; otherwise, lodging and assistance is much less likely.

Having some type of initial contact in a city such as Salta is especially important for the migrant with little formal education and no special skills, because of the difficulty of finding long-term employment. Many migrants feel that they must be able to get jobs quickly since the jobs they do get often pay poorly and last a short time. Unemployment can be disastrous for a family. To avoid it many feel a man should have friends who can function as job contacts, helping him to keep informed about employment opportunities, or even better, helping him to get a job. Many men consider a network of contacts to be the best insurance against long periods of unemployment between jobs. The network's strength is its flexibility, a trait which is a necessity in dealing with resources (information about jobs) which change rapidly. Such networks are regarded as important for gaining some control over job security, but they may be difficult to establish if the migrant does not have friends or family in Salta when he first arrives. Of course, just because a migrant does not know anyone before moving to Salta does not preclude the establishment of a network of friends.

Ethnic Identity and Coping

Given the rising costs of food, clothing, and housing, the insecure jobs and low wages, migrants with limited resources face the threat of hunger, cold, and illness. For them life is precarious. In a sense the men and women are fatalistic, repeatedly noting that much has happened to them that they could do nothing about. It is accepted that hard work is necessary to maintain their families but that it seldom brings a major improvement in their income. Pedro reflects the sentiments reiterated by both men and women: "If I get work, well, I work eleven or twelve hours a day. I work hard and do good work. But what does it get you. The work runs out, the patrón pays little. We are in the hands of God." Men pointed out that hard work must not be the way to earn money, that those who earn the most work the least.

This is not to say that the migrants accept their situation passively. The Bolivians are similar to the low-income population described by Bryan R. Roberts in his study of Guatemala: "What is striking about their behavior is the extent to which they are active in shaping their own destinies. This is not to say that they are successful, either in their own terms or by some objective standard of economic and social development, but it is not for want of trying" (Roberts 1973: 5). The decisions and activities of the migrants are based on a pragmatic and knowledgeable interpretation of the alternatives open to them, and on a conscious resolve to maximize certain possibilities and to accept the potential costs of the decisions. Of course careful assessment of a situation and reduction of risk is harder in a new environment. As indicated in the section on postzafra decisions, migrants attempt to get detailed information about the work and living situation and have very specific questions about the employer, length of work, and pay. The paramount concern for many migrants is developing some degree of control over important aspects of their lives such as housing and income. Individuals often change strategies depending on their personal circumstances and the conditions of alternative work and residence.

The search for security was behind the decision of many migrants to leave Bolivia. Most felt that by migrating to Argentina they could improve their situation. Although the migrants in the sample came to Argentina for a variety of reasons, all of them cited economic factors in their top two motivations. These economic reasons were based on gaining greater control and more dependable income—in other words security—and not on accumulating luxury items. If some came to escape a bad patrón, a creditor, the draft, a brush with the law when they could not afford a lawyer, or political enemies in power, most came because it was difficult to earn a living in Bolivia—without an education or a trade, jobs in the cities were scarce, and they could not buy enough land or water rights in the country with their meager or nonexistent savings.

They came to Argentina with hopes of gaining greater security but did not come with dreams of upward mobility. Argentina, most felt before they came, was worse for the *obrero* (worker) than Bolivia, since there had been no revolution and the oligarchy still owned all the land. But they knew that jobs were available that paid relatively well compared to those in Bolivia, that employers like to hire Bolivians, and that food was inexpensive.

Once in Argentina, Bolivian migrants are often impressed with the wealth of the country. The vast majority of those interviewed feel underpaid and know that their children will be unless they can get an education. They feel that the system of courts, laws, and controls functions against the interest of the worker and in favor of those who have financial resources. Yet most feel there is little they can do about it, especially since they are in a foreign country. For them, the only Argentine politician ever to be interested in the problems of the poor, including the Bolivian poor, was Perón.

Although there is a general appreciation that Argentina encourages Bolivian migration, Bolivian workers feel they are doing jobs Argentines do not want to do. Many migrants resent the attitude of some Argentines that Bolivians are dirty, poor Indians from a backward land and feel the Argentines tolerate them only if they do these difficult physical tasks the Argentines themselves shun; at the same time, they are proud of their ability to do hard physical work which others cannot do.

These views indicate a degree of class consciousness. Equally important, Bolivians often do not emphasize the difference between low-income working-class Bolivians and low-income working-class Argentines. The Bolivians tend to accept their position, not risking confrontation, either because they do not want to be deported or because they feel they could return to Bolivia if their situation became intolerable. This element of the ideology is an important dimension in the value of foreign labor in a class society. It is, as Raymond Wiest (1979: 172) points out, a form of consent.

That many Argentine employers prefer Bolivian laborers has generated resentment on the part of Argentines competing for the same jobs. In a survey conducted by the Oficina de Desarrollo Humano (Office of Human Resources), Villar (1976: 40) recorded a significant amount of negative feelings towards Bolivians. Sixty percent of the sample felt that the Bolivians were not making a contribution to the country. Their primary concerns were that Bolivians were taking jobs from Argentines, lacked education, and had poor health. Those who felt Bolivians were making a contribution viewed the Bolivians as being very hard working and willing to accept jobs shunned by Argentines. Not surprisingly employers felt that Bolivians were making a positive contribution. The highest level of anti-Bolivian feelings were expressed by those competing with Bolivians for jobs. The hiring of Bolivians has reduced pay scales for many types of manual jobs and retarded the formation of strong unions.

Most Argentines do not object to living in the same neighborhood or working at the same jobs with Bolivians, an attitude reflected in the residence patterns and employment structure in Salta. Yet Villar's survey (1976: 39) found that 21 percent of the Argentines would not want their daughter to marry a Bolivian even if he was of the same social position. Thirty-one percent would not oppose such a marriage if they were of the same social position. Five percent would object to such a marriage under any circumstances. The rest did not care or had no opinion. Interpreting these figures is complicated by not being able to relate them to other variables, but they suggest that some Argentines link being Bolivian with being poor because most Bolivians in Salta are low income. There is also an important cultural dimension. Traditional Bolivian highland dress such as the *pollera* (long skirts) and indigenous phenotypic features are looked down on by some Argentines. The myth of European cultural superiority is often used in popular explanations given as the reason Argentina is "advanced" in contrast to Bolivia, where the indigenous imprint has dominated.

Despite these factors, children of Bolivians born in Argentina are Argentine citizens. Language is not as much of a problem for the Bolivian migrants (although some are more fluent in Quechua than Spanish) as it is for many other immigrants to other countries, such as Mexicans in the United States. These factors facilitate the assimilation process. Because most Bolivians work with Argentines and live in the same neighborhoods, friendships commonly cut across nationality.

Ethnicity, defined as cultural national antecedents, is an important dimension of Bolivians' identity and is used according to the situation. *Paisanos* (countrymen), especially those from the same region or village, are often linked by social networks, with mutual obligation to help one another. (These networks are discussed in greater detail in the next chapter.) The presence of paisanos is psychologically important for many Bolivians. Some feel isolated from their families, and the presence of other Bolivians provides psychological support. Most want to stay in Argentina, feeling they have a better opportunity to get work and possibly improve their family's position than if they stayed in Bolivia.

The zafra figures prominently in the migrants' efforts to cope with problems in a new country. Many workers view the zafra as a viable alternative to other forms of temporary employment. Although the pay is low in relation to the profits of a sugar company and the worker realizes that he is being exploited, he sees the zafra as a short-run solution to his family's survival, as well as a possible aid in developing a long-run position of greater security and improved living conditions. At the end of the zafra the zafrero may have a sum of money he can use to help establish himself more securely in the urban environment. For these families, the zafra income which they earn during about 45 percent of the year represents roughly 60 to 70 percent of the family's total yearly income. Families return from the zafra with anywhere from 40,000 pesos to over 100,000 pesos. The mean income from one lote at Ingenio del Norte was over 63,000 pesos, and the people said it had been a good year.

But the sacrifice made in exchange for this sum of money is sometimes substantial. Children may die in the festering environment of the work camps; men may permanently injure themselves, thereby severely limiting their employment opportunities in the future; education may be disrupted, threatening a child's future; families may have to separate for the four or five months. Even without these tragedies and hardships, the zafra is an arduous taskmaster. Its followers must endure all the discomforts of the crowded work camp, the oppressive heat of the later months, the unrelenting insects, and the sheer physical brutality implicit in the nature of the harvest.

The zafra is also a trap. The disruption every six months created by having to return to the plantation may make it difficult to develop either new skills or resources which could lead to a break from work in the cane fields. Furthermore, as already mentioned, children of zafreros are trapped by the educational system and the movement pattern and thereby perpetuate the labor pool of poorly educated individuals competing in a society which generally pays the uneducated relatively little for their labor. Thus the zafreros' efforts to secure short-term gain helps to guarantee a future low-income labor force for those who control the resources. The migrants are aware of the ramifications of their situation and view urban residential stability as a key strategy for themselves and their children to use in breaking out of an eternal cycle of seasonal labor. Yet they also recognize that without the zafra income they lack the resources to gain the necessary stability and controls. As a result, many of them are forced to continue their dependence on the zafra. The fact that the seasonal worker, fully aware of the costs as well as the benefits of the zafra, will nonetheless return to it highlights both the dire condition of the workers and their strenuous efforts to break the shackles of poverty.

8. The Search for Security

Many of the adaptations made by the migrants who had been in Salta for several postzafra seasons are closely associated with the difficulties of gaining access to the resources of the urban environment. The city offers several unique opportunities that they feel enhance their chances of establishing themselves; yet they arrive in the city with no preconceived notions that gaining a foothold in the urban environment will be easy. For this reason they view the plantation and farms in the nearby agricultural regions as resources that they do not necessarily relinquish when they move to the city. Seasonal agricultural work is considered a normal means of dealing with periodic urban unemployment.

Anthony and Elizabeth Leeds (1970: 233) have pointed out that many rural people are prepared for some aspects of urban life. Those who have sold produce in urban markets, for example, are familiar with commercial transactions, with the urban ambience, and with institutions such as transportation, police, bureaucrats, and licensing. Although migrants may adapt quickly to new environments, knowledge of urban life does not in itself provide them with the means to break out of the constraints inhibiting their struggles to attain a higher standard of living. Where long-term employment is rarely available for men with limited education, earning enough money to support a family may be a problem no amount of urban sophistication can solve.

The migrants in the sample have always been handicapped by their socioeconomic circumstances; their problems did not begin when they arrived in the city. While growing up in Bolivia, they had little opportunity for formal education, averaging 2.5 years of schooling. More than half of them had fathers who were migrant agricultural workers, and so the moves to and from the plantations or farms had drastically disrupted their schooling. At that time there were few schools on the plantations for children of migrant workers, and besides, by age ten, the children were expected to help in the fields. For them, school was an impossible dream. Other men grew up as children of peons on isolated haciendas whose patrones did not consider education important. After a few years of school the boys were expected to work. Only two men in my sample came from families who owned enough land themselves that they did not have to work for anyone else. But even then the schools were far off and the children did not continue with their education.

Eight men in the sample had lived in Bolivian cities as children—a percentage I suspect is much higher than for zafreros in general. These men had more years of formal education than had men from rural backgrounds, their mean number of school years being 3.8. More important, six of these men had learned the rudiments of a trade such as carpentry or tailoring, or had had experience with commercial enterprises such as stores; however, none of the men came from families with sufficient resources to help them get established in Bolivia. Five were orphans raised in the city by families for whom they worked.

Despite some differences in education between men of rural and urban backgrounds, neither group had an adequate level of education for a city whose prerequisite for the job of street cleaner was six completed years of schooling. Lack of education and capital put them in a difficult position from early adulthood.

Even migrants with skills particularly suited for the urban milieu encounter difficulty finding dependable employment with a worthwhile return on their labor. In part, this may be due to the large migration of Bolivians with similar skills into a city such as Salta, which is not able to absorb them. Jaime, who had worked as a tailor in Cochabamba, said the competition between tailors in Salta was too great for a newcomer. When he arrived in the city he went to different shops to ask what they paid employees; every place it was the same: the owner of the shop took 50 to 70 percent of each employee's earnings. Jaime talked with Bolivians who had worked like *locos* (crazy men) on a pair of pants and ended up earning practically nothing. Jaime felt he could make more money by working in the zafra than he could in the city. With zafra earnings he could buy land and eventually maybe even start his own tailor shop. Meanwhile Jaime was hired periodically by his brother-in-law, a plumber, to haul and lay pipe. He became friends with a worker at the Coca-Cola bottling company and hoped he might someday get a job at the plant if he did not become established as a tailor. When not working for his brother-in-law, Jaime picked up odd jobs as a laborer on construction projects. He considered himself lucky not to have children and to know something about several different lines of work. Nevertheless, he planned to continue working in the zafra until he could establish himself in the city. Although he did not know how long this would take he doubted he would work more than three or four years longer in the zafra.

In Salta, the most common work sought by migrants without special urban skills is as laborers in construction, where unexperienced men are hired. The pay scales for laborers are low and vary considerably between contractors. For example, at the time of the study, a laborer's assistant was paid 900 pesos, and a skilled laborer between 1300 and 1500 pesos, depending on the size of the company, the inclination of the contractor, and the degree of unionization. There are also systems in which the men are paid *por tanto*, or by the amount of work accomplished, but this is not as common. Temporary construction workers receive neither the salario familiar nor the escolaridad—additional allowances paid to permanent employees for dependents and for children in school. Even though the larger companies do pay these extras, many workers feel that because of them, a man with a large family will be the last to be hired and the first to be fired.

Urban work may also be found in the brick factory. The work is paid por tanto—the workers calculating that they could earn 1000 pesos a day—but there are no additional benefits. Men working as *cargadores*, loading and unloading trucks, earned 500 pesos a day during the time of the research. Ladislao remembers that when he first worked as a cargador near the Salta market in the early 1960s there were only a few men in competition with him. In 1970 there were more trucks, but also many more men hoping to get work. Cargadores often have particular drivers who want their help, but if a man goes off to the zafra every year he has to forfeit his contacts to others. Yet Ladislao felt cargadores earned so little in comparison to what he could earn at the zafra that he could not afford to stay in Salta during the harvest. When asked why others did not go to the zafra, he said they were unfamiliar with the work.

Individuals who earn such wages have little opportunity to save or invest any of their income. In fact, they are hard pressed to maintain even a small family above a subsistence level. As is still true, prices varied from place to place and spiraling inflation kept pushing prices up, while wages often remained stable. In 1969-1970 if a family of four were to have meat twice a day (the Argentine ideal) they had to spend about 500 pesos a day for *puchero*, the cheapest meat —at least half bone—costing 180 pesos per kilo. Daily bread costs were at least 150 pesos for four loaves of French bread. Generally these two foods are considered the staples in the diet. If fruit, vegetables, rice and other starches, cooking fuel, milk or other drinks were also purchased, food costs alone amounted to almost 1000 pesos a day. But somehow other costs had to be met as well. Rent was at least 3,500 pesos a month for a room or shack, unless a family had their own lot or lived in a villa de emergencia, and even there some people paid rent. Round-trip bus fare ran 50 pesos per person from any point in the city. Besides rent and transportation, clothing, medicine, and extras such as school supplies force many low-income families to sacrifice fruit, vegetables, and in some cases meat from their diet. Many families earned less than 1,000 pesos a day when they had work, and most families were larger than four. It is not surprising to find that malnutrition was characteristic of the poor of Salta (Instituto de Endocrinología de Salta 1969: 23).

The above description indicates some of the difficulties experienced by families who find low-paying employment in Salta. Yet there are two other aspects of the employment picture which must be considered. First, most migrants face an almost perpetual threat of unemployment without any type of union subvention fund or unemployment benefits to tide them through these periods. Second, many of the migrants are concerned about employers not paying them on pay day, or not paying the full promised wage. These problems are common to families in both the countryside and the city.

The Strategy of Least Vulnerability

The labor reserve in the city includes a number of structural conditions. For most families in the labor reserve employment is temporary, low paying, and undependable. To make the situation even more difficult, labor laws are seldom enforced, especially in the case of foreign workers. Faced with a structure in which they occupy a precarious position, families are forced to develop multi-faceted means of survival. The assumption underlying these tactics I call a strategy of least vulnerability.

For most of the families a sense of vulnerability permeates their world view. They are painfully aware of the socioeconomic constraints on their efforts to establish a secure livelihood. Although they see Argentina as a land of abundant resources with more employment opportunities than Bolivia, few have found secure niches. Their concerns are reflected repeatedly in conversations which inevitably turn to inflation, the lack of unions, the scarcity of good jobs, the qualities of employers, and work opportunities in other areas. Jokes about how people manage to get back at a bad employer are a great source of mirth. The fear of disabling illness or injury haunts many families that depend on their energy and strength to earn a living. Since employers explicitly state a preference for young men, aging is perceived as a major threat. The Bolivian migrants of the study occupy a middle ground between two extremes described in the literature on Latin America: the fatalistic urban poor on the one hand and the extremely optimistic migrants on the other hand. Most of the Bolivian migrants indicate a confidence in their ability to cope with a difficult situation. They acknowledge their precarious position but feel that by being careful, clever, and hardworking they can survive, and possibly improve their lives over a long period of time.

A variety of factors influence how particular families interpret their situation and subsequently deal with it. Families whose members include illegal immigrants clearly feel the most vulnerable. Many have been threatened with being reported to the police and subsequently deported if they joined unions or attempted to protest substandard wages or failure to pay. This problem is not restricted to the illegal migrants. In a sample of forty legal migrants, fifteen reported employers who still owed them money, and only two felt they would be paid. In some cases the employer came from out of town, hired the workers, finished the job, and left the city without making final payments to his workers or leaving a forwarding address. In other cases, powerful local individuals hired illegal immigrants and either delayed payments or paid extremely low wages. Women as well as men experience a high rate of nonpayment. Four out of thirty women reported being fired without pay, being blamed erroneously for theft or breakage.

Families with large numbers of small children who cannot work and older couples separated from their families feel especially vulnerable. The least threatened are families that have been able to gain some degree of control over their environment. For example, families that have been able to buy a lot and construct a house, however minimal, are more secure than families that are renting or have large debts. Families with more than one member of the household working or in a position to work are better off than families with just one wage earner. If a wage earner has a special skill such as being a tailor or cobbler, the family's position is enhanced. The vast majority of the families are forced to use a series of tactics simultaneously. Tactics explicitly recognized as important include patron-client relationships, formation of friendship networks in Salta to gain information about or access to jobs, small-scale entrepreneurial efforts, holding multiple jobs even if only temporarily available, having as many family members working as possible, maintenance of kin ties and possibly landholdings in Bolivia, gardening, and the raising of animals.

One consequence of these tactics is that activities usually regarded as rural—such as gardening and working as wage labor on farms—are pursued by urban residents. In most cases, both rural and urban, production is individualized (wages are paid to individuals), but food is bought and distributed within the family or household. Wages of family members are often pooled to maintain the family, including those who are unemployed (children, the temporarily unemployed, and the sick). This provides security for the individualized laborer who at any time may or may not be employed.

While these tactics serve to maintain most families, they play an important role in the maintenance and reproduction of the labor reserve. As Douglas Uzzell (1980: 11) points out, "it is the extremity of their needs, the necessity of taking, if not willingness to take, any wage labor that may become available that renders them a pool of reserve labor." The success of so many poor families in sustaining themselves through the creative utilization of minimal resources has perpetuated the labor reserve and capitalist growth without forcing violent mobilization. For example, patron-client ties are an important element in the social relationships of the poor in Salta. Cutting across class divisions, patron-client relationships are used to adapt to the limited mobility which characterizes dependent development (Rothstein 1979: 25). Many workers hope to find a "good" patrón. By working very hard at low wages some migrants feel they can develop a reputation as a reliable, productive, and unobtrusive worker and possibly be kept on the job or rehired. This tactic may also be reinforced by naming the employer as godparent, although urban employers seldom feel this entails strong obligations. When successful, this particular tactic may give the worker some stability, but at the price of lower wages and possibly worse work conditions than he might have in another, less permanent job. At the same time, it gives the employer a high degree of control over the worker at little cost. The vertical ties between the employer and the workers function to make the workers more vulnerable in another sense. They reduce class consciousness and reduce the possibility that horizontal ties will be formed between employees, Bolivian or Argentine, which might lead to organization and pressure for wage increases, additional employee benefits, or possibly movements for even more profound change.

Multiple job holding is an important tactic for survival in an environment in which high-paying, long-term employment is scarce. While it increases a worker's income, it also insures that he will have at least *one* job if the others end— of particular importance to the low-income worker, since few have savings to get them through periods of unemployment. Not many can find enough work to hold two jobs simultaneously (a phenomenon more characteristic of the middle class), but some do hold temporary jobs which overlap at times. For example, Pedro worked during the day as a construction laborer and at night in one of the local movie theaters selling candy. He earned very little at the latter job and eventually gave it up because he was too tired to work. His cousin Manolo found two different jobs within two days of arriving in Salta: he was hired as a daytime waiter in a small restaurant during a holiday period and at night helped load trucks in downtown Salta, where a building was being torn down and the refuse hauled away when the streets were uncrowded.

Neither Manolo's nor Pedro's jobs lasted long, and soon they were searching for new sources of employment. Like many of their fellow migrants, they had to be prepared for the inevitable though unpredictable periods of unemployment, when they could not find work despite endless searching. Periods of unemployment lasting more than a week were common. During the 1970 post-zafra season the men in the sample averaged almost a month during which they looked for work without success. At these times frustration was great and anxiety considerable. There were no unemployment compensations or other federally supported programs to help them weather the hardships of unemployment.

Families often had to pawn some of their treasured possessions, such as kerosene lamps, beds, or bicycles, in order to get money for food. Even the neighborhood stores which commonly gave credit to steady customers were often reluctant to give loans to the zafreros because of their transient presence in the neighborhood.

Because jobs are difficult to obtain, self-employment is often an important aspect of the tactic of multiple job holding. In Salta men and their families often maintain self-employing jobs like cobbling, running small stores, vending fruits or vegetables, gardening, selling newspapers, even construction and tailoring as *secondary* employment—a safety valve to fall back on when jobs dependent upon an employer are unavailable. This safety valve is particularly important when there are no governmental agencies or friends and family to help out when employment opportunities evaporate. Not all self-employed migrants in the study, however, use self-employment as secondary employment. Some are trying to develop viable independent economic bases. Many realize, however, that when other dependable employment is available, little time can be allocated to the enterprise, limiting its possibility for growth. Furthermore, the growth potential is usually already limited by competition and lack of capital; no amount of extra time would make it a dependable, high-return venture.

Another facet of the tactic of part-time self-employment is to reduce dependence on employers. As mentioned earlier, some employers underpay their workers or renege on payments; because of the employment structure in the city, they know they can always find more workers. Others simply leave town without paying when the work project has been completed. Workers, aware of this potential danger, try to reduce the risk by inquiring about employers' reputations. But more importantly, they try to develop work alternatives that can get them through periods when they otherwise might have to work for an employer of unknown or questionable reputation. For this reason, individuals will often work long hours self-employed with meager returns on their labor because it may be better than taking a risk with an employer. In these cases, critical employment problems may lead to an adaptation to avoid exploitation.

At times, self-employment may create additional jobs which can absorb the labor of family members when they are not working. One example is the family store. Although it may bring in scant income, hardly paying for the inconvenience and long hours of waiting for customers who buy little because of prices inflated by their inability to buy in bulk, the store may be maintained; despite the low return on each unit of labor, it represents possible insurance against the inevitable periods of unemployment.

Another type of self-employment is gardening and animal raising. This is often an important responsibility of women who can stay at home with small children. In regional centers such as Salta, low-income residents may own

enough land to grow food for themselves and occasionally for sale; this is usually more difficult in the large primate centers. Like the family store, these require labor-intensive input. In some cases these gardens and animals (fruit trees,
vegetables, chickens, turkeys, ducks, guinea pigs, occasionally goats) are emer-
gency resources which can be used in time of crisis—such as unemployment—to
feed the family and possibly extended kin or friends. Produce is also important
in creating social ties with individuals who will help in times of crisis: one of the
main methods of establishing long-term friendships and reciprocity is the exchange of home-grown produce, which is preferred to buying gifts.

An important conceptual issue is related to this whole discussion. Economists frequently perceive urban labor as being a purely individual transaction.
As a result, the studies, theories, and planning of employment are based on the
individual and not on the family or any other economic group. As the examples
here suggest, however, employment decisions and their implementation are seldom purely individual acts, but instead take into consideration the ability of
family members to be of use, as well as their needs and their noneconomic time
commitments. In some cases an individual can be less dependent upon one employer in the city—having to accept late payment, low wages, or other abuses—
if family members have jobs or a family enterprise.

Women are paid less than men in both the city and the countryside despite
their major inputs into the production process. Although women often work
on the plantations trimming cane leaves, only men are hired and paid by the
owners. On tobacco farms women who work sorting and poling leaves are paid
less than men who work in the fields. The same women earn less than men in
the city, and this is true in other parts of Latin America as well (Bossen 1979).
In Salta jobs are scarce for migrant women with little or no education. It is even
more difficult for women who seasonally leave the city to find jobs as maids or
washerwomen in homes of middle- and upper-class families. Employers want
someone who is dependable and will not be leaving within a few months. It is
more common for daughters to work as maids than their mothers.

Teenage daughters of zafreros usually lack the formal education to get jobs
as clerks in stores but do find employment as maids. In some cases they get
jobs as live-in maids, which despite the low pay relieves their families of providing the space they would occupy in the cramped living quarters and the food
they would eat. For the girls it is a chance to escape from conditions at home,
to have a bed of their own and possibly running water and a bathroom. They
may share part of their earnings with their families. If the girl is still employed
when the zafra begins, she usually stays in Salta instead of leaving with her family.

Women contribute directly to the household income in other ways. Some
buy vegetables and fruits wholesale and sell them door to door. Others raise

chickens and sell them in the market, although generally the Bolivian women have difficulty establishing themselves in the Salta market system. Judith Maria Buechler (1978) has shown how important it is for market women in Bolivia to have kin in the countryside to provide them with produce, as well as kin or village-based ties in the city to establish clients or obtain urban vending sites. The fact that Bolivian women in Salta have not had these resources makes their task extremely difficult.

Some of the women who go to the zafra prepare food for single men on the work camps. Others run small neighborhood stores, or take in washing or sewing. Income from these jobs is a third to a half of what a man could earn in construction. Women, especially when they have large young families, spend much of their time caring for the family and subsequently prefer jobs they can perform at home. Because of the women's low earning power, household work decisions revolve around work opportunities for the men, but the women's income is viewed as critical.

Although some children from the villas sell newspapers and shine shoes, few children of families that go to the zafra do these types of jobs to supplement the family income. The world of the shoeshine boys is tough and highly competitive. Often they have been raised in the city, have known how to get about it from an early age, and have the protection of elder brothers or friends who work in areas close to the plazas. Like their parents, children of migrants need time to learn about the city and to deal with the social order of their age group.

Another important tactic used by some migrants to cope with the employment problem in the city is to do seasonal agricultural work in the hinterlands of Salta, in addition to work in the zafra. In 1970 during the postzafra season more than half of the sample of forty men went to work in the tobacco harvest in Salta and Jujuy and two went to Mendoza for the vegetable and grape harvests. The decision to seek work in the tobacco harvest often depended on the family's job situation at the beginning of the tobacco harvest season. Many of the migrants knew the work and knew where and how to get a job. The rural daily wage at this time was 860 pesos, which was raised shortly afterwards to 936 pesos (Ley 18.886, January 1, 1971), but the required wage was seldom paid. On some fincas where the men were paid por tanto, earnings were slightly higher. If a man were married or had a *concubina* (concubine), the woman could earn another 800 pesos poling the tobacco leaves for drying. Children could also work poling. Three family members working together in the tobacco harvest could earn more than 2,000 pesos a day—considerably more than the husband alone could earn in the city but hardly enough to provide a comfortable living.

Other types of short-term agricultural work are occasionally available for urban residents. After the tobacco harvest, contratistas periodically pass through the villas in trucks to pick up unemployed men who want to work for a day or two on the nearby farms planting, weeding, and doing general clean-up activities. Despite apparent unemployment, the offers are often turned down, like those turned down by the men described by Elliot Leibow in *Tally's Corner* (1967). The wages are low and occasionally not paid, but there are always some men willing to work because of their dire need, thereby enabling employers to maintain low wages.

For those migrants with land in Bolivia, however small, the maintenance of village ties is more than symbolic. For some the possibility of returning to Bolivia is a goal, for others an escape valve in case their efforts in Argentina fail. In the sample of forty, eight of the nine families who once owned land in Bolivia had retained it although only one planned to return. Only twelve families had sent remittances back to parents or children during the year of the sample; although three others suggested they should. Single workers were much more inclined to send money back to Bolivia. (Remittances are usually sent with a relative or a good friend if the migrant is not planning to visit Bolivia in the near future.) Only fourteen, including six of the families who had land, had visited Bolivia during the two years prior to the interview. Other Bolivians living in Salta regularly visit their families in Bolivia for the major holidays. In some cases active commercial activity in contraband products provides a lucrative source of income. This type of linkage is much more similar to what Linda Whiteford (1979) calls an extended community which spreads across Mexican and United States boundaries.

It is not unusual for the urban migrant who is still working in the zafra to have five or six different temporary jobs during the postzafra season, being unable to find one job that lasts the whole period. For most, a key to successful adaptation in the city is developing enough knowledge, contacts, and information about job opportunities so that periods of unemployment can be held to a minimum. A social network that can keep one informed about job opportunities is viewed as being very important in accomplishing this goal. A good social network not only reduces one's vulnerability to a bad employer, it also reduces one's vulnerability to the whims of the economic system.

For individuals without friends or relatives in Salta when they arrive, networks are often difficult to develop. Meeting new friends and maintaining contacts is further complicated when migrants and their families leave the city for five months every year. As a result, some families are unable to develop extended social networks. The potential for strong networks is enhanced if the migrants make contact in Salta with fellow Bolivians, especially from the same region in Bolivia and of the same socioeconomic background. The Bolivian fiesta complex, to be discussed later, is one event in Salta that facilitates this process. Men also meet at work, or while visiting with friends on weekends. Residential proximity, similar personality, and length of residence also promote the development of mutually supportive networks. Argentines with similar backgrounds may become good friends with the Bolivian migrants, but generally the closest friends are fellow migrants from Bolivia.

There are different levels of intensity and expectation in friendships. On the most intimate level they are a source of amusement and enjoyment, but they also have an important economic function. As Lomnitz (1973: 63) points out, for the poor in Mexico City "the networks of reciprocal exchange. . . are functioning economic structures which maximize security and their success spells survival for large and important sectors of the population." When one of the families does not have work, it is common for others in the network to help them with gifts of food. But for this to happen families must have *confianza* (confidence) in each other, a feeling that the same will be done for them in times of family crisis. This type of confidence takes time to develop. Of course, the help cannot extend for too long without overtaxing the resources and patience of the benefactors.

On another level it is important to have a network of *contactos* (contacts). Differing from the networks of families which have a reciprocal exchange of goods, contactos are relationships established between men, usually strengthened by periodic drinking together. The men are often from the home community in Bolivia, friends from former jobs, or friends made in the neighborhood. Although sometimes a few close friends may exchange labor in projects such as house building, most contactos have a loosely defined concern for each other and can be depended upon to help one another learn about employment opportunities.

Information about job openings is often all that a contacto can offer. If he can offer more he is regarded as a *cuña* (wedge). To get some jobs it is almost essential to have a cuña or an "in." A migrant who is particularly successful in establishing a set of contactos is known to be *muy bien relacionado*, meaning he has good connections. In a situation of short-term employment, being muy bien relacionado is a reflection of a successful strategy. Although cuñas may often be vertical ties, the reciprocity networks are usually horizontal ties. An individual must make an effort to keep in touch with his contactos, occasionally dropping by their homes on a Sunday afternoon with a little wine or a small gift. For contactos of the same economic position, sharing job information is crucial in coping with the economic nature of the city.

Of course, just because a migrant does not know anyone before moving to Salta does not mean he cannot establish a network of friends. There are mechanisms which help introduce new migrants to the more established Bolivian migrants. One such mechanism is the fiesta complex.

The Role of Associations

To my knowledge there are no village or regional associations of Bolivian migrants in Salta. Village or regional associations were first reported in the anthropological literature on urbanization in Latin America by William Mangin (1959). They were described as a type of club in the primate city organized by and for migrants from specific provinces, districts, or towns in the city's hinterland. Mangin found that the connection between the club in Lima and the town from which the migrants had come was often very strong, and that the clubs played an important role in the acculturation of migrants in Lima.

Part of the reason regional or village associations have not evolved in Salta among Bolivian migrants may be because there are not enough migrants living in the city from any one village or small region to maintain frequent communication with a distant homeland. As already pointed out, some migrants did not come from a village and others lost contact with theirs during their lengthy sojourns in Argentina. Furthermore, because the migrants are foreigners in Argentina they are not active politically. In Lima some of the regional associations with middle-class migrant members actively helped the village or town through the political system based in the city. Obviously this would be impossible for Bolivian migrants in Salta.

In Salta a fiesta organization takes the place of the regional association and has some of the same functions. The adaptive importance of fiesta systems in Bolivia has been pointed out by Hans Buechler (1970: 62), who states that "the adaptability of the fiesta system has furnished a large segment of the population, both Indian and Mestizo, with a language with which to express social relations."

The Bolivian population in Salta does not constitute a separate enclave, but instead is scattered throughout the city, maintaining social relations through interlocking friendship networks. Some villas have a larger percentage of Bolivians than others, but none is 100 percent Bolivian. Lower-income Bolivian migrants, though sharing many of the same problems and competing for scarce jobs with low-income Argentines, tend to interact socially more with fellow Bolivians.

The fiesta complex is a pan-Bolivian institution, symbolically reinforcing national identity and solidarity. It offers migrants from different regions of Bolivia an opportunity to meet and socialize with one another. Shared status as foreigners from the same country facing similar socioeconomic problems overshadows regional cultural differences and rivalries. Within this framework individuals of more similar backgrounds may meet. Although the fiesta complex does not have any explicit functions for social betterment for the group as a whole, it has an important adaptive value in facilitating the establishment of interpersonal relations for new migrants.

The fiesta complex consists of nine annual fiestas. Being Bolivian, regardless of department of origin, is the most important principle governing participation. Invitations are sent only to Bolivians, most of the rituals and celebrations of the fiestas are conducted behind closed doors, and people without invitations are not allowed to attend. Some adult children of Bolivians, born and raised in Argentina, will occasionally attend fiestas. Aside from the traditional Bolivian *chicha* (fermented corn liquor) which is regularly poured on the ground to the *pachamama* (Earth Mother), the *pollo picante* (highly seasoned chicken), and the Bolivian music and dances, there are symbolic aspects of the fiestas as well. Bolivian flags often adorn the invitations and a large stuffed condor (the national bird of Bolivia) and Bolivian silver work are displayed on top of rented taxis in the religious procession which transports the image of the saint to the church where it is blessed and returned to the fiesta site. The purpose of the fiestas is to honor important Bolivian saints, many of whom are unimportant in Argentina. All of this serves to reinforce the participants' shared identity as Bolivians. The extent of Bolivian participation in the Salta fiesta complex is difficult to estimate. There are Bolivians in Salta who have never gone to any of the fiestas, but it would be difficult to find one who neither knew about the complex nor had a friend actively involved. The size of the individual fiesta ranges from one to two hundred guests. The core of regular participants numbers about twenty to thirty couples. Generally these are long-term Salta residents who have had some economic success in the city in a variety of activities—often engaging in several small businesses at the same time, such as small stores, butcher shops, low-rent hotels, and game rooms. Characteristic of the core group is a strong pride in being Bolivian and an economic interest which rests with the Bolivian population of Salta. Their clientele is predominantly Bolivian and may learn about a particular business through informal communication networks. For many of the entrepreneurs, the fiestas bring them into contact with paisanos (countrymen), who may be potential customers or employees, as well as possible business associates. Out of this core group come the people who organize and give the fiestas.

There is another, more peripheral group of about forty to fifty people who attend a majority of the fiestas but who make little pretense of planning to give one. In general, they hold temporary jobs or work in the lowest-paying sectors of the Salta economy, collecting tickets at movie theaters, making bricks, or waiting tables in restaurants with low-income clientele. It is not uncommon for these people to seek an employee-employer relationship with the people in the fiesta group described. A third group that participates in the fiestas is made up of invited teenagers who live in the barrio or villa where the fiesta is given. Another group includes either temporary visitors to the town or migrants who come with friends who have been officially invited. For these people the fiestas provide an opportunity to make contacts and to learn about job and housing possibilities.

The reasons for participation in the fiesta complex in Salta vary considerably. The most immediate function of the fiesta complex is providing an opportunity for the participants to enjoy good food, live music, and each others' company. For some of the more established Bolivian residents, the fiestas are an opportunity to develop new clients for their business, or in some cases to find employees. More importantly, those with the resources to sponsor the fiestas are looking to their paisanos for prestige in a traditional activity, rather than looking to Argentine society for recognition. For the recent migrant the fiestas offer an opportunity to participate in ongoing social activities with countrymen in a city in which there is no ethnic enclave. Some find the resulting sense of belonging and opportunity to meet new people highly beneficial.

Another organization in Salta which supports Bolivian identity is the Club Boliviano, but its members are mostly at a higher income level than the proletarians who work or worked in the zafra. Bolivian food is served, and national Bolivian holidays are celebrated in parties that are open to the public. These functions are occasionally attended by low-income Bolivians. To some extent the Club is interested in promoting the image of Bolivia and Bolivians in the Salta community, and it has the support of the Bolivian consul.

The migrant may have access to two other types of organizations which have adaptive value in the city. Participation in these organizations is not based on nationality. The first are unions. In Argentina some unions are very powerful and play an important role in the political process. If the migrant can find a job with a large construction company, a large store, or factory, he may well benefit from the power of a union. But despite the presence of important unions in Salta, only two of the forty migrants in the sample had union affiliation. Unionized jobs are very difficult to obtain; most types of temporary urban employment are not unionized.

The second potentially important type of organization for migrants is the villa association. Villa associations are organized in almost all villas in Salta to give the residents more influence with municipal officials. They are joined together in a federation. The residents of each villa elect a president, who represents them at the federation meetings. He is a powerful figure in the villa, not only because he has been allocated power by villa members, but also because he is occasionally delegated power from the city government. The villa associations have some influence with the city government. The president of the federation may have frequent visits with the mayor of the city, depending on the situation and the orientation of the mayor. The associations petition for a wide variety of needs, such as paved streets, extension of city water pipes and electricity, and child-care centers, and are used by urban residents to gain access to city services and facilities which otherwise might remain unavailable to them. The families that work in the zafra may be members of villa associations but generally are not active participants because of their seasonal absence and their status as foreigners.

Squatments, Housing, and Control

Land ownership for the poor in Salta is an important first step in gaining some modicum of control in the urban environment. It is also regarded as an investment. Inflation steadily increases costs for the poor while their income increases slowly, if at all; Salta land values, however, may increase more rapidly than inflation. Families who plan to remain in Salta try to purchase lots on the outskirts of the city in the villas that have been opened for development, both as an investment and an escape from rising rent.

The migrant families have many reasons to own their own homes, even if they do not plan to live year around in Salta. Having some type of dwelling where the family can stay after the zafra, even if it plans to move on to another area during the postzafra season, saves money and reduces insecurity. Generally a home in Salta is a base of operations while the family either works in the city or looks for employment in the city or countryside. Without a home the family could be forced by unemployment to sleep in the streets; or, if engaged in rural work during the postzafra season, they could be laid off at the whim of the farm owner or manager and find themselves homeless. For some, a home serves another important function: it may enable a man to leave his wife and youngest children in Salta when he goes to the zafra; the children can attend school and not be exposed to the unhealthy environment on the plantations.

A general survey by the Salta government of recognized villas de emergencia found that only a small percentage of the male residents were Bolivian, and only a few of these worked in the zafra. Several conditions explain this. New squatments or invasions of land are almost nonexistent in Salta, and the government has an active program prohibiting new building on existing squatment land without the consent of the owner. In some cases the owner is the railroad, a private club, the city, or an individual. Squatment residents in major cities such as Buenos Aires can often successfully pressure government officials into selling or giving the land to them, because of the size of the squatments and the resulting power of their leaders. In contrast, residents of the relatively small, isolated squatments in Salta have almost no influence and feel they will never own the land on which they live. They hope only to stay as long as possible, or until they have a better alternative. For newcomers, getting permission to move into a villa de emergencia in Salta often requires special ties with its president, who then deals with the city government.

Today people are being moved off the villas de emergencia and some are being given the opportunity to move into new "low income" housing built by the government on the far outskirts of town. There is little enthusiasm for such housing because many fear they will not be able to afford what the government considers low monthly payments. For low-income families without secure work, required monthly payment is a very threatening prospect. The men who work in the zafra want to build when they have money and want to have the security of knowing they will not be evicted if they are unemployed for a prolonged period. Therefore, if they can buy land with good access by bus or bicycle to employment sites, it is a preferable alternative to living in the villas de emergencia. The men in this sample who live in villas de emergencia have very large families and are not in a position to allocate any of their earnings to housing. They need the money for food and clothing, at least until they can develop a more or less dependable postzafra income. If this does not happen they do not see how they will be able to buy a lot.

As already indicated, the villas de emergencia in Salta are unlike those of the larger cities in Latin America such as Lima (Mangin 1967, Uzzell 1972, Dietz 1969, Doughty 1970, Matos Mar 1968), Rio de Janeiro (Leeds and Leeds 1970), or Buenos Aires (Friedman 1969). They are very small, generate little internal economic activity, are less heterogeneous in terms of distribution of income (which is low), have less internal power, and are dominated by city government. The insecurity of tenure, the low income of the residents, and the government restrictions prohibiting further growth combine to make squatments in Salta very sterile ground for anyone interested in starting a small store or shop. People interested in starting their own enterprises and who have some flexibility about where they live, as do some who work in the zafra, move to the developing villas. I know of one exception: the president of a squatment who developed monopoly store rights in his villa de emergencia. His store is highly lucrative, and the presidency position gives him considerable power when dealing with other people who want to open competing operations. For most people, however, these small villas de emergencia in Salta offer little economic opportunity and even less security.

A migrant with zafra earnings who plans to settle in Salta is eager to increase his security and possibly his economic position by buying a lot in a villa on the outskirts of the city. Once the down payment is made, income earned in future zafras helps to complete the payments and contributes substantially to financing building materials and eventually basic furniture. This is especially true when large payments are required. Accumulation of funds would be almost impossible without the concentrated earnings made at the plantation. For those who migrate to Salta without capital, the process is much more difficult. Furthermore, due to the low wages and meager employment opportunities, it is extremely hard for them to accumulate enough capital after arrival in the city.

To purchase a lot of 30 x 50 meters in the new villas, an initial down payment of 30,000 pesos is needed. In 1969 the total cost of a lot of this size was approximately 180,000 pesos. In some cases, a lot purchased at this price could have been sold six months later for 250,000 pesos. There are many payment plans; some require seven payments within a two-year period, others allow for a more gradual rate of payment. Smaller lots of 8 x 30 meters range from 120,000 to 160,000 pesos, depending on the villa, with a down payment of 20,000 pesos and bimonthly or monthly payments of 3,000 to 6,000 pesos.

For someone with a small income, construction material is also a financial strain. Bricks cost 8 pesos apiece and the tin roofing strips cost 1,000 each. One informant who built two rooms approximately 5 x 6 meters estimated the building materials alone cost 60,000 pesos for one room. He did the building himself, and the house is still without running water and electricity. Not all build their homes out of such solid material, but the advantage of having cash to make basic purchases for housing is obvious and tremendous.

Of the forty men who worked in the 1970 sugar harvest, the sum they took home at the end of the zafra varied between 100,000 and 40,000 pesos. The average was 63,000 pesos. The two extremes were due to a number of factors listed earlier, the most important being the differing amounts of help from family members as well as differences in health. Use of the money also varied considerably. Large families with young children had to spend more money on clothing and reserve more for food needed during periods of unemployment. In cases where men or families could not stay with friends or relatives and did not own a home of their own, rent consumed a substantial part of their savings. These families found it difficult to meet costs and at the same time buy land or building materials. Blankets, beds, bikes, lanterns, chairs, and radios were also purchased by most of the families, but usually only one or two of these could be bought during one postzafra season. Three men were making payments on one-room dwellings in the central city. Eighteen allocated some money to either the purchase of land or to buy building materials for their home.

All but two of these families live on land they are paying for in one- or two-room structures. The most common building material used is inexpensive rough brick and tin roofing strips, although several families used burlap or tar paper for siding if they could not afford the bricks. All but four of the homes have dirt floors, and only two have glass windows. Two families have electricity and three have a well or pipe in water of their own, in contrast to those who have to take their water from spigots in the villa. Cooking is done outside under protective covering, usually over wood or charcoal. Most lots in the villas are large enough for summer gardens, which can make an important contribution to the diet and budget. In many cases the conditions are not substantially better than those in the villas de emergencia But the residents feel they have greater security in owning their own land and house and are consequently not as vulnerable to government eviction and regulation.

The families that were not in the process of buying land or building houses are divided between those unable, because of other expenses, to make long-term financial commitments to housing, even with earnings from two or three zafra seasons, and those not yet ready to commit themselves to staying in Salta. Included in the former group were families who needed all of their zafra earnings to pay debts and living expenses. This is particularly true of large families with young children, or families that had experienced prolonged illness or injury of the major breadwinners. In the latter group were individuals and families who decided not to continue returning to Salta after the zafra and those who were considering the possibilities of settling but did not feel they were ready to make a financial commitment. Of course, among those who were buying land some felt it was a good investment despite the fact they might not remain in Salta. It is very possible that for some of these migrants, Salta is not a final destination, but only a stop in their migration toward larger cities such as Buenos Aires.

In three exceptional cases families had pooled resources with relatives and used part of their income to purchase a vehicle, such as a truck or taxi, which would generate income during the postzafra period and possibly when they quit the zafra. Two other men invested individually in their own small business.

Table 7
Major Planned Allocations of
1971 Zafra Income

Use of Money*	Number	Percentage of Total
Land	12	30.0
Building materials for home	6	15.0
House payments	2	5.0
Articles for home—bed, stove, etc.	5	12.5
Development of own business	3	7.5
Truck or taxi	2	5.0
No major purchases	10	25.0
Savings	0	0.0
Total	40	100.0

*Individuals or families could plan to allocate money to more than one category, but they were asked to suggest major uses.

When asked how they would spend money from the next zafra most migrants had already planned specific uses. Although four families did not know at the time if they were going to return to the zafra, table 7 indicates a continuation of the pattern established the year before. Sometimes unexpected crises occur, making it difficult for families to follow through on their plans. It is significant that none of the families felt it was either possible or worthwhile to save their earnings for another year.

The above discussion suggests the importance of zafra earnings in the migrants' strategizing. Only one in the sample had made all of the payments for his land and home, and even he planned to expand his dwelling the following year. Migrants who planned to settle out of the migrant stream placed high priority on control of housing, although because of the constraints they were not always able to achieve what they desired. They received no governmental help in terms of credit or inexpensive materials. Although the standard of housing was low, and the houses often lacked important facilities, the control of housing was an important goal in developing a degree of security for the migrant families.

9. Different Perspectives of the City

Each year when the zafra is about to begin, families again reconsider their needs, resources, and alternative courses of action. The migrants described in the previous chapters, by working both in the countryside and the city, utilized resources in a niche which transcends rural-urban boundaries. Yet the occupation of this niche has a high cost in terms of personal inconvenience and possible deleterious effects on the family. The pressures against returning to the plantations vary according to the age and physical condition of the parents, the age, sex, and number of children, the family's resources and skills, and the immediate employment alternatives.

Although the migrants have little control over these personal circumstances, they consider them carefully when deciding whether to move. If they decide not to return to the zafra it will be very difficult to get rehired because of the increasing implementation of company policy to hire only men who worked in the zafra the year before. As a result, men do not give up the option of working in the zafra until they have established what they consider at least minimal control in the city to insure a degree of security and reduced vulnerability. If this seems impossible in Salta, men and their families continue their seasonal trips between Salta and the plantations, or possibly move on to other areas of Argentina or Bolivia.

This chapter examines the types of adaptations and subsequent controls families develop before they feel confident about remaining in the city year around. Together they depict the migrants' perceptions of the potentials and pitfalls of a particular type of urban environment. Most migrants have some flexibility in deciding whether to remain in the city. Because they are not forced to become entirely dependent for the whole year on an income developed in the city, they feel they may have an opportunity to develop the controls they perceive are necessary for "making it" in the city as full-time urbanites. Although some families are able to accumulate enough controls to settle out of the migrant stream, others continue moving from one locality or region to another, in search of work as rural proletarians.

There are cases in which migrants break from the zafra before they have developed the desired controls. For example, a man may become sick or injured just prior to the zafra and be unable to handle the hard physical work of the harvest. In other cases, acting spontaneously without establishing control, families may remain in the city because of their dislike of work on the plantation. Another pattern which is not a result of long-term strategy includes individuals or families who through a series of events have gained jobs with long-term potential. In these cases the family may decide to stay in Salta and skip the zafra, but it is a difficult decision unless other urban controls have been developed. With little margin for error the new urban resident is reluctant to give up the zafra, his only dependable source of income, even if it is only seasonal.

The material in this chapter is based on a sample of fifty former zafreros and their families living in Salta. They live scattered throughout the city in villas and barrios, ranging from the poorest villas de emergencia to some of the relatively prosperous new land divisions that are springing up on all sides of the city. Some have new homes with television, while others live without electricity and cook over firewood brought from the hills.

The detailed life histories of former zafreros living in Salta revealed significant differences in their reasons for breaking with the zafra and their urban adaptations at the time of their break. Three-fifths of the sample came to Salta as unskilled laborers hoping to find in the city some degree of security. Ten of these were forced to look to the city as a place of refuge, since age and failing health made it impossible for them to find jobs in the countryside. Their ages ranged from forty-eight to fifty-five at the time they stopped working in the zafra; they had little education and few urban skills. Twenty-four men broke from the zafra for a variety of reasons associated with their growing families. Of these nine had an employable urban skill. These plus eleven other men with similar skills such as marketing, cobbling, or tailoring had worked in communities of more than two thousand in Bolivia and viewed the city as a better place to practice their trade. Five of the men who did not have urban skills at the time of their break were single with few responsibilities. They felt no compelling reasons to settle, but disliked the zafra and preferred life in the city.

The City as a Locality for Residential Stability

As we have seen, a variety of factors pressure individuals and families to settle. In some cases they settle after having made adaptations in the city which give them some control; in other cases they may be forced to settle without first developing controls. The pressure to settle, as well as the families' strategizing flexibility, depends on the family cycle. The establishment of conjugal relationships, with or without formal marriage, raises the issue of settling. If either the man or woman has settled parents who can be depended upon for help in terms of lodging, the couple could decide to break out of the migrant stream. In the sample of former zafreros, forty-four were working in the zafra when they married or formed a common-law union, and only four stopped working in the zafra. In each of these latter cases the couple settled only temporarily in a rural community where one or the other had parents, returning to the zafra within the next three years. The vast majority continued to work in the zafra, but with the help of their spouse.

With the birth of children, the pressure to develop more residential stability increases. Children are expensive to feed, transport, and clothe; they hinder travel and more importantly are susceptible to diseases and possible injury if exposed to too much travel and the poor living conditions on the labor camps. The movement from job to job makes it impossible for them to finish the school year in the same school—often causing them to fail a grade. Parents are particularly concerned with education because they feel a lack of education is part of the trap inhibiting their access to better jobs. These considerations pressure many migrants to attempt to settle or at least to have a place where the women can live with the children while the man works in the zafra.

Families pressured to settle by the needs of their children worked in the zafra five to ten years. Like most Bolivian zafreros they lacked marketable urban skills when they first came to the city. As a result, their flexibility in settling in Salta was highly influenced by their ability to *develop* skills or resources in the urban environment.[1] The process of acquiring these skills or resources varies considerably. A series of little decisions and opportunities may eventually lead to the opportunity to break from the zafra. As indicated earlier, the skills and resources are seldom the product of long-term plans or strategies but result from actions taken to maximize control in the urban environment, such as reducing the uncertainty of employment, housing, and payment of wages.

Antonio did not want to be a seasonal laborer all his life but for several years came with his family from Bolivia to work in the zafra. When he was twenty he went with a hometown friend to Río Negro to pick apples after the sugar harvest and on the way back spent time in Buenos Aires trying to find work. It was not as easy as they had anticipated, and after a week without success they decided to return to Bolivia. When the zafra began again they returned to the plantation but with hopes of getting jobs in a city later on. Antonio met a girl on the lote, who after the zafra went with him to the city of Jujuy, where they had relatives, to look for work. He got a temporary job mixing cement, another hauling bricks for a mason, and another as a substitute waiter. But all of the jobs were of short duration, and by January the couple decided they could earn more money working in the tobacco harvest than in the city. They soon afterwards found work on a finca. The owner was impressed with the work of the couple during the harvest season and asked them to stay on. They accepted on the condition that they could return to the zafra every year.

Five years passed and the family grew to six. Then Antonio was fired from his job on the tobacco finca for fighting while drunk. The tobacco harvest was over and it was too late for them to find work on farms in Mendoza or Río Negro; suddenly they were without a roof, without an income, and without any viable job alternative. They decided that Jimena would go to Salta where her family then lived to ask if they could move in temporarily. Her parents consented although their house had only two rooms. After five days of looking for work Antonio was taken to the central market by a friend of his father-in-law, where he was hired to unload trucks. It was not a dependable source of income, but Antonio continued to go to the market at four or five o'clock in the morning. The Garcías could not save enough money to move out of their family's house, a change everyone would have appreciated. When the zafra began in late May it was almost a relief for Antonio and Jimena to leave Salta.

While discussing Salta at the lote, Antonio met several other men who lived in the city. One told him he had a brother who was a foreman in a Salta cement factory that produced telephone poles. He told Antonio that they hired periodically and that he might get a job after the zafra. During the last month of the zafra, when many families who owned land were leaving early to plant their crops, Antonio's friend received a letter from his brother saying that the cement company had just been given a large order and would be hiring within the week. The next day Antonio and his friend went by bus to Salta; two days later they were hired at the plant. When they returned to the zafra the contratista was displeased with their absence and with their decision to leave before the end of the harvest. The families had intended to ride back to Salta on the train chartered by the plantation, but because the men quit early they were not allowed to. Instead they rented a truck to take them to the bus station. On arrival in Salta, the Garcías again stayed with Jimena's family.

The job worked out well for Antonio. Being employed immediately after the zafra and not having to pay rent enabled him to use his zafra earnings to buy a lot near his in-laws and some materials to put up temporary housing, which he built during the weekends. When the new order at the factory was finished, Antonio was laid off. Fortunately at one of the Bolivian fiestas in Salta he had met a man who told him he would soon be needing laborers for a construction project. Antonio looked him up and was soon employed; the job lasted almost until the zafra began again.

This time after the zafra the Garcías were certain they would return to Salta. They owned land and shelter there, and Antonio knew at least two potential employers. He felt confident that he had the skill to do some of the jobs in the city, a factor which had troubled him earlier. Before long he was employed as a laborer for a friend of the man who had hired him the year before. Although the job did not last long, Antonio now knew where to go and whom to contact when he needed work. It never came easy, and seldom quickly, but he felt he could now manage in the city.

Three more years passed during which the Garcías annually migrated to the zafra and back to Salta. As the next zafra approached, the family considered whether to return. Antonio and Jimena hated living on the plantation. The family had grown to seven, and the eldest children had started school; however, the year before they had not gone to school on the lote, which troubled their parents. Furthermore, two of the children had become very ill at the zafra, and Jimena was distressed because the little boy in the neighboring room had died during the harvest. By now Antonio had enlarged his house in Salta to two rooms, had a set of good friends, and belonged to the construction workers' union. They decided that they would not return to the zafra and remained in Salta.

When Antonio and Jimena first moved to Salta an entire year in Salta dependent upon urban employment seemed a bleak alternative. Yet they decided to return to the city a second year after the zafra because they felt they could make ends meet for a limited period and possibly have their own home.

Over a period of postzafra seasons in Salta they were able to make a series of adaptations which reduced their vulnerability in the city. Through Jimena's family they met several other migrant families from the village of San Lorenzo in Tarija, Bolivia, and established themselves in a network of friends. In times of crisis these families helped one another with small loans and gifts of food. Antonio was also able to get work through his father-in-law and made friends with fellow workers, especially the Bolivians. Over time he developed a network of contacts with more than fifteen men who could help him find work. During the next two years Antonio obtained seven jobs that he learned about through friends. Finally, through two of his friends he managed to get a construction job on one of the major building projects in the city with a company that hired union labor. Once in the union, his wages were higher and the possibility for employment with companies that hired union labor increased. Although neither he nor Jimena had a permanent job with long-run prospects, these adaptations significantly reduced their vulnerability in the city so that, with the lot and building materials now paid for, they felt in a position to stop working in the zafra.

Families like the Garcías that were pressured to settle by the growth of their family needed a number of years to develop the adaptations necessary to reduce their vulnerability. The migrants with special skills spent a shorter period in the rural-urban proletarian pattern, averaging a little over three years before giving up work in the zafra. Those without specific urban skills averaged over five years in the rural-urban mode before settling year round in Salta. They had also worked an average of three years longer in the zafra before moving to Salta. These differences suggest that those with skills used the zafra as a stepping stone to the city, whereas the unskilled were less direct in moving to the city, in many cases hoping to find year-round employment in the countryside instead. Only when unsuccessful did they turn to the city.

The most common tactics for the unskilled migrants with young families were the two types of networks—the network of contacts and the small networks of close friends (commonly extended family)—and buying land and constructing a dwelling.[2] At the time of the break all but two families owned their own house, half had electricity and more than two rooms; only two families were still making payments on the land. Just one family had started its own business. Although only one man had two jobs at the time of the break, several had held two jobs shortly before breaking from the zafra, and in eight cases more than one family member was working at the time. These adaptations suggest that most families waited to settle permanently in the city until they felt they had made certain adaptations to conditions in the city which would give them some control over housing and employment. These tactics served to reduce their vulnerability to both employers and to fluctuations in the labor market in Salta at the time. Without these adaptations the migrants did not feel they were in a position to give up the security of dependable employment in the zafra.

Urban-rural linkages may be very important in the development of urban-based economic enterprises. In some cases cutting cane has evolved into other economic activities on the plantation, involving both the husband and wife. This in turn may have a feedback effect on the migrant's urban economic activity, as the following case shows. It also illustrates how the city may replace the village as the base of residence for seasonal rural workers.

Julio is tall and slim. He wears new clothes neatly pressed. Born on a small farm near Tarija, he initially came to Argentina when he was seventeen to work in the zafra. That was nineteen years ago. For the first two years he returned to the farm to help; but he had many brothers and sisters, and the third year, after talking with the family, he decided to remain in Argentina to look for work after the zafra. Today Julio is considered a successful man by his peers and also by his own evaluation.

Julio actively pursued two strategies, one directly connected to the plantation environment and the other to the urban setting of Salta. Actually these strategies did not evolve until he married and settled with his wife and children in Salta. The first years he actively learned about Argentina and the Northwest. He remembers best the problems of getting work after the zafra, of spending money without any coming in, and of not knowing how he could earn more. The first postzafra season in Argentina he went with a friend from Bolivia who claimed to know where to find work. Turned away from several tobacco farms, they decided to seek work at construction sites. On the second day they found a job, but were laid off after the first week with only half their earnings. Not knowing how to protest, they left town the next day.

Julio's wife Juana grew up in Cochabamba, Bolivia. After her father died, her mother María started selling vegetables to make a living; later they moved to Oruro, where her mother and brother worked in a mine. When the Bolivian revolution began, María took her two daughters and son, who was in the army at the time, to Argentina. They moved to Salta, where she had a sister, and they have remained there ever since, except during the zafra season, when they all went to one of the ingenios to work in the cane fields. When they arrived in Salta the first time, her mother agreed to work as a cuarta for a friend of her sister's. She prepared his meals and helped him in the cane fields.

When Julio married Juana he changed his orientation as they decided there were several ways to earn more money at the plantation than by cutting sugar cane. Juana's mother had earned money cooking for one man; Juana decided to cook for as many men as she could, although realizing others were also doing the same. Several factors forced food prices up and made it difficult to make a good living giving pensión. Since the lotes were isolated food prices were high, especially for meat and vegetables, which had to be trucked into the lote every day. On some lotes a few women went to town every few days to purchase these goods, but the process was long and drawn out since the buses ran irregularly. By pooling their money, the family managed after several years to buy an old truck, which Juana's brother-in-law used to deliver meat from the nearby town. For years he had been trying to work out a trucking agreement with a local butcher. With his truck he delivered meat during the morning to two lotes and brought meat and vegetables at reduced rates to Juana. The family was so successful it was able to purchase a newer truck the following season. Two years later, Julio himself bought a truck. With two trucks the family had increased mobility, which opened new possibilities for profit. They charged for transporting people to the train or to town; they hauled firewood for other zafreros as well as themselves, which also cut down the cost and time of preparing food for the pensión. Gradually Juana cut her prices, and her boarders increased to forty-six men. Julio also had a job on the side—fixing bikes, the most common mode of transportation for zafreros. Tires and bicycles are always in need of repair because of the heavy wear from the rough gravel roads. Meanwhile Julio continued to work as a zafrero because people not working for the company are not allowed to live on the lote. Through these efforts the family members were able to develop four sources of income on the plantation in addition to work in the cane harvest: providing meals for workers, selling meat at the work camp, charging workers for trucking services, and repairing bicycles.

There was one more important source of income and control that Julio did not develop in the beginning, but which he was quick to take advantage of when the opportunity presented itself. The contratista who recruited for Julio's lote brought over five hundred men to the ingenio every year. He hired four or five mayordomos to help him recruit and to help supervise in the fields. As indicated earlier, a mayordomo has usually worked in the zafra and commands respect of the workers. He must also be able to write and do simple arithmetic. Within a five-year period Julio and his family had built up a large network of contacts and were regarded by fellow workers as examples of how working hard pays off. The contratista had his food prepared by Julio's wife at a reduced rate and was well aware of the growing success of the family. When an opening for mayordomo developed, the contratista felt Julio would be a useful assistant: he had a truck and because of his mobility could be a big help in recruiting workers; he was well known by the workers and could read and write. Julio accepted the position, removing himself from the difficult work in the fields. Although he received a lower wage, there were compensations.

As described earlier the mayordomo is in a unique position of control. He is asked for many favors and in turn receives favors or direct bribes. This had a positive effect on family business: people did business with the family in hopes of getting favors from Julio. The favors he could now hand out ranged from assigning good rows of cane instead of poor rows to assigning rooms. As mentioned before, both are important to a worker. A poor row of cane may yield a worker one-third less income for the same amount of work. Rooms are important, for the people try to avoid crowding and hope to live near friends or relatives. Julio could also deny zafreros work at the beginning of each year. These new powers he exploited to the fullest.

When people speak of the family they do so with a touch of envy, but also a strong feeling of bitterness. For example, they tell about how at the end of the harvest one year Juana refused to pay her two teen-age helpers the amount she had originally promised. Instead she paid half the amount, suggesting that they had been poor workers. The girls complained and their families were upset, but it did no good. Julio was the mayordomo, who is usually supposed to arbitrate these matters.

Meanwhile, the family's financial success on the plantation had a profound effect on their strategies in Salta. After completing their truck payments they bought adjacent lots in Salta and constructed three houses for themselves. Then they bought another two lots and gradually over the next two years built two houses with zafra earnings, which they rented eventually. Both were in the neighborhood they lived in but were better houses. Julio's brother-in-law worked trucking but had submitted an application to become a taxi driver. Meanwhile, Julio did construction on jobs where his truck would be helpful. He was regarded by many as having key information about jobs because of his contacts with small builders. The builders in turn looked to him for temporary laborers, which he could usually find through his zafra contacts.

Generally a zafrero's opportunity to gain any type of control on the plantation or lote is very limited. Yet for a small minority of workers the lote environment offers unique means of gaining some control and often capital. Important elements in the individual's success seem to include: (1) enough education to do limited supervision; (2) a family network with economic influence; and (3) growing capital. Julio's strategies changed over time but were interrelated, with important feedback effects. For example, the success of the pensión program was helped considerably by the family's truck; the meat-selling concession, also made possible by the truck, helped cut meat prices for the pensión program. All of these contributed to Julio's rise to mayordomo, which in turn opened new sources of income and functioned to strengthen the pensión program as well as other business. Together these resources and profits allowed the family to buy land in Salta—a long-term investment of resources, first for housing and then as a source of rental income. Furthermore, land is a safe investment in an inflationary economy. The family strategy of establishing another year-round source of income in Salta led to buying a taxi. They felt if their urban efforts failed they could always go back to the zafra. Meanwhile, increased mobility gave Julio access to information about labor needs and job openings and allowed him to work as a construction contratista, controlling work opportunities on one hand and labor on the other.

The City as a Last Resort

Another factor that pressures migrants to settle is their inability to continue the grueling work in the zafra. This is usually due to advancing age or declining physical health.[3] The work becomes increasingly arduous for older people, many of whom have suffered injuries, illnesses, and malnutrition during their lives.[4] Some companies have stopped hiring men over fifty because the administrators feel they are less productive than young men. Ten of the former zafreros, all with families, gave up or were forced out of work in the zafra because of problems associated with age. Their plight is sad because despite many years of year-round work in harvests in Bolivia and Argentina these men do not usually receive jubilación (retirement pay). This is because they have worked much of the time as temporary laborers for many employers. The men studied averaged fifty-one major moves from one region (and occasionally city) to another between their initial departure from Bolivia and their present stay in Salta. In the course of constant traveling, many lost or badly damaged their booklets with their employment records. Others have no records because for much of the time they were illegal immigrants and no records were kept. Even men who have worked in the zafra for more than thirty years receive no help from the companies and little aid from the unions in claiming retirement pay.

For these men and their families, the city was a last resort, a place to make a stand, taxing both their remaining physical strength and their meager resources. Much of the literature on urbanization suggests that migrants to the city are positively selected, meaning that the best-educated and most-ambitious young adults in the village move to the city (Balán 1968; Balán, Browning, and Jelin 1973). Yet the city draws another type of migrant as well: the most marginal. Having few alternatives, these migrants are often forced to settle in the city before they have established the controls they feel are minimally necessary. Five of the men had adult children in Salta who could help them; the others settled in the city because they could not get jobs in the countryside. In those cases where the migrants had family in Salta, they were able to stay with them during part of the rural-urban stage and all but one bought land. Three of the migrant families that did not have relatives in Salta had to rent and later purchased a shelter in a villa de emergencia; one managed to buy a lot and put up a primitive one-room shack. Another family rented a room off an alley in downtown Salta, where they have continued to live.

The same socioeconomic structure which limited these migrants' opportunities in the countryside, and to which they adapted by being temporary agricultural workers much of their lives, extended to the city as well. None of the migrants had a long-term job at the time of his break. Their networks of contacts were limited. Many mentioned that they had hoped to establish a type of patron-client relationship but had not been successful. None belonged to a union.

The migrants' occupations in Salta range from shining shoes to gardening, but in all cases the jobs are temporary and low paying. Many are forced to take light seasonal rural work on tobacco farms to increase their meager earnings. Unlike younger unskilled workers, who may eventually develop new skills in the city, the older men seldom can risk the time nor are they offered the opportunity to learn new skills.

Concepción, age fifty-four, has worked in the zafra almost every year since he was seventeen years old. This is the first year he has not gone to the harvest; the plantation where he worked lowered the maximum working age to fifty. Concepción is fully aware how difficult it is for a man his age to work in the zafra and wishes he were younger, as "there is good money to make in the zafra." He has worked on all of the plantations in the Ramal as well as on several in Tucumán. His brother, his wife's brothers, and his two sons-in-law all work in the zafra. Juan, his only son, worked in the zafra until recently but is now in Buenos Aires, where he went after the last harvest. Concepción had hoped he would return and they could work together in the zafra—Concepción working as a helper—but he did not have his son's address and for all practical purposes contact between them has been broken.

From the time he began working in Argentina at age seventeen until he was thirty years old, Concepción returned every year to the small farm run by his mother in Bolivia (his father had died when he was very young). When Concepción was thirty the patrón turned them off the land to put it into pasture, and Concepción, his wife, and two children left Bolivia permanently. During the postzafra seasons he worked mainly on tobacco farms in the area of Perico. He did not have proper work papers. Although a farm owner or manager would hire him without documents, he was seldom paid a wage equivalent to Argentine workers. Bitterly he remembers five or six employers who paid only half the wages they had promised; but he had little recourse and they knew it. During this period one of his children died and another two were born. He would have liked a farm of his own, but his low income compounded by the needs of the precarious postzafra season made this impossible. He did not look for urban work, feeling his experience made it easier to get rural jobs. One postzafra season Concepción went to Mendoza in search of employment—a trip he continued to make for many years. In Mendoza he usually found work harvesting grapes, onions, tomatoes, mint, and apples. Although each harvest was of short duration, combined they lasted almost until the zafra began again. For several years he went to Río Negro for the apple harvest. The trips to Mendoza and Río Negro were expensive and left the family of five with little money when they returned to the North. Concepción recalls bitterly the insecurity of having to look for work and the frequent moves of the family.

When Concepción realized his zafra years were limited, he decided to move to Salta, where there would be more work opportunities and where he had friends who also worked in the zafra. The first year the family came to Salta an old friend helped Concepción get a job in the brick factory. The owner was pleased with his work, even though his production was impeded by his bad limp, the result of an accident while loading cane at the zafra. He was paid by the number of bricks finished and by working longer hours was able to earn almost as much as other men. But the daily income was at least 1000 pesos less than he could make in the zafra. Furthermore, when there were no orders for bricks the employees were temporarily unemployed. With his zafra earnings, Concepción decided to buy a lot and build a home with rejected bricks from the factory, located nearby. He felt fortunate to have a relatively steady job, but did not know how long he could continue with the heavy work. Furthermore, the pay was very low and he and his aging wife were just scraping by. They raised vegetables in the spring and summer and had some chickens, which fended for themselves most of the time.

For men like Concepción age and health are the main reasons they decide to settle and to abandon work in the zafra. Generally, if given the strength and opportunity to continue working in the zafra they would choose to do so. As indicated earlier, families do not return to harvest cane for the love of it, but rather because of their dire straits or their desire to improve small aspects of their lives. Declining physical strength, inability to write, and the lack of special urban skills combine to greatly curtail their flexibility in establishing themselves in the urban environment. Concepción regards himself as particularly fortunate in finding the job in the brick factory, a job which strains his physical condition but which he can handle for awhile. Few are so fortunate. Most of the men forced by age to settle had been rural mobile proletarians much of their lives, failing to accumulate capital, losing touch with some family members, and highly dependent on the zafra as a source of income. Only when the zafra was denied them were they forced to look elsewhere for employment. What confronted them was a bleak prospect.

Breakdown Before Urbanization

The preceding sections make clear the role of friends and relatives in the migrants' adaptation. All of the migrants interviewed acknowledged that it is important to have help upon arriving in the city, and 94 percent felt that a family needed friends to survive the unavoidable periods of unemployment in the city.[5] Yet only 40 percent of the Bolivian migrants who came to Salta after the zafra and planned to return to the zafra the following season actually received help from relatives or friends from a home community; and only 63 percent of the unskilled former zafreros received help. These figures are low when compared with percentages given in studies describing urban migration in other parts of Latin America. For example, in a sample of over two hundred migrants from the Mexican village of Tzintzuntzán, Robert V. Kemper (1974: 84) found that more than 90 percent settled in Mexico City with the aid of relatives or friends. Mario Margulis (1968: 150) reported that village migrants from the province of Catamarca, Argentina, received extensive support in their adjustment in Buenos Aires. Eighty-one percent received some help; of these 77 percent stayed with friends or relatives upon arrival, and 72 percent had help in finding jobs.

What accounts for the comparatively low percentage of migrants receiving aid from friends and relatives in Salta? The size of the city may be a variable: migrants may feel it easier to adjust to a smaller city than to a larger, more complex one and try it in the absence of friends or family. Another possible explanation may be that the Bolivian migrants described here were not as dependent on the city as were some migrants, because they could count on the stable, relatively well-paying zafra employment. As a result they could afford the risk of trying to settle without contacts. Still another explanation could be that the migrants had few actual contacts on arrival in Salta. This phenomenon could be explained in two ways: that there was a small Bolivian population in the city, or that the migrants in the sample were pioneer migrants from their home villages. But the Bolivian population in Salta is relatively large and migration from southern Bolivia has a long history.

As I pursued the question it became clear that two other processes were more important in the explanation. Some migrants have lost contact with relatives or friends because of multiple moves from one work site to another within Bolivia and Argentina. In these cases the friends and relatives are often itinerant rural workers as well, which compounds the difficulty of maintaining communication—addresses are unknown, mail service to work camps is nonexistent, and many of the workers are illiterate. Furthermore, the vast number of farms and the great distances between agricultural areas in Argentina reduces the migrants' expectations of ever meeting acquaintances again. Although some families annually reunite in plantation work camps or return year after year to the same farm after the sugar harvest, they are constantly threatened by the possibility that this regularity will be disrupted, because they do not own the housing or the source of employment. In addition, it is common for families or children to take a job at a time when they would be expected back at the plantation. The above factors impede communication, and as a result nuclear families may become socially atomistic units whose lack of contacts is a major disadvantage if they migrate to the city.

Although these factors are helpful in explaining why certain families interviewed in Salta had lost contact with children and extended kin in Argentina, they constitute only part of the explanation. Extended periods of migration over great distances seldom result in permanent loss of contact with kin and friends. For example, Raymond Wiest (1979) documents the importance of remittances sent back to the home village by Mexican workers in the United States. Labor migration from the Tlaxcala, Puebla region of Mexico "increased the incidence of the extended family household" (Nutini and Murphy 1970: 97). James Watson (1975) has shown the integration of Chinese migrants in London with life in their home villages. My own data contain ample evidence of Bolivians who return regularly to their home communities, often sending remittances while in Argentina. What seems to distinguish a significant number, twenty-eight, of the migrants without contacts in Salta is that they were itinerant rural workers without what they regarded as a home community in Bolivia. Most had been children of highly mobile rural workers, spending their formative years on a variety of farms and plantations in both Bolivia and Argentina, and therefore not identifying with any community. In three other cases, migrants had lost contact with their home community because of years of living in Argentina and family tragedy at home.[6] This was especially true if they had no access to community or family land—an important inducement for migrants in many parts of Latin America to maintain ties with the village and remain at least somewhat active in village affairs. Without this incentive, and as the length of time the individual resided in Argentina increased, his knowledge about the exact location of fellow village migrants from Bolivia tended to decrease, as did his ability to assume that he could count upon supportive aid if he moved to an Argentine city where they lived.

In contrast to migrants lacking ties to stable communities, it appears that migrants coming from a stable community of origin and who migrate relatively directly to the city, such as the Tzintzuntzeños in Mexico City, usually arrive in the city with a network of potentially supportive contacts, the earlier migrants from the same village—what Charles Tilly (1973: 3) calls a "non-territorial community network."[7] Most village migrants who become established in a particular city have been preceded—and helped—by pioneer migrants from the same village who arrived in the city with few contacts. In the sample, thirty-two of thirty-six migrants from villages received some help with housing or employment from friends or relatives.

Because of the size of the sample on which this discussion is based, no conclusive statement can be made, but it is possible to suggest that breakdown of kin ties before urbanization may occur for migrant families continually forced to migrate in search of work. As shown earlier, individuals and families try various strategies to eliminate the uncertainty and insecurity of this life style and are often successful. But when unsuccessful, breakdown can result. Because of erratic movement patterns, low income, and the short time spent in work camps, the families may make few enduring friendships and may lose track of their own kin. This process could be called "rural proletarianization with breakdown." Although it has been suggested that the proletarianization of rural people might be regarded as a preadaptive phase facilitating their urbanization, there are also deleterious effects which cannot be ignored.

Even with many family members simultaneously working in different parts of Argentina, Bolivians demonstrated a remarkable ability to maintain contact. As Alison MacEwen (1973) found in her research in southern Argentina, under conditions of high mobility and economic instability the kinship system becomes the most important source of social relationships. But if families or individuals are unable to develop and maintain a home base during critical periods of the family cycle, it becomes very difficult to maintain contact with members of the extended family and sometimes even with one's own adult children. Life histories of the Bolivians in Salta who settled out of the migrant stream because they could no longer get rural work reflect this mobility and its consequences. In one case a family moved all of their belongings seventy-two times in a twenty-year period. Ten families averaged forty-nine moves from the time they last left Bolivia to the time they moved to Salta. Seven of these families had one or two adult children with whom they had completely lost contact. Not knowing where their children were nor feeling their children could find them caused great sadness and frustration for the parents.

The combination of rural proletarianization, poverty, and great geographic mobility resulting in loss of contact with kin has some interesting implications for one of the old issues in the urbanization literature: urbanization with or without breakdown. The traditional bases of social solidarity were once presumed by sociologists to disappear with urbanization (Wirth 1938). This view had a profound influence on Redfield (1941, 1947) when he developed his concept of the rural-urban continuum. The influence of the city was perceived as leading to personal and social disorganization of immigrants. Oscar Lewis (1952) led the attack against this view with his study of migrants from Tepoztlán in Mexico City in which he showed for his sample no social breakdown but instead the transfer of rural institutions to the city. Since that time various studies in Latin America have tended to reiterate the theme of the migrants' "successful adjustment to urban life," and numerous cases document the importance of continued contact with family and village friends. Most of these studies, however, were of individuals who were villagers and who moved to cities or towns that were relatively close to their original home base.

The manner in which an individual copes with the constraints and takes advantage of resources, however minimal, depends to a considerable degree not only on his unique skills and resources but also on the social capital he or she brings to the city or is able to develop in the city. Social capital here means the ties with friends and relatives both in the city and in the rural areas. In order to cope with unstable, short-term job opportunities in a provincial city such as Salta, an individual needs a highly flexible social network in which a variety of people can help him learn about and possibly get various jobs over the year, thus reducing the periods of unemployment. But if breakdown has occurred in the countryside, successful urban adaptation is much more difficult since the individual begins working without social capital. In these cases individualization is not caused by the city, but instead by the forces of capitalism and the resulting rural social structure, which have led to rural proletarianization and atomistic adaptations in the countryside.

Unskilled migrants arriving in Salta without friends or ties there have more difficulty making social adaptations the migrants consider necessary to cope with the socioeconomic structure of an industrialized city.[8] Included in this category are seven families who settled-out due to family pressures and four families who settled-out due to age. Half had tried cities before in their search for security and had encountered the same types of problems in the city as in the countryside.

All eleven families took longer to move from the rural-urban migration pattern to "permanent" urban residence than did the families who, otherwise similar, had important social resources of friends or family. The eleven families spent much longer in other migration patterns, in particular the rural mobile proletarian pattern. In Salta their incomes were lower, they had longer periods of unemployment, and as a result they lived more often in villas de emergencia. If they did own a home it was usually a one-room structure, very crowded, without electricity or running water. Seven families continued to do some type of seasonal rural work after the break from the zafra. The most common social adaptation (five cases) was the establishment of weak patron-client relationships with an employer who paid substandard wages. In six other cases no significant adaptations focusing on employment security had been made at the time of the break. They continued to be highly vulnerable to employers (rural and urban) and to fluctuations in the economy.

The City as the Best Place To Work

Some of the Bolivian migrants who had worked in the zafra and settled in Salta had special skills more marketable in the city than in the countryside. Almost all of the men were cobblers, tailors, mechanics, or carpenters in Bolivia, although they had worked at many other tasks as well, and they hoped to establish themselves in these fields in Argentina. They came as young men in their twenties or early thirties, using the zafra as a stepping stone into Argentina. By signing up with a contratista to work in the zafra they were able to get free transportation into Argentina and were assured immediate employment for a definite period of time. During their first postzafra season they moved to Argentine cities, sustaining themselves with money earned in the harvest while they looked for jobs in their own fields.

Towns and cities in Latin America usually have a large service sector including, among other occupations, service trades such as cobbling and tailoring. Presumably, competent individuals have the option of individually setting up a shop or working for others. The former takes capital and involves considerable risk; the latter, in some places, entails a risk of another type—the risk of not being paid and low returns on work.

After learning about the employment situation in Salta and in neighboring cities, many skilled migrants wanted to work on their own. But it is difficult to set up a shop without capital. Some of the capital could be earned in the zafra. If they found postzafra jobs soon after the zafra ended, and limited their expenses, within a period of three or four years they could establish themselves in Salta, spending a shorter time in the rural-urban adaptive mode than the unskilled workers. Although they did not always achieve the desired independence, their jobs tended to have greater security than those of other migrants.

Typical of the skilled group is Pedro, father of four. Pedro grew up as an orphan in Tupiza, where he learned to work as a cobbler. Not able to find enough work, he left Bolivia in 1952, when only eighteen, and went to Argentina with a friend to work in the zafra at a Salta plantation. After the harvest his friend returned to Bolivia, but Pedro, having no family in Bolivia, decided to remain in Argentina, finding work in vegetable farms in the area of Fraile Pintado in the sugar zone of Jujuy. He was fortunate and managed to get work on several farms in the area until the zafra began again; this time he went to Ingenio del Norte. Ten years passed during which Pedro did not visit Bolivia. His postzafra search for work took him to the cities of Jujuy and Salta, where he failed to get work as a cobbler but found temporary employment in construction. He also worked a few years in the Jujuy tobacco harvest and even went to Mendoza to harvest grapes, returning each year to the zafra at Ingenio del Norte. At twenty-five he married a girl he knew from his home town in Bolivia who came annually to the zafra with her family.

By the time he was twenty-eight Pedro had saved some money from the zafra and purchased a lot in Salta, on which he built an inexpensive one-room shack out of wood scraps. Having heard much about the high-paying jobs in Buenos Aires, he decided to go there with a friend to get work after the zafra. Pedro and his wife decided that he would go alone, the family joining him when he found enough work to support them. In the meantime, Serafina would stay in Salta with the children and try to get work as a housemaid. Pedro quickly found work in Buenos Aires as a construction laborer and shared a room with his friend in one of the big villas miseria. He enjoyed the exciting atmosphere of the big city and liked seeing the major soccer teams play on the weekend, but he quickly realized that he would never have the income needed to buy or rent a house outside of the villas miseria. Although he felt they were acceptable for a grown man, he was appalled at the thought of raising children in the squalid environment of mud, garbage, sewage, flies, and loose morals; he feared that his two sons would grow up to be gunmen. Moreover, he did not like the long trips between the villa miseria and his work site. For a man who did not have much money and did not like living in crowds, Salta was a better place to raise a family, Pedro felt. When the zafra began again he decided to return to the Northwest to be with his family.

After returning from the zafra, Pedro bought bricks and built an addition to his shack. He found work in a large cobbler's shop in downtown Salta, where he received 60 percent of the income from his labor. Some days he earned up to two thousand pesos but on others he earned as little as two and three hundred pesos. To supplement his salary he worked nights as an usher in a movie theater. By this time he had two more children and his income barely supported his family. Unable to save the considerable amount needed to rent a room and set up his own shop in the business district, Pedro contemplated opening a shop in his new room at home, but this was far from even the center of his own villa and his neighbors were poor. Furthermore, he needed capital to buy materials.

Although the zafra promised a relatively high income, Pedro was reluctant to return to the plantation because he felt the environment—the heat, insects, and crowded conditions—was bad for his children and wife. He had seen too many children get sick at the lotes, and he wanted his eldest son to get a good education. Yet he knew he was not earning enough in Salta to ever establish his own shop. Pedro contemplated leaving his family in Salta and going alone to the zafra, but he knew a man needed the help of his wife if he were to make money. The family finally decided to return to the zafra one more year.

After the zafra Pedro found a room in Salta that rented for nine thousand pesos a month and seemed well located for a cobbler shop. It was within twenty minutes of his home by bicycle and was located on the edge of a small business section in one of the peripheral areas of the city. He decided to rent it, paying two months' rent and buying the necessary materials with his savings from the zafra. Although he would be unable to make any additions to his home, he would be in business on his own. Additional materials, including some extra tools, cost him twenty thousand pesos. He owned a small work bench but had to make a storage rack and hire a truck to haul it to his shop, which cost him another twenty thousand pesos. Finally, after painting his sign, he was in business.

But as often happens, business did not start rapidly. By the end of the month Pedro had to pay rent again, plus a five-hundred-peso electric bill. A city collector informed him that ten thousand pesos were due for a business permit and tax. By now his zafra savings were dwindling rapidly since his postzafra income did not meet his family's needs. Fortunately he had no more lot payments to make and did not have to pay rent for his house. The two boys got jobs delivering and selling newspapers, working in the morning before they went to school. At first they only sold twenty a day, but within three weeks their sales had increased. On weekends they managed to sell around eighty, and when Pedro joined them they sold over one hundred, making a profit of sixteen pesos per paper. Although Serafina tried to get work as a maid, people were unwilling to hire her because she had a young baby she would have to bring with her. Pedro was able to borrow some money against his land to keep the shop going another month.

In the second month business picked up and Pedro had enough to keep him working late into the evening. As his reputation of being a good cobbler who charged reasonable prices and delivered punctually spread throughout the neighborhood, his business continued to improve. By working long hours he was able to establish a secure income and maintain payments on his shop. Pedro has never had to return to the zafra. During some winter months he feels it may be harder to work as a cobbler than as a zafrero. On a cold Salta day, working in an open shop without heat leaves his fingers numb. At times he becomes ill. When work is slack he does not earn as much as he would at the zafra; and when work is abundant he must work all day and long into the night. But at least he knows he does not have to move his family twice a year and he has control of his own labors.

Pedro's story points out the importance some migrants attach to saving capital which can be used to secure housing and to set up a work base. The low pay of most types of work available to migrants, coupled with rising living costs, make it difficult to save enough money to establish oneself in any type of self-employment. In Pedro's case, not only was an initial investment of 58,000 pesos necessary to cover business expenses for the first two months, but an additional 30,000 pesos were needed to cover living expenses during this time, with housing already paid. Although Pedro's zafra earnings were enough to set up his business, they could not last long enough for him to become well established. Fortunately his business suddenly began to draw customers, and he was able to *dar la vuelta* (turn the corner). Others have not gotten past that critical point and have lost both their zafra earnings and their businesses.

Like most in this group of former zafreros who had marketable skills when they arrived in Salta, Pedro was able to contemplate moving to an urban environment early in his migration career and felt confident that he would be able to leave the zafra forever. As mentioned earlier, however, the opportunities for craftsmen such as cobblers or tailors are not great in Salta. Unless one has his own shop, the return on labor may be so low that having a special skill is almost negated as an opportunity. Because of fluctuations in demand the hired helper of a tailor or cobbler is likely to be laid off, and he cannot be sure of getting paid for his labor. For these reasons, Pedro felt he would have difficulty breaking from the zafra unless he had his own shop. Like most of the skilled group, Pedro decided to continue working in the zafra, where he received higher and more dependable wages than he could earn in Salta working for someone else, until he was able to be his own boss. For Pedro, the strategy of reduced vulnerability meant not being dependent on employers or landlords. The zafra was perceived as the best source of the capital necessary to gain this independence. He felt strongly that a man should not get "too involved with others"; they would eventually let him down because their interests do not always correspond with his. He did not try to establish the same type of social network as the unskilled migrants. He knew where he had to look to find work if it were available, and many of his contacts were of the same profession. This was true of most of the skilled migrants.

At the time they broke from the zafra, ten of the twenty skilled workers had established their own shop or business and felt they could make a go of it. Three had become partners with other Bolivian migrants in a business enterprise such as a tailor shop. This too took an investment of capital. In contrast to the unskilled, a greater percentage of the skilled migrants developed a type of patron-client relationship. Either they worked as an employee in their trade for an employer whom they trusted or they became supervisors. Four of the workers held more than one job at the time they quit the zafra. Although these employment adaptations are distinctly different from those made by the unskilled migrants, they continue to reflect a strategy of least vulnerability. Their housing at the time of the break was no better than that of the unskilled, and a lower percentage owned their own housing. They were more concerned with establishing the basis of their livelihood, which often required capital, than they were in developing control over their housing. Only nine of the men had bought land; of these only three had built houses.

Summary

The density of jobs and the availability of relatively inexpensive land within easy commuting distance of job sites were perceived by many migrants as important resources in Salta. But the temporary nature of most employment and the low wages were significant problems. As foreigners, perhaps without the proper work papers, the migrants were vulnerable to employers who might not pay them the going wage, as well as to the fluctuating economy and inflation. Making a living in the city entailed developing one or more tactics of a strategy of least vulnerability before giving up their only source of secure seasonal employment: the zafra. Income from the zafra gave the migrants some flexibility in their efforts to adapt to the city, but pressures such as age or a growing family with educational and health needs limited the length of time families felt they could occupy the transitional niche of the rural-urban adaptive mode. Some of the urban migrants had skills which gave them greater flexibility in settling in the city, but they too were concerned about reducing their vulnerability. Their tactics were different from those of the unskilled because they could establish independent shops, patron-client relationships in which they had some power, or could get more than one job at a time. Because they needed zafra-generated capital for employment-related investment, control over housing at the time of the break was less important than it was for the unskilled migrants. The unskilled migrants who had family or friends in Salta when they arrived had an advantage in establishing two types of networks: one of work contacts and another of close friends.   Families who had spent very long periods as rural temporary workers in adaptive modes such as the rural mobile proletarian mode had the most difficult time making important adaptations to reduce their vulnerability.   Breakdown before urbanization did reduce adaptive flexibility in the city.

10. Conclusion

Most studies of urbanization in Latin America deal with the migration of rural villagers to the city, and the basic spatial models of the urbanization process account for only this particular pattern of migration. These models generally depict migrants moving from villages to increasingly larger towns and cities in various steps and time periods. They do not account for the many migrants who move to the cities via rural wage work rather than directly from villages or towns, an unfortunate omission because the number of these rural proletarians in Latin America is already large and growing rapidly (Feder 1971, Greaves 1972).

In parts of Latin America the poor peasants or tenant farmers faced with increasing rent, deteriorating land, and other problems of production have no alternative but to leave the land. Some move to the city. For those who prefer rural life to the uncertainties of the city a second option is sometimes available. In areas such as Northwest Argentina, capitalist commercial agriculture offers seasonal work, and so for many migrants employment as a rural worker is seen as a clear alternative to moving to the city and more attractive because of their familiarity with agricultural work. Others perceive wage work on the plantation as a stepping stone to the city.

In this study I have tried to place migration in a historical context. This is based on the assumption that forces stemming from dependent capitalism have shaped the patterns of uneven development in Argentina and Bolivia. Migration is both a symptom and a product of this process. The plantations of the Norte initiated labor migration to the cane fields by using coercive methods of obtaining and maintaining an inexpensive labor force. The recruitment of Bolivian workers was but one of a series of efforts to accomplish this goal. For years most Bolivian workers migrated between the plantations and their home communities. Yet the contradictions inherent in sectoral dualism led to a break in the circular migration as an increasing number of families could no longer sustain themselves in Bolivia for even part of the year. Once in Argentina, many decided not to return to Bolivia after the harvest but remained in Argentina, working on farms and in cities scattered throughout the country.

Although the migrants disliked the work and dismal living conditions of the plantations, much to my surprise many saw another dimension to work. In struggling for a livelihood, families attempted to use the zafra work to establish themselves in Argentina. The steady employment during five months of the year when other sources of agricultural work were scarce represented a unique situation. In addition, payments were dependable and compensations required by law—but seldom paid on other jobs—were usually granted. The workers' view of the positive aspects of plantation work reflects the degree of their plight, the resilience of their hope even when faced with the obstacles described herein, and their victimization by capitalist agriculture, which extracted so much labor with so little pay.[1]

Bolivians living on the plantation work camp actively seek information about various kinds of postzafra work situations. Since most of the migrant workers find postzafra work harvesting another crop, it is vital for them to get specific reports on the quality of the crop, length of the harvest, living conditions, salaries, and dependability of payments; on availability of schools, stores, garden plots, and medical facilities; on transportation costs to and from the farm area; and on additional sources of work in the region. Those contemplating moving to towns or cities in search of work need specific information about job sources, housing, and the like.

Where a worker or family decides to go after the zafra, a crucial part of their strategy, depends on their circumstances: not all workers have the same alternatives since not all share the same problems, resources, and opportunities. Some own land, however meager, in Bolivia; some, homes in towns or cities of Northwest Argentina. Others have never owned land and may have only the few material possessions they take with them on their nomadic journeys in search of work. Some have special skills or several years of schooling; others cannot read or write. The men range from eighteen years old with no family to almost fifty with a large family to support. They also vary considerably in the degree of contact they maintain with nuclear and extended kin. Some pool their resources and make joint investments with relatives, meeting seasonally in the work camp or sharing postzafra housing with them. Those at the other extreme have lost contact even with their own children, and their kin ties have eroded or atrophied entirely.

Besides such individual considerations, there are many constraints that affect the migrant's struggle to meet basic needs. The seasonality of much of the rural work, the short duration and low pay of urban jobs, the high risk of being trapped in jobs where the contratista or patrón does not pay regularly, and the threat of illness or injury without compensation put the migrant and his family in a precarious position. With good reason, maximizing security is the great concern of the migrants, especially as their families grow and they become older. They hope to reduce the risk and uncertainty of their existence primarily through greater control of housing and stability of employment.

Many of these families eventually seek work in cities as well as in the countryside. But far from being attracted by the "inevitable pull of the city," the migrants with little education and few resources often regard life in the provincial capital of Salta as having many of the same problems as life in the countryside. Since Salta has developed neither a large industrial sector nor a job-opportunity structure which permits migrants to find secure, long-term employment easily, for many migrants the problems of low pay, jobs of short duration, and difficulty in finding employment know no rural-urban boundaries.

The move to the city is often depicted in social-science literature as a permanent transfer from one way of life associated with agriculture to another life where employment is earned strictly in urban activities. In this book I have attempted to show that by moving to the city many migrants do not in fact shift from one form of socioeconomic structure to another but remain part of a labor reserve that transcends rural-urban borders, as does the capitalist mode of production. Few households in a labor reserve have a single dependable source of income that sustains them through the year. Instead, they are forced to combine a variety of strategies over the year to maintain themselves, often at a subsistence level, and to reduce their vulnerability. These strategies are critical to the perpetuation of the labor reserve in both the countryside and the city.

Not all families are equally capable of developing the same tactics. Family size and the age and preparation of family members as well as their resource base play an important role in their adaptation to the city. The ability to develop social networks is influenced by other factors also, such as having friends or family already present in the city on arrival. Proletarianization, extended periods of spatial mobility, and the temporary nature of rural work can reduce the ability of some families to maintain ties with kin and friends, making it harder for them to develop networks in the city.

Many of the tactics used by migrants—marketing, gardening, owning small stores, and building their own homes—have been classified in the social-science literature as pertaining to the informal sector. According to Keith Hart (1973), formal and informal income opportunities can be distinguished by one being wage labor and the other self-employment. Rob Davies (1979: 88) makes an important analytical distinction, pointing to the structural differences between the two sectors. In the formal sector, means of production are controlled by a small class and operated by workers for the benefit of the owner class; division of labor is vertical. In the informal sector, means of production are owned by those who do the work; division of labor is horizontal. As we have seen, activities in the informal sector play an important role in the lives of many migrants. In combination with a series of social ties based on culturally appropriate expectations, the families described in this book used mixed strategies which link the two sectors. At any one time a family may have members working in both the informal and the formal sectors. Work in the formal sector is viewed as unstable and highly risky yet necessary. At the same time family members usually take jobs in the informal sector when they become available. Thus the two sectors are linked by families in the labor reserve.

As the discussion of the families that dropped out of the migrant stream suggests, some individuals do not seek work in the formal sector but attempt to become self-employed, with what they regard as sufficient security and income. The process of capital accumulation suggests the considerable stratification in the informal sector.

Specific urban characteristics in Salta make urbanization a viable strategy for Bolivian families. In the city the migrant has an opportunity to gain a degree of control over certain aspects of his life, often not possible as a rural worker. First, because employment opportunities are concentrated, the migrant family can settle in one place and still have access to a variety of jobs. Second, the low-income migrant to Salta generally encounters more opportunities to cooperate, to coordinate his activities with others, than he did in most rural work situations —he can participate in more networks and belong to powerful organizations, such as unions. These two factors give the migrant greater potential control over his employment situation. Third, in a city such as Salta, where a migrant can still buy land and build a home close to most of the major sources of employment and where neighborhood associations are important, the individual has greater control over his housing than would be possible in the rural environment. Finally, because of the variety of stores in the city, many families feel they can buy food and other necessities there for less than from a farm-owned monopoly store. Thus, from the point of view of many Bolivian migrants a city like Salta, by its very nature, offers better prospects for increased security through greater control over important aspects of their lives. In this sense the city is qualitatively different from the rural environment of the migrant families.

The pace of urbanization is continuing in Argentina and an increasing number of rural laborers are moving to the city. The low-income neighborhoods where many of the migrants settle in cities such as Salta are beginning to replace villages as the locale of family subsistence maintenance. It is in the neighborhoods that families use mixed strategies as their forefathers had used family labor in the countryside in an attempt to cope with poverty. The families remain part of a process which maintains and reproduces a class of people who provide short-term labor for both rural and urban capitalist enterprises while they support themselves through periods of unemployment. As a social class, they are not being slowly integrated into a greater share of the benefits of the modern economic and social sectors of Argentina or Bolivia. This change must await the transformation of the economic and political structures in which their lives are embedded.

Notes

Chapter 1: Introduction

1. An alternative approach to what Larissa Lomnitz has called the modernization paradigm is that sparked by the work of Latin American social scientists of the Working Group on Internal Migration (Lomnitz 1973). The approach has been called historical structuralism. Historical structuralism not only places migration in a historical context, but it expands the analysis to focus on the nature of capitalist development and dependency, linking them to unequal development which in turn generates the migration (Muñoz and Oliveira 1972). A series of new studies have followed, linking migration patterns to national development strategies. These have been called economy specific models (Downing 1979).

In line with many similar concerns of the historical structuralist, I will consider migration as a symptom of basic regional differences in resources (employment, health, education, physical security, and social environment). Instead of studying the symptom, it is of greater significance for the social scientist to analyze the processes responsible for the character of the regions or localities. Migration then becomes one of the processes interacting with others in locality change and can be studied in the context of the social change from which it is generated and to which it contributes.

2. In a recent article, John Walton (1979: 164) suggests "what is called for, and beginning to emerge in recent urban research, is a new unit of analysis based on distinctive vertically integrated processes passing through a network from the international level to the urban hinterland." This is the orientation taken in this book.

3. In Latin America the massive movement of people from the countryside to the cities generated a series of studies during the 1960s and 1970s by social scientists. In the major Latin American studies, marginality became an important concern, along with the social organization of the poor. A series of important studies of slum settlements—*favelas, pueblos jóvenes, villas miseria,* and *tugurios*—were conducted by anthropologists (Mangin 1967, Leeds 1969, Uzzell

1976, M. Whiteford 1976), political scientists (Cornelius 1975, Collier 1976, Perlman 1976) and sociologists (Eckstein 1977). The analyses showed a highly dynamic element in the social organization and pointed out the need to view neighborhoods within the wider context of the political economy of the city and nation.

Questions of a different nature were raised by another group of researchers, some of whom were anthropologists. Particular attention was given to "motivations of individual migrants, the characteristics of their origin and destination and their adaptation problems in the new and usually urban environments" (Kemper 1979: 11). Many of these issues can be traced back to questions raised by Robert Redfield, who, although not studying urbanization, developed the classic folk-urban continuum and postulated a law of culture change. Strongly influenced by the writings of Louis Wirth and Emile Durkheim, Redfield suggested that population concentration, heterogeneity, and the complexity of urban life led to secularization, individualization, and disorganization. These studies contributed a rich micro-analysis of family organization, adaptation, and the migration process, yet they have been criticized for their failure to put migration into a broader context.

4. "Marginality theory" has been criticized by various authors. Janice Perlman (1977: 244-245), for example, points out that "the 'marginality' paradigm is based on an equilibrium model of society . . . . Marginality theory assumes that in a functioning system the interconnections between sub-portions tend to be mutually satisfactory and beneficial to all. It is perfectly possible, however, to have a stable system which is balanced to the advantage of some precisely through the explicit or implicit exploitation of others. Exploited groups in such a situation are not marginal but very much integrated into the system, functioning as a vital part of it." For further discussion and alternative perspectives, see Peattie 1974 and Babb 1979.

Several dependency theorists, equally critical of that perspective, speak of marginality in terms of the labor reserve (Babb 1979, Murmis 1969, Nun 1969, and Quijano 1974). They place this marginalized labor reserve as a socioeconomic formation—or form (or mode) of production—separated from, yet dependent upon, the dominant capitalist system. In contrast, in the perspective taken here, the labor reserve is not marginal; that it appears to be so is the result of its contradictory class position, in which it provides cheap labor, goods and services to capitalism in a similar fashion as the "full" proletariat yet is denied full incorporation into the capitalist relations of production, and its crucial position within capitalism is constantly negated by that system.

5. It should be noted that though the internal organization of this population and its articulation to the greater economic structure enable it to function as a labor reserve within the framework of capitalism, we are not implying that this function was its raison d'être; in other words, its function alone does not explain the cause of its existence.

6. For an in-depth view of the life of a Bolivian migrant in Argentina, partic-

ularly Buenos Aires, see *Eloy Quiroga: El obrero que desafió su mundo* by Betty Adams (1974).

7. One of the most famous studies was by Oscar Lewis, who published the results of his research on migrants from the village of Tepoztlán to Mexico City in an article entitled "Urbanization Without Breakdown" (1952). Lewis found a continuation of rural institutions and behavior in the city. Furthermore, he discovered that the migrants did not become individualized but maintained contact with each other and with the village. More recent studies done throughout the developing world have shown that the anonymity and uncertainty of rural migrants in the city is reduced through their networks with relatives, fellow village migrants, and their home community.

Chapter 2: Historical Context of Bolivian Migration

1. As noted, resources here are broadly defined to include employment, education, health, physical security, and social environment. Large-scale migration is a reflection of people's perceptions of locality differences, real or imagined (a data-gathering and evaluative process is discussed later). Of course, individuals define resources differently, and those resources available to some in one locality may not be available to others in the same locality. Furthermore, specific localities do not necessarily have a monopoly on all types of resources.

2. This is not an original conclusion, although arrived at independently. Castro (1970), Mármora (1973), and Villar (1972) make the same point in different ways. The purpose here is to show that Bolivian migration is a product of a process that has had a long history in Argentina.

3. The term *cabecita negra* comes from the name of a common Argentine sparrow. During Juan Perón's first government, use of the term was forbidden.

4. "The term was first used by the well-to-do to depreciate the urban rabble that assembled in a mass demonstration in the Plaza de Mayo on October 17, 1945, to demand the release of Perón from arrest by certain military groups. Perón subsequently seized upon the term as a rallying cry for the common man" (Scobie 1964a: 233).

5. It is interesting to note that in the previous census, of 1914, almost 93 percent of the Bolivian migrants in Argentina were in provinces of Salta and Jujuy. The decrease in the percentage in 1947 indicates an increase of Bolivian migration into Argentine areas further from Bolivia (Recursos Humanos 1973: Chart 7).

6. Both of the latter figures appear to be high, considering that the total number of employed *zafreros* in the Norte (which hires more Bolivians than does Tucumán) was estimated in 1970 to be no more than 24,000 men. This estimate was based on figures provided by the head *contratistas* (labor recruiters) of three of the five major plantations, their estimates of the labor needs of the other two plantations, and an estimate of labor needs of the independent sugar growers by the general secretary of the Cañeros Independientes del Norte (Independent Cane Growers of the North).

7. Once again the figure appears to be high. According to the census of 1960, over 70 percent of the Bolivians in Argentina were in the Northwest; Hicks' figure of 500,000 has well over half of the Bolivians living in Buenos Aires. Aguiló and Saavedra also state that they disagree with authors who claim that over 300,000 Bolivians live in Buenos Aires (1968: 9).

8. These figures have not been broken down by nationality. Unfortunately, at the time of this writing official 1970 census figures for the country as a whole have not yet been released.

9. There is much to be said for the figure given by the migration official on the number of illegal Bolivian migrants in Salta, and the figure could well be higher in Jujuy. In my research I found that more than half of the men interviewed who lived in the city of Salta had initially entered Argentina without documents. Because I was focusing on zafreros, and the plantations required papers beginning in the mid-1960s, almost all of these men eventually got papers. In the course of the research, however, I met others without documents (who are particularly vulnerable to exploitation by employers). Upon returning to Argentina in 1974, I found that Perón (in his second term) had taken major steps to help migrants obtain documents and to reduce the expense of the process.

10. As already noted, estimates may vary considerably, but these figures at least give a good indication of the comparative percentages.

Chapter 3: Sugar Production and Seasonal Labor

1. The seasonality of the rainfall is an important factor influencing sugar production in the Norte. At the southernmost part of the valley, where cane can be grown commercially, rainfall averages only 500 millimeters (20 inches) per year. At the northern tip bordering Bolivia rainfall is more plentiful, averaging 1,200 millimeters (48 inches) (Jones 1975: 124). Rains begin in October and last until May. Little precipitation falls during the harvest period, an advantage for the plantations. Because rainfall is not sufficient in most parts of the Ramal, irrigation is required.

2. Focusing on the general patterns of labor control that have evolved in the Norte does not deny some variations between the five major plantations. More detailed studies in the line of Raúl H. Bisio and Floreal H. Forni's 1976 study of specific plantations and their impact on neighboring economies are needed. But there are enough parallels in the recruitment of seasonal labor to justify a general overview of the labor-recruiting mechanisms which have articulated the plantations with other regions of Northwest Argentina and Bolivia. A more detailed history of Jujuy is presented in an excellent study by Ian Rutledge (1975).

3. For a description of fighting between the Matacos and Tobas on another plantation in the region, see Muir 1947: 323-33.

4. One example that illustrates the wealth and power of plantation owners: between 1930 and 1949 the owner of the plantation San Martín de Tabacal pur-

chased seven haciendas totaling 930,236 hectares (Rutledge 1977: 216).

Chapter 4: Recruiters, Canecutters, and the Work Camp

1. I have not used the real name of the plantation in order to protect informants who might be recognized by their position and work camp. Within anthropology it is a common practice to use fictitious names for towns and villages of study to protect informants; yet I apply the practice here with great reluctance because using the actual name would have contributed to comparison
among plantations within Argentina, which vary in organization, size, and productivity. Of course, the processes described in the study are not specific to
the single plantation and relate to the development of large-scale capitalistic
agriculture in the Ramal. Ingenio del Norte is the fifty-first largest firm in Argentina and the sixth largest privately owned firm. More than 20,000 acres are
owned directly by the company. The refinery can produce 1500 tons of sugar
a day. Cane yields average 90,000 kilograms per hectare. The pulp from the
cane combined with wood fiber is made into paper. Alcohol is also made from
the cane. Loans from the Export-Import Bank and City National Bank have
been used to import advanced processing technology. In 1965, 196,409 tons
of sugar were harvested, at that time the largest amount ever harvested by one
firm. Estimated annual sales are approximately forty million dollars a year (1965).

2. Names of all informants are fictitious.

3. John S. Schockley, in a paper titled "Migrant Labor and the Chicano Re-
volt in a South Texas Town," points out the radical potential of the migrant
worker. Since the migrant workers did not depend on the Anglo employers in
Crystal City or in the surrounding countryside, they could afford to vote for
more radical candidates than could other Mexican-Americans who were dependent upon a single Anglo employer and feared losing their jobs. In contrast to
the case described by Shockley, in Argentina at the time of the study migrant
workers did not have an option in terms of political party, much less a radical,
ethnically based political party.

4. To load a zora in the nonmechanized harvest the men carry a load of
trimmed cane weighing up to 140 pounds over their shoulders and, without
using their hands, climb up home-made ladders with the load. Loading is the
most exhausting and dangerous work in the zafra.

5. When we returned to the lote in 1974 we found that some efforts to improve housing and sanitation were under way. The governor of the province and
the plantation owner had met in Buenos Aires with the national minister of labor; after prolonged disagreement the session ended in a decision regarding the
changes to be implemented on the plantation in response to a law passed in
1973. Included in the agreement was a section on seasonal workers. The plantation was to improve the housing for the temporary workers and to provide
electric lighting, safe drinking water, showers, and bathrooms with sewers.

6. In some regions, such as south Texas, the development of corporate agriculture has increased class differences within the population which traditionally

is a source of migrant labor. One consequence of this process is that individuals with health problems are not able to get local employment and are forced to become migrant workers while healthier workers are employed locally (Spielberg 1979).

7. Michael Taussig (1977) and June Nash (1972) have examined cases in Colombia and Bolivia where wage workers are believed to sell their souls to the devil to increase productivity. Taussig, writing about Colombian workers, notes that "It is only when they become proletarianized that the devil enters the scene in this way. While the imagery of God and good, or the spirits of Nature and the ancestors, dominate the ethos of labor in the peasant mode of production the devil permeates the local metaphysics with the capitalist mode of production" (p. 136). The same analysis seems to hold for the families described in this volume. It also reflects a concern for the human price paid by the workers and their families in order to earn the zafra income.

8. Although no studies document the long-term consequences of prolonged exposures to different types of pesticides, laboratory evidence suggests a relationship between exposure and high rates of malignancy.

9. It is possible that people who contract an infectious disease on the plantation carry the illness back to their homes in Bolivia or Argentina after the zafra. The role of seasonal migration in the dissemination of shigellosis, a dysentery with a high fatility rate for untreated patients, is shown in a study by Mendizábel-Morris, Mata, Gangaros and Guzmán (1971).

Chapter 5: Working in the Fields, the Union, and Postharvest Planning

1. A zafrero may be impressed with how much money he can earn at the plantation, but in fact he may be paid for the combined labors of several family members and maybe hired helpers. Per capita income is low indeed. For example, if a man earns 1,500 pesos for a ton and a half of cane, he has received a relatively high daily wage in relation to what he might earn on other jobs. But if one considers the possibility that had the help of his wife and maybe a helper (cuarta), the company is getting the work of three persons and paying relatively good wages to only one. Nevertheless, the zafrero does not see it this way. If his female companion came to the lote, there are few other ways she can earn an income. He is interested in the total amount of money he can accumulate by the end of the season, not in what each member of his family should receive for his or her work.

2. In a questionnaire given to a small sample, I asked how children could get ahead in the world; 90 percent of the responses suggested that education was the key. I also asked what the respondents wanted their children to be when they grew up. Both the contratista and the enfermero on the lote were sure that the majority would answer, "zafrero." Instead, the answers were much less exact, many zafreros responding only negatively, saying that they did *not* want their children to have to work in the cane fields. Education was suggested as a means of escaping zafrero status.

3. Unfortunately, I have been unable to document this break and have received conflicting interviews on the relationship of the local union to that of the CGT. It deserves further study.

4. There were skilled temporary workers, but they were usually hired by individual contratistas and had little contact with the zafreros. They did not belong to the union.

5. Based on life histories of both active zafreros and former zafreros who were living in the city of Salta in 1970, it appears that during the late 1940s and early 1950s many of the Bolivians who came to Argentina obtained their first Argentine employment on the sugar plantations. The zafra provided a definite job for which they could sign up before even crossing the border. The occupational composition of zafreros working on the plantations during the 1940s and 1950s is not known, but the life histories suggest numerous cases of skilled workers—such as cobblers, carpenters, and tailors—working a few years in the zafra to earn the capital needed to set up shops and establish themselves. Work in the zafra was more readily available and higher paying than work in the city. Reymón, for example, left Bolivia during the revolution of 1952. He had been a cobbler in Tupiza, but left all of his tools behind. For four years he toiled in the zafra and other agricultural jobs before he had enough money to buy tools and to rent a room in Salta to set up his shop. He was successful and never returned to the zafra.

Chapter 6: The Multiple Faces of the Labor Reserve

1. Families that participate in a particular pattern do not become a particular type of family, nor do workers involved with labor associated with a specific pattern become differentiated from others. Furthermore, the patterns examined here are artificially frozen; in fact they are dynamic and fluid and include a range of variation. It is the types of problems and adjustments made by families involved in each pattern that make the differentiation of patterns analytically useful. Taken as a whole, such differentiation helps show important features of the labor reserve. Percentages of families or individuals participating in each pattern are impossible to calculate, but Juan Villar's figures suggest that only 25 percent of the seasonal workers return to Bolivia after the zafra (Villar 1975) and thus a conservative estimate would identify 60 to 70 percent of the Bolivians as workers participating in patterns other than the semiproletarian pattern.

2. Many of the workers who seasonally go to the plantations from Bolivia have temporary work permits, which officially allow foreign laborers to work in Argentina for six months. These papers are arranged by the plantations. Fewer of the Bolivian workers hired within Argentina had official work papers. Villar's government study (1974: 49) found that 35 percent of the workers hired entered "without being asked for papers" and 2 percent entered secretly. Another 7 percent had tourist permits, and 2 percent had permanent residence papers. Residence papers allow a person to work in the country and elapse only

when they stay out of Argentina more than two years. The Argentine government has been trying to make it easier to become a legal resident. The large numbers of workers without "proper work papers" reported in Villar's survey corresponds with my figures, although I found more than 50 percent without proper documentation.

3. There is an important debate in the literature on peasants about the nature of proletarianization and semiproletarianization. As Richard Harris (1978: 4) points out, there is disagreement "about the degree to which the development of capitalism in rural areas has dissolved and proletarianized the peasantry." The debate stems from important conceptual issues. There is disagreement over whether the peasantry can be considered a separate precapitalist mode of production. There is disagreement over the nature of peasant family or household organization and how it is influenced by incorporation in the capitalist mode of production. The complexity of the family organization and the participation of individual members in different forms of production is succinctly made clear by several social scientists. Angel Palerm's analysis (1977) shows that a peasant family may go through stages or cycles in which they depend predominately on the production of subsistence agriculture; later they may depend on the sale of their labor; and still later the family may become commercial producers. The analysis suggests that members of the same household may be involved in a number of different forms of production at the same time. Arturo Warman (1972) makes a similar point, explaining how many families may retain access to land without actually owning it, through a series of ties with extended family. These points support the position that studying the family as "a unit attempting to maintain itself is fundamental in the analysis of proletarianization" (Singlemann 1979: 3). Sidney Mintz (1974) and Luisa Paré (1977) also provide further insight on the topic.

4. In "Rural Labor" Richard N. Adams (1964: 61) differentiated between semirural proletarians, mobile rural proletarians, and rural proletarians.

5. In order for the machines to operate at their maximum efficiency, the fields must be especially prepared for the use of machines and all aspects of the harvest must be carefully coordinated. At the time of the study this had not yet been achieved, and as a result the machines were replacing less than half the manpower expected.

Chapter 7: Urbanization and Seasonal Migration

1. There are an increasing number of studies of regional centers in Latin America. Rubén Reina's (1973) study of Paraná, Argentina, and Andrew Whiteford's (1964) study of Querétaro, Mexico, and Popayán, Colombia, are insightful for their analysis of social class in these cities. Michael Whiteford's (1972) ethnography of a barrio in Popayán is also of interest for comparative purposes. In some cases these centers are referred to as *secondary cities*. This term is used to contrast them with primate cities, such as Buenos Aires, Mexico City, Rio de Janeiro, and Lima, which have been the sites of most of the major studies of

urbanization. Yet the term seems to include towns and cities of such a range in size and national importance that it has little value for comparison. There is a need to develop a better comparative framework, one which includes population size and the occupation structure of the population.

2. As indicated in the introduction, it was impossible to select a random sample of Bolivians living in Salta. Forty Bolivian families from the department of Tarija in Bolivia who live in Salta but work in the sugar harvest were studied in depth. These families had spent an average of six years in Salta. Questionnaires were administered and life histories were collected from heads of households of all forty families. Some of these families we knew from the plantations; others we met for the first time in Salta. Bolivians from other departments of Bolivia were interviewed but not included in the sample of forty. Ethnographic data was gathered over a ten-month period.

3. There is some evidence, although not conclusive, that Bolivian migrants who used the zafra to migrate to Salta came in waves that reflected changing political and economic conditions in Bolivia and Argentina. Migrants who came during different time periods possibly had different socioeconomic characteristics. There were more skilled migrants in the cohort sample of migrants who left Bolivia in the 1950s than those who left in the 1960s.

4. The *villas de emergencia,* or villas miseria, are low-income neighborhoods usually built on land not owned by the residents. They lack paved streets and basic city services. The former term is used more commonly by policy makers, whereas the latter is a stronger, evocative term more commonly used by the public.

5. This figure might be misleading since many Bolivians without papers are reluctant to admit that they are foreigners, fearing arrest and possible deportation. Friends cover for them when a study is conducted.

Chapter 9: Different Perspectives of the City

1. In some cases urban migrants do not develop adequate controls in the city and return to rural work. Here they often remain dependent upon the zafra for employment for many years.

2. The term *network* is used to indicate the social relations which include some reciprocal exchange between one individual and his or her significant others. This exchange may be of a physical commodity or of information. I did detailed analysis of several networks in terms of density of linkages, size, degree of connection, content and structure, and other characteristics. Although the variation between networks is important and worthy of further research, such analysis is very time consuming and would have precluded other more germane aspects of the study. The important question here is whether individual migrants in the course of the interview defined and discussed the role of specific friends and relatives in their urban adjustment. My being able to observe through participant observation the role of this reciprocity in many of the cases helped verify the migrants' interpretations.

3. Many Bolivians in Salta are at first reluctant to use public-health facilities. They tend to depend on Argentine or Bolivian *curanderos* (traditional curers), on herbs and plants they purchase in the market or from vendors who visit the neighborhood, or on the treatment recommended by the local pharmacist. For the very poor, hospitalization and medicine are free. Although the migrants appreciate inexpensive medical care, many are suspicious of doctors and fear being hospitalized. Estela Cornjeo San Millán (1973: 13) reports the following figures for Bolivians treated in a major Salta hospital in 1972: "1,106 cases of tuberculosis (mostly contracted in Argentina); 876 of animal bites; 741 of blennorrhagia; 536 of syphilis; 486 of *chagas* disease (trypanosomiasis—a type of sleeping sickness), mostly contracted in Bolivia; and 374 of malaria."

4. The plight of the aged zafrero deserves a few extra remarks. Inevitably illness and time take their toll, and the security based on strong limbs is lost. In a traditional society the old have some insurance and often can begin to do a different kind of work, usually with diminished prestige but still contributing to the welfare of the group. In a changing society characterized by high spatial mobility and unequal incomes and access to power, the aging laborer who cannot return to a home community or family may suffer the ignominy of a final dismissal.

5. It has been noted by Germani (1967: 179) and Kemper (1972: 3) that the help of fellow villagers may facilitate the early adjustment of new migrants, but not necessarily their assimilation into urban culture. Dependence upon fellow villagers seems to decline quickly in some situations, although in others the ties remain strong over a considerable period. Factors that could influence solidarity of migrants from the same village are the opportunity structure of the city, the resources controlled by the village migrant population, and the cultural "fit" of the migrant population with the native population.

In some cases the move to the city is used by migrants to break free of the social control of villages and kinsmen. Bernard Gallin (1978) notes this pattern for some migrants to Taipei in Taiwan but found most felt a need for the identification and security of fellow villages and lineage relatives.

6. Three men had contacts in Salta whom they had met in the course of their travel and work, but they received minimal help from them.

7. A stable community does not necessarily have to be an independent peasant village. Some migrants try to maintain an identity with a community or even a plantation, but it may not be a functional identity based on friendship and kin ties with people still residing in the community. Permanent workers on plantations and large farms may be part of a stable, relatively cohesive community. However, the fluidity of farm labor is not conducive to developing lasting supportive ties between workers; even when a family spends considerable time as rural proletarians on one farm year round, they may not be able to develop a useful network of contacts.

8. Obviously the presence or absence of friends or family in the city is not the only factor which influences migrants' ability to make social adaptations.

Many migrants are gregarious and make friends quickly, especially if there are institutions such as the fiesta complex, work, and bars which draw people toge-ther. Furthermore, as already pointed out, Bolivians in Argentina are more in-clined to be friendly and helpful to countrymen, even those not from their own village, than to native migrants. Thus an individual's status as a foreigner may help him develop social ties. In some cases, extended families follow the origi-nal migrant to the city. Although the initial migrant may not receive help at first, when other extended family members join him they may establish net-works together. Some migrants are much less dependent on social adaptations than others, even in a city like Salta and particularly if they have a uniquely marketable skill. This is the case of the skilled migrants who used the zafra as a stepping stone into Argentina. Yet these migrants too had an easier time if they received some help.

Chapter 10: Conclusion

1. Because of the labor surplus in Argentina, plantations no longer recruit intensively in Bolivia. In fact, the surplus led to the deportation of Bolivians in 1977 and 1978 (*Visión* 1978: 57). The deportation of Bolivians, many of whom worked in the zafra, was an unprecedented step in Argentina. At the same time it appeared that Bolivian migration was slowing because of the devel-opment of new opportunities in Bolivia, particularly in the Oriente (Eastern lowlands). This region has attracted seasonal workers for both the sugar and cotton harvests (Stearman 1973, 1979); colonization projects have attracted additional migrants from the highlands. While the development of the Oriente was attracting families from the highlands, in 1977 West Germany was attempt-ing to settle in this region as many as 150,000 whites of German and Dutch ex-traction from Namibia, Rhodesia, and South Africa. The West German govern-ment suggested that Bolivia would benefit from the technological expertise, ex-perience, and capital of the settlers and offered to make a loan to instigate the project (Goff 1977: 28).

Bibliography

Adams, Betty H.
   1974   *Eloy Quiroga: El obrero que desafió su mundo.* La Paz: Editorial
           Los Amigos del Libro.
Adams, Richard N.
   1964   Rural labor. In *Continuity and change in Latin America*, ed. John
           J. Johnson, pp. 49-78. Stanford, Calif.: Stanford University Press.
   1967   *The second sowing: Power and secondary development in Latin
           America.* San Francisco: Chandler Publishing Co.
   1970   Brokers and career mobility systems in the structure of complex so-
           cieties. *Southwest Journal of Anthropology* 26: 315-327.
Aguiló, P. Federico, and Luis Llano Saavedra
   1968   *El contingente de bolivianos en el exterior.* La Paz: Editorial Don
           Bosco.
Antezana, Fernando
   1969   *The braceros of Bolivia: The human tragedy of thousands of Boli-
           vian migrant workers in Argentina.* A summary of research on inter-
           nal migration in Latin America. Geneva: World Council of Churches.
Babb, Florence E.
   1979   Market women and Peruvian underdevelopment. Paper presented
           at the annual meetings of the American Anthropological Association.
Balán, Jorge
   1968   Are farmers' sons handicapped in the city? *Rural Sociology* 33:
           160-174.
   1976   Regional urbanization under primary-sector expansion in neo-colo-
           nial countries. In *Current perspectives in Latin American urban
           research*, ed. Alejandro Portes and Harley L. Browning, pp. 151-179.
           Austin: Institute of Latin American Studies, University of Texas.
Balán, Jorge, Harley L. Browning, and Elizabeth Jelin
   1973   *Men in a developing society: Geographic and social mobility in
           Monterrey, Mexico.* Austin: University of Texas Press.

Banco Industrial de la República Argentina
 1960   *La industria azucarera Argentina.* Buenos Aires.
Barraclough, Solon, ed.
 1973   *Agrarian structure in Latin America: The resumé of the CIDA Land Tenure Studies.* Lexington, Mass.: D.C. Heath and Co.
Beckford, George L.
 1972   *Persistent poverty: Underdevelopment in plantation economies of the Third World.* New York: Oxford University Press.
Best, Lloyd
 1968   Outlines of a model of pure plantation economy. *Social and Economic Studies* 22: 283-335.
Bisio, Raúl H., and Floreal H. Forni
 1976   Economía de enclave y satelización del mercado de trabajo rural: El caso de los trabajadores con empleo precario en un ingenio azucarero del Noroeste Argentino. *Desarrollo Económico: Revista de Ciencias Sociales* 16, no. 61: 3-56.
Bohning, W. R.
 1972   *The migration of workers in the United Kingdom and the European countries.* London: Oxford University Press.
Boissevain, Jeremy
 1974   *Friends of friends: Networks, manipulators and coalitions.* Oxford: Basil Blackwell.
Bossen, Laurel
 1975   Household work patterns in an urban shantytown in Guatemala. Paper presented at the annual meetings of the American Anthropological Association.
Bromley, Ray I., and Chris Gerry, eds.
 1979   *Casual work and urban poverty in Third World cities.* New York: Wiley.
Brunton, Anne Marjorie
 1971   The decision to settle: A study of Mexican-American migrants. Ph. D. dissertation, Washington State University.
Buechler, Hans C.
 1970   The ritual dimension of rural urban networks: The fiesta system in the northern highlands of Bolivia. In *Peasants in cities: Readings in the anthropology of urbanization,* ed. William Mangin. Boston: Houghton Mifflin Company.
Burawoy, Michael
 1976   The function and reproduction of migrant labor: Comparative material from South Africa and the United States. *American Journal of Sociology* 81: 1050-1087.
Caldwell, John C.
 1969   *African rural-urban migration: The movement to Ghana's towns.* London: C. Hurst and Company.

Carrón, Juan A.
  1979   Shifting patterns in migration from bordering countries to Argentina, 1914-1970. *International Migration Review* 13, no. 3: 475-487.
Castles, Stephen, and Godula Kosack
  1973   *Immigrant workers and class structure in Western Europe.* London: Oxford University Press.
Castro, Donald Steven
  1970   The development of Argentine immigration policy. Ph. D. dissertation, University of California, Los Angeles.
Centro Azucarero Argentino
  1954   *Annual reports on sugar production.* Buenos Aires.
CIDA (Comité Interamericano de Desarrollo Agrícola)
  1965   *Land tenure conditions and socio-economic development of the agricultural sector: Argentina.* Washington, D.C.: Organization of American States.
Cliffe, Lionel
  1978   Labour migration and peasant differentiation: Zambian experiences. *Journal of Peasant Studies* 5: 326-346.
Collier, David
  1976   *Squatters and oligarchs: Authoritarian rule and policy change in Peru.* Baltimore: The Johns Hopkins University Press.
Colson, Elizabeth
  1960   Migration to Africa: Trends and possibilities. In *Population in Africa,* ed. F. Lorimer and M. Karp, pp. 60-77. Boston: Boston University Press.
Consejo Federal de Inversiones
  1967   *Plan de emergencia para el N.O.A.: Diagnóstico.* Buenos Aires.
Conteris, Hiber
  1970   The Bolivian braceros and the provisional committee on their behalf. *Migration Today* 14: 50-56.
Cornelius, Wayne
  1975   *Politics and the Migrant Poor in Mexico City.* Stanford, Calif.: Stanford University Press.
  1978   *Mexican migration to the United States: Causes, consequences, and U.S. responses.* Center for International Studies. Cambridge: Massachusetts Institute of Technology.
Cornejo San Millán, Estela
  1973   The situation of Bolivian immigrants in Salta, Argentina. *ICMC Migration News* 22, no. 5: 11-15.
Courtenay, Phillip P.
  1965   *Plantation agriculture.* New York and Washington: Frederick A. Praeger.
David, Pedro Rubens
  1963   The social structure of Argentina. Ph.D. dissertation, Indiana University.

Davies, Rob
1979   Informal sector or subordinate mode of production?   A model.
In *Casual work and poverty in Third World cities,* ed. Ray Bromley and Chris Gerry, pp. 87-104.   New York: John Wiley &
Sons.
de Janvry, Alain
n.d.   The agrarian question and reformism in Latin America.   Ms.
Delich, Francisco J.
1970   *Tierra y conciencia campesina en Tucumán.*   Buenos Aires: Edicio-
nes Signos.
Denis, Pierre
1922   *The Argentine republic: Its development and progress.*   Translated
by Joseph McCabe.   London: T. Fisher Unwin, Ltd.
Devons, Ely, and Max Gluckman
1964   Introduction and conclusion: Modes and consequences of limiting
a field study.   In *Closed systems and open minds,* ed. Max Gluckman, pp. 13-19, 158-262.   Chicago: Aldine Press.
Díaz Santana, Arismendi
1976   The role of Haitian braceros in Dominican sugar production.   *Latin
American Perspectives* 3, no. 1: 120-132.
Dietz, Henry
1969   Urban squatter settlements in Peru: A case history and analysis.
Journal of Inter-American Studies 11: 353-370.
Dirección Provincial de Estadística
1970   1970 Producción agrícola de la provincia de Salta.
Dirks, Robert
1972   Networks, groups and adaptations in an Afro-Caribbean community.   *Man* 7: 565-585.
Donahue, John
1975   Circular and return aspects of labor migration in southern Colombia.   Ph.D. dissertation, Columbia University.
Downing, Theodore E.
1979   Explaining migration in Mexico and elsewhere.   In *Migration across
frontiers: Mexico and the United States,* ed. Fernando Cámera and
Robert Van Kemper, pp. 159-167.   Institute of Mesoamerican Studies, State University of New York, Albany.
Doughty, Paul L.
1970   Behind the back of the city: "Provincial" life in Lima, Peru.   In
Peasants in cities: Readings in the anthropology of urbanization,
ed. William Mangin, pp. 30-46.   Boston: Houghton Mifflin Company.
Eckstein, Susan
1977   *The poverty of revolution: The state and the urban poor in Mexico.*   Princeton, N.J.:   Princeton University Press.

El Tribuno (Salta)
1971   Desempleo en el Norte. June 25: 10.
Erasmus, Charles J.
1969   Land reform and social evolution in Southern Bolivia: The valleys
        of Chuquisaca and Tarija. In *Land reform and social revolution in
        Bolivia*, ed. Dwight Heath, Charles Erasmus, and Hans Buechler,
        pp. 61-165. New York: Frederick A. Praeger.
Feder, Ernest
1971   *The rape of the peasantry: Latin America's landholding system.*
        Garden City, N.Y.: Doubleday and Co.
Ferrer, Aldo
1967   *The Argentine economy: An economic history of Argentina.* Berke-
        ley and Los Angeles: University of California Press.
Frank, Andre Gunder
1972   The development of underdevelopment. In *Dependence and under-
        development: Latin America's political economy,* ed. James D.
        Cockcroft, Andre Gunder Frank, and Dale L. Johnson, pp. 3-17.
        Garden City, N.Y.: Doubleday and Co.
Friedl, John, and Noel J. Chrisman
1975   *City ways: A selective reader in urban anthropology.* New York:
        Thomas Y. Crowell Company.
Friedland, William H., and Dorothy Nelkin
1971   *Migrant agricultural workers in America's Northeast.* New York:
        Holt, Rinehart and Winston.
Friedman, Herbert D.
1969   Squatter assimilation in Buenos Aires, Argentina. Ph.D. disserta-
        tion, Massachusetts Institute of Technology.
Gallin, Bernard
1978   Rural to urban migration in Taiwan: Its impact on Chinese family
        and kinship. In *Chinese family law and social change in historical
        and comparative perspective,* ed. David C. Buxbaum. Seattle: Uni-
        versity of Washington Press.
Gamson, William G.
1968   *Power and discontent.* Homewood, Ill.: The Dorsey Press.
Garbett, G. K., and Kapferer, B.
1970   Theoretical orientations in the study of labour migration. *The New
        Atlantis* 2: 179-197.
Gatti, Luis María
1975   Plantación, campesinado y manufactura: Un caso de análisis de la
        articulación de clases en el Noroeste Argentino. Paper presented at
        the third conference of the working group Procesos de Articulación
        Social. Consejo Latinoamericano de Ciencias Sociales, Quito.
Germani, Gino
1955   *Estructura social de la Argentina.* Buenos Aires: Raigal.

1966   Mass migration and modernization in Argentina. *Studies in Comparative International Development* 2, no. 11: 165-182.
1967   The concept of social integration. In *The urban explosion in Latin America*, ed. Glenn H. Beyer, pp. 179-188. Ithaca, N.Y.: Cornell University Press.

Goff, James
1977   Bolivia: Transplanting apartheid. *NACLA's Latin America and Empire Report* 11, no. 6: 28-29.

Graves, Nancy B., and Theodore D. Graves
1974   Adaptive strategies in urban migration. In *Annual Review of Anthropology* 3: 117-152. Ed. Bernard Siegel. Palo Alto, Calif.: Annual Reviews, Inc.

Greaves, Thomas C.
1972   The Andean rural proletarians. *Anthropological Quarterly* 45: 65-83.

Guillet, David, and Scott Whiteford
1974   A comparative view of the fiesta complex in migrant adaptation. *Urban Anthropology* 3: 222-242.

Guy, Donna J.
1973   Politics and the sugar industry in Tucumán, Argentina 1870-1900. Ph. D. dissertation, Indiana University.

Haigh, Roger M.
1968   *Martín Güemes: Tyrant or tool?* Fort Worth: Texas Christian University Press.

Haney, Jane B.
1978   Migration, settlement pattern, and social organization: A Mid-West Mexican American case study. Ph. D. dissertation, Michigan State University.

Harris, Richard L.
1978   Marxism and the agrarian question in Latin America. In *Latin American Perspectives* 5, no. 4: 2-26.

Hart, Keith
1973   Informal income opportunities and urban employment in Ghana. *Journal of Modern African Studies* 11: 61-89.

Heath, Dwight B.
1973   New patrons for old: Changing patron-client relationships in Bolivia. *Ethnography* 12: 75-98.

Heath, Dwight B., Charles J. Erasmus, and Hans C. Buechler
1969   *Land reform and social revolution in Bolivia.* New York: Frederick A. Praeger.

Herrán, Carlos A.
1976   Migraciones y estructura social en el valle de Santa María, Provincia de Catamarca. Paper presented at the third conference of the working group Procesos de Articulación Social. Consejo Latinoamericano

de Ciencias Sociales, Quito.

Heyduk, Daniel
1974   The hacienda system and agrarian reform in highland Bolivia: A re-evaluation. *Ethnology* 13: 71-81.

Hicks, Frederic
1972   Making a living during the dead season in sugar-producing regions of the Caribbean. *Human Organization* 31: 72-81.

Hollander, Frederick
1976   Oligarchy and the politics of petroleum in Argentina: The case of the Salta oligarchy and Standard Oil, 1918-1933. Ph. D. dissertation, University of California, Los Angeles.

Instituto de Endocrinología de Salta
1969   Memoria anual. Serie Memorias Anuales No. 12. Salta: Publicaciones del Instituto de Endocrinología.

Johnson, Allen W.
1971   *Sharecroppers of the Sertão: Economics and dependence on a Brazilian population.* Stanford, Calif.: Stanford University Press.

Jones, David
1975   Shifting patterns of sugar production in Northwest Argentina. Ph.D. dissertation, Michigan State University.

Kemper, Robert V.
1971   Rural-urban migration in Latin America: A framework for the comparative analysis of geographical and temporal patterns. *International Migration Review* 5, no. 13: 36-46.
1972   Social adaptation of Tzintzuntzán migrants in Mexico City. Paper presented at the 71st annual meetings of the American Anthropological Association, Toronto, Canada.
1973   Social factors in migration: The case of Tzintzuntzeños in Mexico City. Paper presented at the IX International Congress of Anthropological and Ethnological Sciences, Chicago.
1974   Tzintzuntzeños in Mexico City: The anthropologist among peasant migrants. In *Anthropologists in Cities*, ed. G. M. Foster and R. V. Kemper, pp. 63-92. Boston: Little, Brown and Company.
1979   Frontiers in migration: From culturalism to historical structuralism in the study of Mexican-U.S. migration. In *Migration across frontiers: Mexico and the United States,* ed. Fernando Cámera and Robert Van Kemper, pp. 9-24. Institute of Mesoamerican Studies, State University of New York, Albany.

Klein, Herbert S.
1969   *Parties and political change in Bolivia, 1880-1952.* Cambridge: Cambridge University Press.

Knight, Rolf
1972   *Sugar plantations and labor patterns in the Cauca Valley, Colombia.* Anthropological Series No. 12. Department of Anthropology, Uni-

versity of Toronto, Canada.

Kritz, Mary M., and Douglas Gurak
1979   International migration in Latin America. *International Migration Review* 13, no. 3: 407-427.

Laks, Nathan
1971   Argentina. In *The urban development of Latin America 1750-1920*, ed. Richard M. Morse, pp. 22-35. Stanford, Calif.: Center for Latin American Studies, Stanford University.

Lattes, Alfredo E.
1973   Migration, population change, and ethnicity in Argentina. Paper presented at the IX International Congress of Anthropological and Ethnological Sciences, Chicago.

Lattes, Zulma L. Recchini
1967   Demographic consequences of international migratory movements in the Argentine Republic, 1870-1960. In *World population conference* 4: 211-215. New York: United Nations.

1969   *Migraciones en la Argentina: Estudio sobre las migraciones internas e internacionales basado en datos censales 1869-1960.* Buenos Aires: Editorial del Instituto Torcuato di Tella.

1963   El proceso de urbanización en la Argentina: Distribución, crecimiento y algunas características de la población urbana. *Desarrollo Económico: Revista de Ciencias Sociales* 12, no. 48: 867-886.

Leeds, Anthony
1965   *Men, culture and animals: The role of animals in human ecological adjustments.* Washington: American Association for the Advancement of Science.

1969   The significant variables determining the character of squatter settlements. *América Latina* 3: 44-86.

Leeds, Anthony, and Elizabeth Leeds
1970   Brazil and the myth of urban rurality: Urban experience, work, and values in the "squatments" of Rio de Janeiro and Lima. In *City and country in the Third World: Issues in the modernization of Latin America*, ed. Arthur J. Field, pp. 229-285. Cambridge: Schenkman Publishing Company, Inc.

Lewis, Oscar
1952   Urbanization without breakdown: A case study. *The Scientific Monthly* 75: 31-41.

1965   Observations on the urban-folk continuum and urbanization with special reference to Mexico City. In *The study of urbanization*, ed. Philip M. Hauser and Leo F. Schnore, pp. 491-503. New York: John Wiley and Sons.

Liebow, Elliot
1967   *Tally's corner: A study of Negro street corner men.* Boston: Little, Brown and Company.

Lomnitz, Larissa
  1973   The survival of the unfittest. Paper presented at the IX Internation-
          al Congress of Anthropological and Ethnological Science, Chicago.
  1977   *Networks and marginality: Life in a Mexican shanty town.* New
          York: Academic Press.
MacEwen, A. M.
  1972   Stability and change in a shanty town: A summary of some re-
          search findings. *Sociology* 6: 41-57.
  1973   Kinship and mobility on the Argentine pampa. *Ethnology* 12: 135-151.
McEwen, William J.
  1969   *Changing rural Bolivia.* New York: Research Institute for Study of
          Man.
McWilliams, Carey
  1939   *Factories in the fields: The story of migratory farm labor in Cali-
          fornia.* Boston: Little, Brown and Company.
Mafeje, Archie
  1973   The fallacy of dual economies revisited. In *Dualism and Rural De-
          velopment in East Africa.* Copenhagen: The Institute for Develop-
          ment Research.
Mandle, Jay R.
  1972   The plantation economy: An essay in definition. *Science and So-
          ciety* 36: 49-62.
Mangin, William
  1959   The role of regional associations in the adaptation of rural popula-
          tions in Peru. *Sociologus* 9: 23-36.
  1967   Latin American squatter settlements: A problem and a solution.
          Latin American Research Review 2, no. 3: 65-98.
Margulis, Mario
  1968   *Migración y marginalidad en la sociedad Argentina.* Buenos Aires:
          Paidos.
Mármora, Leleo
  1973   El estudio histórico estructural de los movimientos de poblaciones
          en América Latina: Su aplicación al caso Argentino. In *Imperialis-
          mo y urbanización en América Latina,* ed. Manuel Castells, pp. 57-
          96. Barcelona: Editorial Gustavo Gili.
Marshall, Adriana
  1979   Immigrant workers in the Buenos Aires labor market. *International
          Migration Review* 13, no. 3: 488-501.
Matos Mar, José
  1968   *Urbanización y barriadas en América del sur: Recopilación de estu-
          dios realizados entre 1956 y 1966.* Lima: Instituto de Estudios Peruanos.
Mayer, Philip
  1961   *Tribesmen and townsmen: Conservation and the process of urbani-
          zation in a South African city.* London: Oxford University Press.

Mendizábel-Morris, César, Leonardo J. Mata, Eugene J. Gangarosa, and Guillermo Guzmán.
 1971   Epidemic shiga-bacillos dysentery in Central America: Derivation of the epidemic and its progression in Guatemala, 1968-69. *American Journal of Tropical Medicine and Hygiene* 20, no. 6: 927-931.
Merkx, Gilbert W.
 1968   Political and economic change in Argentina from 1870-1966. Ph.D. dissertation, Yale University.
Miller, Solomon
 1964   The hacienda and plantation in northern Peru. Ph.D. dissertation, Columbia University.
Mintz, Sidney W.
 1956   Cañamelar: The subculture of a rural sugar plantation proletariat. In *The people of Puerto Rico,* ed. Julian Steward, pp. 314-417. Urbana: University of Illinois Press.
 1974   The rural proletariat and the problem of rural proletarian consciousness. *The Journal of Peasant Studies* 1: 291-325.
Mitchell, Clyde J.
 1969a   *Social networks in urban places.* Manchester: Manchester University Press.
 1969b   Structural plurality, urbanization and labour circulation in Southern Rhodesia. In *Migration*, ed. J. A. Jackson, pp. 156-180. Cambridge: Cambridge University Press.
Muir, J. H.
 1947   *Hoo hooey: An Argentine arcady and how I came there.* London: Country Life.
Municipalidad de Salta
 1970   *Estudio completo de la selección de adjudicatavios de vivienda para erradicación de villas de emergencia.* Salta.
Muñoz, Humberto, and Orlandina de Oliveira
 1972   Migraciones internas y desarrollo: Algunas consideraciones sociológicas. *Demografía y Economía* 6, no. 2: 248-260.
Murmis, Miguel
 1969   Tipos de marginalidad y posición en el proceso productivo. *Revista Latinoamericana de Sociología* 5: 2 (July).
Nash, June
 1972   The Devil in Bolivia's nationalised tin mines, *Science and Society* 26: 221-233.
Nelkin, Dorothy
 1970   Unpredictability and life style in a migrant labor camp. *Social Problems* 17: 472-487.
Nun, José
 1969   Sobrepoblación relativa, ejército industrial de reserva y masa marginal. *Revista Latinoamericana de Sociología* 4 (2): 178-237.

Nutini, Hugo G., and Timothy D. Murphy
    1970   Labor migration and family structure in the Tlaxcala-Puebla area,
            Mexico. In *The social anthropology of Latin America: Essays in
            honor of Rolf Leon Beals*, ed. Walter R. Goldschmidt, pp. 80-103.
            Los Angeles: University of California Press.
Orellana, Carlos L.
    1973   Mixtec migrants in Mexico City: A case study of urbanization. *Hu-
            man Organization* 32: 273-283.
Ortiz, Sutti
    1967   The structure of decision making among Indians of Colombia. In
            Themes in economic anthropology, ed. Raymond Firth, pp. 191-
            228. London: Tavistock.
Padilla, Elena Seda
    1956   Nocorá: The subculture of workers on a government-owned sugar
            plantation. In *The people of Puerto Rico*, ed. Julian Steward, pp.
            265-313. Urbana: University of Illinois Press.
Palerm, Angel
    1959   Comments. In *Plantation systems of the New World* (Papers and dis-
            cussion summaries of the seminar held in San Juan, Puerto Rico), ed.
            Vera Rubin, pp. 99-103. Washington, D.C.: Pan American Union.
    1977   Sobre la fórmula M-D-M y la articulación de modo campesina de
            producción al sistema capitalista dominante. Cuadernos de La Casa
            Chata, Centro de Investigaciones Superiores del Instituto Nacional
            de Antropología e Historia, Mexico City.
Panettieri, José
    1970   *Inmigración en la Argentina*. Buenos Aires: Ediciones Macchi.
Paré, Luisa
    1977   *El proletariado agrícola en México: Campesinos sin tierra o proleta-
            rios agrícolas*. Mexico City: Siglo Veintiuno Editores.
Payne, William, and Charles T. W. Wilson
    1904   *Missionary pioneering in Bolivia*. London: H. A. Raymond.
Pearse, Andrew
    1975   *The Latin American peasant*. London: Frank Cass.
Peattie, Lisa Redfield
    1968   *The view from the barrio*. Ann Arbor: University of Michigan Press.
Perlman, Janice
    1976   *The myth of marginality: Urban poverty and politics in Rio de
            Janeiro*, Berkeley: University of California Press.
Provincia de Salta
    1969   *Censo tabacalero*. Directed by Aida A. Falcone. Salta: Ediciones
            San Bernardo.
Quijano Obregón, Aníbal
    1974   The marginal pole of the economy and the marginalized labour
            force. *Economy and Society* 3, no. 4: 393-428.

Reboratti, Carlos E.
1974   Santa Victoria: Estudio de un caso de aislamiento geográfico. *Desarrollo Económico: Revista de Ciencias Sociales* 14, no. 55: 481-506.
Recursos Humanos: Oficina Sectoral de Desarrollo
1973   *La inmigración desde países limítrofes hacia la Argentina.* Análisis Estadístico: Buenos Aires.
Redfield, Robert
1941   *The folk culture of Yucatán.* Chicago: University of Chicago Press.
1947   The folk society. *American Journal of Sociology* 52: 293-308.
Reina, Rubén E.
1973   *Paraná: Social boundaries in an Argentine city.* Austin: University of Texas Press.
Roberts, Bryan R.
1973   *Organizing strangers: Poor families in Guatemala City:* Austin: University of Texas Press.
1979   *Cities of peasants: The political economy of urbanization in the Third World.* Beverly Hills: Sage Publications
Rocheau, Mons. Jorge, Jozef Perridón, and Padre Lino Pedisic
1969   *Inmigrantes Bolivianos, Chilenos y Paraguayos en Argentina.* Buenos Aires: Comisión Católica de Inmigración.
Rothstein, Frances
1979   The class basis of patron-client relations. *Latin American Perspectives* 6, no. 2: 25-35.
Rutledge, Ian D.
1975a   El desarrollo del capitalismo en Jujuy 1880-1960. Serie Estudios de Cuadernos no. 8 del Centro de Investigaciones en Ciencias Sociales. Buenos Aires.
1975b   Plantations and peasants in northern Argentina: The sugar industry of Salta and Jujuy, 1930-43. In *Argentina in the 20th century,* ed. David Rock, pp. 88-143. University of Pittsburgh Press.
1977   The integration of the highland peasantry in the sugar economy of northern Argentina, 1930-43. In *Land and labour in Latin America: Essays on the development of agrarian capitalism in the 19th and 20th centuries,* ed. Kenneth Duncan and Ian Rutledge, pp. 205-228. New York: Cambridge University Press.
Schaedel, Richard
1972   Variations in patterns of contemporary and recent urban-rural (macro-microsocietal) linkages in Latin America. Paper presented at 40th Congress of Americanists, Rome.
Schleh, Emilio
1921   *La industria azucarera en su primer centenario: 1821-1921.* Buenos Aires: Ferrari.

Schmid, Lester
    1967   The role of migratory labor in the economic development of Gua-
            temala. Ph. D. dissertation, University of Wisconsin.
Schockley, John S.
    1974   Migrant labor and the Chicano revolt in a south Texas town. Paper
            presented at a symposium on comparative peasant movements,
            Michigan State University.
Scobie, James R.
    1964a   *Argentina: A city and a nation.* New York: Oxford University
            Press.
    1964b   *Revolution on the pampas: A social history of Argentine wheat,
            1860-1910.* Latin American Monograph No. 1, Institute of Latin
            American Studies. Austin: University of Texas Press.
Scott, C. D.
    1976   Peasants, proletarianization and the articulation of modes of pro-
            duction: The case of sugar cane cutters in Northern Peru, 1940-69.
            Journal of Peasant Studies 3: 321-341.
Sindicato de Obreros y Empleados de Azúcar
    1964   *Estatutos.* Jujuy: Talleres Gráficos.
Singelmann, Peter
    1972   On campesino movements in Latin America. Ph. D. dissertation,
            University of Texas at Austin.
    1979   Peripheral capitalist development and the transformation of rural
            class relations: The role of peasant cane growers in the Mexican
            sugar industry. Discussion paper presented at the national meeting
            of the Latin American Studies Association, Pittsburgh.
Solari, Juan Antonio
    1937   *Trabajadores del Norte Argentino.* Buenos Aires: Talleres Gráficos
            de la Vanguardia.
    1940   *Parias Argentinos: Explotación y miseria de los trabajadores del
            país.* Buenos Aires: Talleres Gráficos de la Vanguardia.
Solberg, Carl
    1970   *Immigration and nationalism: Argentina and Chile, 1890-1914.*
            Austin: University of Texas Press.
Spielberg, Joseph
    1979   Illness and disability as factors promoting dependence on seasonal
            migratory farm labor among chicanos. Paper presented at the 4th
            Annual Cíbola Anthropological Society Meetings.
Stavenhagen, Rodolfo
    1978   Capitalism and the peasantry in Mexico. *Latin American Perspec-
            tives* 5, no. 3: 27-37.
Stearman, Allyn Maclean
    1973   Colonization of Eastern Bolivia: Problems and prospects. *Human
            Organization* 32: 285-294.

1979   Migrantes andinos en el oriente boliviano: El caso de Santa Cruz.
        América Indígena 39, no. 2: 381-400.
Steward, Julian H.
1955   *Theory of culture change.* Urbana: University of Illinois Press.
Taussig, Michael
1977   The genesis of capitalism amongst a South American peasantry:
        Devil's labor and the baptism of money. *Comparative Studies in
        Society and History* 19: 130-155.
1978   Peasant economics and the development of capitalist agriculture in
        the Cauca Valley, Colombia. *Latin American Perspectives* 5, no. 4:
        62-90.
Thorn, Richard S.
1971   The economic transformation. In *Beyond the revolution: Bolivia
        since 1952,* ed. James A. Mallory and Richard S. Thorn, pp. 157-
        216. Pittsburgh: University of Pittsburgh Press.
Tilly, Charles
1973   Do communities act? Working Paper No. 92. Mimeo. Ann Arbor:
        Center for Research on Social Organization.
Torrado, Susana
1979   International migration policies in Latin America. *International
        Migration Review* 13, no. 3: 428-429.
Uzzell, [John] Douglas
1972   Bound for places I'm not known to: Adaptations of migrants and
        residents in four irregular settlements in Lima, Peru. Ph.D. disser-
        tation, University of Texas at Austin.
1976   Ethnography of migration: Breaking out of the bi-polar myth. In
        New approaches to migration, ed. David Guillet and Douglas Uzzell,
        pp. 45-54. Houston: Rice University.
1980   Mixed strategies and the informal sector: Three faces of reserve la-
        bor. *Human Organization* 39: 40-49.
Verlinden, Charles
1970   *The beginning of modern colonization.* Ithaca and London: Cor-
        nell University Press.
Vessuri, Hebe
1977   La estructura socioeconómica local en una colonia agrícola Tucuma-
        na: Campesinos y empresarios. Serie Reimpresiones Z. Centro de
        Investigaciones en Ciencias Sociales. Buenos Aires.
Villar, Juan Manuel
1972   Historia y significación de la migración boliviana en la Argentina.
        Tesis Facultad de Sociología. Buenos Aires: Universidad Católica.
1974   Los migrantes de países limítrofes bolivianos en los ingenios azuca-
        reros de Salta y Jujuy. Oficina Sectorial de Desarrollo de Recursos
        Humanos.
1975   Los migrantes de países limítrofes: Bolivianos en las fincas tabaca-

leras del norte. Buenos Aires: Oficina Sectorial de Desarrollo de
Recursos Humanos.

1976   Los migrantes de países limítrofes: Estudio de actitudes de los habi-
tantes de la ciudad de Salta sobre migrantes bolivianos. Buenos
Aires: Oficina Sectorial de Desarrollo de Recursos Humanos.

Visión

1978   El retorno de unos pacos, 50, no. 2: 57.

Walton, John

1979   From cities to systems: Recent research in Latin American urbanization. *Latin American Research Review* 14: 159-169.

Warman, Arturo

1972   *Los campesinos, hijos predilectos del régimen.* Mexico City: Nues-
tro Tiempo.

Watson, James L.

1975   Emigration and the Chinese lineage: The Mans in Hong Kong and
London. Berkeley: University of California Press.

White, Ernest William

1882   *Cameos from the silver-land: A young naturalist in the Argentine
republic,* vol. 2. London: John Van Voorst Publisher.

Whiteford, Andrew H.

1964   *Two cities of Latin America: A comparative description of social
class.* Garden City, N.Y.: Doubleday and Company.

Whiteford, Linda

1979   The borderland as an extended community. In *Migration across
frontiers: Mexico and the United States,* ed. Fernando Cámara and
Robert Van Kemper, pp. 127-140. Institute for Mesoamerican Studies, State University of New York, Albany.

Whiteford, Michael B.

1972   Barrio Tulcán: Colombian countrymen in an urban setting. Ph. D.
dissertation, University of California, Berkeley.

1976   *The forgotten ones: Colombian countrymen in an urban setting.*
Gainesville: University Presses of Florida.

Whiteford, Scott

1976   Migration in context: A systematic historical approach to the study
of breakdown before urbanization. In *New approaches to the study
of migration,* ed. David Guillet and Douglas Uzzell, pp. 147-162.
Houston: Rice University.

Whiteford, Scott, and Richard N. Adams

1975   Migration, ethnicity and adaptation: Bolivian migrant workers in
Argentina. In *Migration and ethnicity: Implications for urban policy and development,* ed. Helen Safa and Brian M. des Toit, pp. 179-
200. The Hague: Mouton Publishers.

Whiteford, Scott, and Luis Emilio Henao

1980   Irrigación decentralizada, desarrollo y cambio social: Un caso de organización y división en el campesinado mexicano. *América In-dígena* 40, no. 1.

Wiest, Raymond
  1979   Anthropological perspectives on return migration: A critical com-mentary, *Papers in Anthropology* 20, no. 1: 167-188. Norman: University of Oklahoma.
  1979   Implications of international labor migration for Mexican rural de-velopment. In *Migration across frontiers: Mexico and the United States,* ed. Fernando Cámara and Robert Van Kemper, pp. 85-100. Institute for Mesoamerican Studies, State University of New York, Albany.

Wirth, Louis
  1938   Urbanism as a way of life. *American Journal of Sociology* 44: 1-24.

Wolf, Alvin W.
  1970   On structural comparisons of network situation and social networks in cities. *Canadian Review of Sociology and Anthropology* 7, no. 4: 226-244.

Wrigley, G. M.
  1916   Salta: An early commercial center in Argentina. *Geographical Re-view* no. 2: 116-133.

Index

Adams, Richard N., 10, 43-44
Adaptation, social: definition, 8; in the city, 158 n.3, 166 n. 8; on the plantation, 69
Agricultural labor (nonsugar plantation), 75, 78, 82, 86-87; sources of information concerning, 71, 73-75. *See also* Tobacco farming
Argentina: colonial period, 18; economic growth, 18, 20; immigration to, 17-18, 22, 105; political parties, 20-21

Beckford, George L., 29
Best, Lloyd, 29
Bolivia: bracero program, 25-26, 37; history of, 17, 19; and migration to Argentina, 18-19, 25-26
Buechler, Hans C., 120
Burawoy, Michael, 4, 7

Calchaquí Valleys, Salta: as a source of plantation labor, 33, 47
Children, 81; and the cuarta system, 58-59; and urbanization, 116-117; and the zafra, 58, 79. *See also* Organization of plantation work
Circular migration, 5-6, 84, 151, 157 n. 1

Class consciousness: and plantation labor, 77
Cliffe, Lionel, 7
Compadrazgo: contratistas and, 45

Debt peonage, 34
Decision making, migrant, 8; at the end of the zafra, 71, 73; and the move to Argentina, 80; and pressures to settle in the city, 100-101, 130-131; and reproduction of labor reserve, 113
De Janvry, Alain, 6, 81
Denis, Pierre, 32-34 passim
Dependent capitalism, 5, 157 n. 1
Development theory, 5
Dirks, Robert, 9
Donahue, John, 5
Downing, Theodore E., 157 n. 1

Ecology: seasons, 31; and sugar-cane areas, 13-14; and sugar production, 30, 57-58
Education: of harvesters, 61; opportunities in Bolivia, 109; on tobacco farms, 85; and urban employment, 110
Employment in the city. *See* Urban employment

Erasmus, Charles J., 23
Ethnicity, 68, 107; ethnic relations between plantation workers, 38, 69; Bolivian ethnic identity, 122

Families, migrant, 142; size, as it affects migration, 81; and urbanization, 112-113
Fiesta complex, 120-122
Folk-urban continuum, 158, n. 3
Functional Dualism, 5-6, 81, 157, n. 1

Gatti, Luis María, 35
Germani, Gino, 166 n. 5
Growers associations. *See* Sugar industry

Hacienda system: in Bolivia, 22-23; government ownership, 35; hacienda-plantation relations, 5, 34; and organization of labor, 33-34
Hart, Keith, 153
Health: diseases on the plantation, 56; health care, 49-50; infant mortality, 56; pesticides, 55; and settling out, 137
Herrán, Carlos A., 34
Heyduk, Daniel, 24
Hicks, Frederick, 31
Historical structuralism, 157 n. 1
Hollander, Frederick, 32
Housing: government, 124; on the plantation, 51, 68; urban, 123-126
Humahuaca, Quebrada de, Jujuy: as a source of plantation labor, 33, 47

Industrialization, 20; in Salta, 48
Informal sector, 144, 153-154
Information. *See* Decision making, migrant

International migration, 4, 17, 22; and the expansion of capitalism, 4-5; illegal immigration, 26, 36-38, 47, 84, 112-113; regulation of, 24; and ties to the Bolivian homeland, 118
Irrigation, 31, 160 n. 1

Kemper, Robert V., 140, 158 n.3, 166 n. 5
Kritz, Mary M., and Douglas Gurak, 4

Labor-control mechanism, plantation, 36, 62
Labor legislation, 59, 63; Estatuto del Peón, 35; violations, by plantation, 35; minimum-wage law, 59
Labor migration, 4, 17; and life cycle, 78; and migrant lifestyle, 7; patterns of, 37, 77-79, 81-84, 86-87; rural-urban, 6. *See also* International migration
Labor Recruiters (*contratistas*): and postzafra employment, 74-75; relations with workers, 44-45; role of, 41. *See also* Organization of plantation work
Labor reserve: and labor-market fluctuations, 83; role in the urban capitalist economy, 6, 99; seasonal workers as, 6; transcending rural-urban boundaries, 6
Leeds, Anthony, and Elizabeth Leeds, 109
Lewis, Oscar, 143
Lomnitz, Larissa, 9, 119, 157 n. 1

MacEwen, A. M., 28, 142
Mangin, William, 120
Marginality, 7, 157 n. 3; theory of, 158, n. 4
Mechanization of agriculture, 39; on

the plantation, 38, 164 n. 5; of
vegetable and tobacco farms, 82-83
Medical care. *See* Health
Merchants, 45, 54
Merkx, Gilbert W., 18, 20-21, 25
Methodologies, research, 10-11
Migration. *See* International mi-
gration; Labor migration
Miller, Solomon, 62
Mintz, Sidney, 62
Modernization paradigm, 5
Muñoz, Humberto, and Orlandina de
Oliveira, 157 n. 1

Networks, 8, 118, 165 n. 2; and
ethnicity, 107; as a form of urban
security, 104, 118, 157 n. 7;
function, 9; types, 118-119. *See
also* Urbanization, migrant

Oligarchy, Salta's, 32, 95; and land-
tenure system, 14, 29, 32, 63,
95
Organization of plantation work, 57,
59; *cuarta* system, 51, 59, 79;
chain of command, 57; and migrant families, 58; and permanent
workers, 67; and relations between
seasonal and permanent workers, 68.
See also Children; Plantation (Ingenio del Norte)

Padilla, Elena Seda, 62
Palerm, Angel, 29, 164 n. 3
Patron-client relationships, 71-72, 85,
148; and employment strategies,
85; as information sources, 74;
and social mobility, 114
Patrón Costas, Robustiano, 21
Perlman, Janice, 158 n. 4
Perón, government of, 21, 63; and
documentation for Bolivian migrants, 160 n. 9; Peronism, 21; and
support for rural workers, 62. *See*

also Unionization
Plantation (Ingenio del Norte):
described, 60, 161 n. 1; description of work on, 58, 61, 67;
economy of, 29-30; and land-
tenure system, 14, 29, 32, 63,
95; management of, 62-63;
organization of work of, 46,
61, 63; and political parties,
44, 62. *See also* Organization
of plantation work
Plantation labor: foreign (Bolivian) labor, 5, 36; Indian labor,
33; labor-recruitment mechanisms, 34, 160 n. 2; and need
for cheap labor, 5; peasant labor, 33-34, 47, 78; wage system, 54. *See also* Labor Recruiters (*contratistas*); Organization of plantation work
Power relationships, 10, 43-44;
and migrant labor, 31, 58, 61.
See also Patron-client relationships
Primate cities, 164 n. 1
Proletarianization, rural, 88, 164
n. 3; and semi-proletarians, 5,
90, 164 n. 3

Railroads, 19, 94; transporting
migrants, 47-48, 50
Ramal, described, 3, 12; and health
conditions, 55; as a sugar zone,
13. *See also* Ecology
Redfield, Robert, 143, 158 n. 3
Regional associations, 120; and
fiesta complex, 120-122; and
villa associations, 122-123
Roberts, Bryan R., 7, 9, 105
Rural-urban linkages, 6, 20, 77,
134, 158 n. 3; and the rural-
urban continuum, 143;
Rutledge, Ian D., 32, 34-36 passim

Salta (City): described, 14, 91-
92, 103; economy of, 103;
history of, 93-94; immigration and population growth,
97; level of employment, 99
Salta (province), 12; agricultural economy of, 98-99
Schleh, Emilio, 33
Schooling. *See* Education
Scobie, James R., 21-22
Seasonal labor. *See* Labor Migration
Secondary cities, 164 n. 1
Service sector. *See* Informal
sector
Settling out. *See* Urbanization,
migrant
Solari, Juan Antonio, 34-36 passim
Squatments in Salta, 102, 123-
124, 165 n. 4; and marginality, 157 n. 3
Stavenhagen, Rodolfo, 5, 7
Strategies: kinds of vulnerability, 31, 61, 75, 88, 148; of
least vulnerability, 6, 9, 112,
148, 153; for maximizing family security, 123-127 passim,
153; rural vs. urban, 8; and
search for postzafra employment, 71, 73-76, 152; and
self-employment, 154
Sugar industry: growers associations, 64; history of, in Northwest Argentina 12, 18-19, 26-
27

Tobacco farming, 85; history of,
in Northwest Argentina, 24,
26, living conditions for workers, 85; and migrant work, 37,
71, 78-79; as postzafra employment, 75; process of cultivation, 84. *See also* Agricul-

tural labor (nonsugar plantation)
Transportation, for migrants, 47, 54
Tucumán, sugar industry of, 12, 64

Unionization, rural: under Perón, 21,
35, 37, 63; and plantation management, 62; and seasonal workers, 31
Unions, rural, 22, 37; CGT (Confederación General de Trabajo), 64;
FAR (Federación Azucarera Regional), 63; legislation, 59, 65; and
mechanization of plantations, 38;
organization of, 65-66; and seasonal workers, 61, 65-66, 68, 71;
and strikes, history of, 36, 63, 69.
See also Labor legislation
Urban employment: kinds of, 110-
111; and mixed household strategies, 6, 115; and multiple job holding, 114; self-employment, 115,
154; and short-term agricultural
work, 117-118; and urban constraints on migrants, 112, 152.
See also Informal sector; Strategies
Urbanization, process of: history of,
in Argentina, 154. *See also* Rural-
urban linkages
Urbanization, migrant: and breakdown, 143, 149; and difficulties
of adjustment, 103, 111-112, 143;
and employment difficulties, 112;
and land ownership, 123-124; settling out, 137. *See also* Adaptation, social; Networks; Rural-urban
linkages; Urban employment
Uzzell, Douglas, 7, 113

Villar, Juan Manuel, 84, 106

Walton, John, 157 n. 2
Warman, Arturo, 164 n. 3
Wolf, Alvin W., 9

Women: and employment in the city, 116; and the zafra, 58

Work conditions. *See* Plantation (Ingenio del Norte)

Work camps: living conditions in, 51, 53-54, 161 n. 5; merchandizing on, 45, 54; lack of privacy in, 52; strategies for control of the environment, 41, 52